CONTRACT AND CONTROL IN THE ENTERTAINMENT INDUSTRY

Contract and Control in the Entertainment Industry

Dancing on the Edge of Heaven

STEVE GREENFIELD AND GUY OSBORN
Centre for the Study of Law, Society and Popular Culture,
University of Westminster, London

Ashgate

DARTMOUTH

Aldershot • Brookfield USA • Singapore • Sydney

Published by
Dartmouth Publishing Company Limited
Ashgate Publishing Limited
Gower House
Croft Road
Aldershot
Hants GU11 3HR
England

Ashgate Publishing Company
Old Post Road
Brookfield
Vermont 05036
USA

British Library Cataloguing in Publication Data
Greenfield, Steve
    Contract and control in the entertainment industry :
    dancing on the edge of heaven. - (Studies in modern law and policy)
    1.Contracts - England 2.Contracts - Wales 3.Music trade - Law and legislation -
    England 4.Music trade - Law and legislation - Wales 5.Leisure industry -
    Law and legislation - England 6.Leisure industry - Law and legislation - Wales
    I.Title II.Osborn, Guy
    343.4'2'078'79

Library of Congress Cataloging-in-Publication Data
Greenfield, Steve, 1960-
    Contract and control in the entertainment industry : dancing on
    the edge of heaven / Steve Greenfield, Guy Osborn.
        p.   cm.
    Includes bibliographical references.
    ISBN 1-85521-561-6 (hb)
        1. Entertainers–Legal status, laws, etc.–Great Britain.
    2. Performing arts–Law and legislation–Great Britain. 3. Artists'
    contracts. I. Osborn, Guy, 1966-   . II. Title.
    KD3720.G74   1998
    344.73'097–dc21
                                                                98-3170
                                                                    CIP

ISBN 1 85521 561 6

Printed and bound by Athenaeum Press, Ltd.,
Gateshead, Tyne & Wear.

Contents

REFERENCES

Preface

When the news broke in the NME of a contractual dispute between the group, The Stone Roses, and their recording and publishing company, our first thoughts were of the implications for the group itself - would we ever see the second album? However, at the same time, we were also teaching contract law to undergraduates and saw this as an interesting and apposite way of investigating some particular contractual issues. Simultaneously it enabled us to foray into the burgeoning research culture that was developing in higher education, albeit, on a fairly small scale in the polytechnic sector. For us it was a case of being involved with something professionally that interested us personally and was something that was eminently researchable - the sort of thing we probably would and did talk about in the pub. Our interest and focus grew from here and began to embrace other areas where similar issues and events had occurred or were taking place; the sheer dynamism was itself enthralling. Fortunately these areas - film, music, boxing, cricket, football etc were also central to our personal lives, labours of leisure rather than labours of love. This book effectively arose out of our very first conference paper, given at the Socio-Legal Studies Association Annual meeting at Exeter in March 1993 (our first conference breakfast was unforgettable) and expertly chaired by Ralf Rogowski. We are of course eternally grateful to Ralf for providing us with the vehicle to expand and elaborate on the issues that were first raised as 'In Defence of Pop Music: Inequality of Bargaining Power and the Creative Artist' during that Conference, to John Irwin for his help and confidence in us early in our academic career and to Ann Newell for patiently explaining the intricacies of publishing.

We hope that this text will be of interest to academics, students (especially those on our own Entertainment Law course!) and to anyone who is curious as to how areas within the entertainment industry have placed restrictive controls on the raw material of the industry - the creative artists themselves. Above all, we hope that it will provide some small impetus for others to take up arms and begin research in areas that really interest them and touch, in some way, their lives. This book would not have been written were we both not passionately interested in music and sport - we are lucky that we are able to let our work and play collide. It is perhaps useful in terms of wider orientation to list some of our passions at this point; this is not our list of thanks and acknowledgments but a list of some of the inspirations that have fired our interest. Thanks then, in no particular order, to Birmingham City Football Club, The Jam, The Smiths, The Stone Roses, John McEnroe, Steve Ovett, George Best, Viv Richards, The Clash, Barca, Warwickshire County Cricket Club, Middlesex County Cricket Club, the Welsh Rugby Union team of the 1970s, Milan A.C., Stiff Little Fingers, Cape Fear (both versions), Young Mr Lincoln, Eric, Abdul Qadir and Shane Warne, Tiny, Marabou Stork Nightmares, The Name of the Rose and many more besides. Above all, thanks for the belief and passion of the Manic Street Preachers (proving rock 'n' roll can be intelligent and empowering) and respect for the genius of Richard Edwards.

For ease of reference we have referred to cases by an italicised name and these are listed in the reference section at the end of the book. We chose to do this as we feel that it makes the work as a whole read so much better but offer our apologies for the undoubted breach of legal protocol.

This book could not have been written without the help, time and support of Steve Redhead, Lawrence Harrison, Jonathan Ebsworth, Martin Edwards, Graham ex Rezzillo in Barcelona, Simon Conroy, John Sugden, Martin E. Silfen, Simon Block, Dave Wibberley, Glenys Williams at the MCC Library, Tom Huff, Dave McArdle, Alan Tomlinson, Horace Trubridge, John Kennedy, Ray Clemence, Mick McCarthy, and 'Obi Wan' who has provided a guiding light and voice of measured reason in the fight against the dark side - may the force be with you! Apologies to those we have undoubtedly overlooked, the fault for this, as with any errors within the book rest with the authors. Our thanks also to our long suffering partners, Allison and Delyth, although you will probably never read this unless under duress! Thanks are also due to John Osborn who has read much of the original work contained here as it has evolved beyond the bounds of any parental duty, and to Rosemarie Osborn who has provided support in so many ways over many years and who truly deserves the title 'star'. Thanks to Roy Greenfield for his meticulous proofreading and critical comments and to June Greenfield for her general support and encouragement.

This book is dedicated to Keir and Aneurin - keep right on!

*The true view at the present time I think, is this: The public have an interest in every person's carrying on his trade freely: so has the individual. All interference with individual liberty of action in trading, and all restraints of trade of themselves, if there is nothing more, are contrary to public policy, and therefore void. That is the general rule. But there are exceptions: restraints of trade and interference with individual liberty of action may be justified by the special circumstances of a particular case. It is a sufficient justification, and indeed it is the only justification, if the restriction is reasonable - reasonable, that is, in reference to the interests of the parties concerned and reasonable in reference to the interests of the public, so framed and so guarded as to afford adequate protection to the party in whose favour it is imposed, while at the same time it is in no way injurious to the public (Lord Macnaghten, **Nordenfelt**, 1894, p.565).*

*The common law of England has for centuries recognised that a man has a right to work at his trade or profession without being unjustly excluded from it. He is not to be shut out from it at the whim of those having the governance of it. If they make a rule which enables them to reject his application arbitrarily or capriciously, not reasonably, that rule is bad. It is against public policy. The courts will not give effect to it (Lord Denning M.R., **Nagle**, 1966, p.644-645).*

1 Of Human Bondage[1]

do you wanna get out,
do you wanna give in,
do you wanna be contained,
do you wanna be restrained,
do you wanna be enforced by the laws that are made,
do you wanna be deprived, do you wanna be advised,
do you wanna be controlled,
wanna be patrolled,
do you wanna be designed to accept all the time,
do you wanna be bored,
or do you wanna be broke,
do you wanna be conned,
do you wanna be robbed,
do you wanna have to beg for the price of a smoke.
(ManBREAK 'Ready or Not', Rondor Music (London) Ltd, 1997, from the album
'Come and See', written by Swindelli).

CONTROL and its (non) existence is the essential fulcrum of this work. As an artist[2] if you're 'hot' and in demand you've got it (at least to some extent) whilst without it contractual terms will reflect this lack of bargaining power in a contract that may be weighted heavily in favour of the party that holds the bargaining leverage.[3] This leverage will fluctuate not only according to talent, but also to the prevailing market demand. Artists may sign an initial deal as an unknown commodity, if they become more valuable, they will wish to improve terms. Even a well established artist such as George Michael may want to seek variations to equate with a growing superstar status. The essence of this book is a tale of artists and those who buy and control talent; tales of resistance and tales of conflict. Without some element of compromise this conflict may end up in the High Court[4] and beyond, as both sides strive for ultimate control, or more accurately, the legal right to control. There are certain distinct problems that are confined to individual areas, for example a crucial dimension to the boxing disputes (chapter four) has been the structure of the professional game and the inter-relationship between managers and promoters raising questions of conflicts of interest. By the same token in all four areas that we dissect, a significant factor has been the use of standard form agreements to determine the basic contractual terms and this is put in a broader context in the concluding chapter. In the area of sport this has been developed by the relevant controlling body as a means of ensuring overall standardisation and control. The music industry is similarly affected by the use of general terms although these are ones that have developed as industry standard rather than being imposed from above by an overall governing body. As the conclusion to that chapter indicates, attempts are being made by at least one major company to alter some of the substantive terms of recording contracts and perhaps more importantly the bargaining process itself. This is symbolic of a number of approaches to self-policing and internal regulation that have been made.

This introductory chapter is an orientation to issues of contractual control within the entertainment industry and utilises, in particular, the film industry as an example of themes that underpin the book as a whole. This industry is a prime example of an arena in which attempts were made to regulate and control entertainers and where the first inroads towards artist freedom were later seen. How far this is replicated within other spheres of the entertainment industry will be examined in the main body of the work, but this chapter will examine the development of some of the basic principles that have affected contractual relations within the entertainment industry as whole. Whilst the doctrine of restraint of trade[5] will be dealt with at various points in the text, this is not intended to be a book charting solely the development of restraint of trade - our remit is far wider. We are interested in examining how the various parties are bound together and how contracts have been altered in response to a number of external and internal factors. That said, there is inevitably some historical detail in terms of how various challenges have been made to contracts in these areas and consequently how the position of the artists has altered as a result of this. Whilst in some of these areas litigation has proved the catalyst (see for example chapter five), in others there are separate devices that have been utilised such as a more traditional notion of trade unionism in the successful campaign by the Professional Footballers' Association to remove the maximum wage provisions (see chapter two). We have also sought to chart the changes hinted at by legal intervention where the outcome is not fully resolved; the issue of joint promoting and managing of boxers that we deal with in chapter four being a good example of this. Underpinning all of these interventions are some basic contractual principles regarding the enforceability of agreements. The rest of this chapter deals specifically with two aspects of this; firstly, the so-called doctrine of restraint of trade and secondly, the enforcement of personal service contracts. In addition to this, the issues we alluded to at the beginning of the chapter; control, bargaining power and leverage will become motifs that are hinted at throughout all the chapters and this key to the work will be dissected in the conclusion.

Restraint of trade and reasonable restrictions?

> The emphasis of freedom of contract is on the parties' freedom of choice. First, the parties should be free to choose one another as contractual partners (ie partner-freedom). Like the tango, contract takes two. And, ideally the two should consensually choose one another. Secondly, the parties should be free to choose their own terms (ie term-freedom). Contract is about unforced choice (Adams & Brownsword, 1987, p.208).

The quote above is an expression of a traditional market-individualist position, one in which the contract is a 'sacred text', agreed between the parties and incapable of external fracture. Such a position is not one for which much support could now be garnered (as Adams and Brownsword argue) as it would be construed as anachronistic and oblivious of a number of important factors. Contracts are now governed not only by the parties but also through a number of extraneous devices, including statute. In particular, far from being a sanctified and untouchable document, a contract may be subject to judicial scrutiny and intervention in a number of circumstances. For example, Lord Denning MR in *Nagle* spoke (rather optimistically) of a 'right to work', a concept that has sporadically appeared as a justification for granting relief in exceptional and often controversial circumstances. In *Nagle* all three of the judges drew upon this notion, though it is Salmon LJ who gives the notion more credence; 'The principle that courts will protect a man's right to work is well recognised in the stream of authority relating to contracts in restraint of trade' (*Nagle,* 1966, p.654). It is primarily this latter area (restraint of trade) with its long and significant history that has been used to sever freely made contractual relations in many parts of the entertainment industry.

The doctrine of restraint of trade is a well-established one. Superficially however, it appears to run contrary to the principle of freedom of contract; a principle that was part of the *laissez faire* ideology that prevailed in England broadly between 1770 and 1870. This philosophy had, at its root, an adherence to notions of individualism and self-sufficiency, which saw paternalist ideology as being inimicable to the growth and development of an industrial society. During this period the so-called 'classical contract theory' was fashioned. This contractual theory is based on consent - that parties are free to enter into bargains and to negotiate the terms of such an agreement. Such a theory took little or no account of external features such as necessity (economic or personal) or relative bargaining positions but was concerned solely with the enforcement of contractual agreements. If an individual did not want to be bound by the terms of a contract he would not have agreed it in the first place. The prevailing situation of the time is lucidly outlined by Atiyah (1995, p.14):

> Freedom of contract meant that you could choose whom you wanted to contract with, and you could arrive at the terms you wanted by mutual agreement. Even in the nineteenth century this was only true in a narrow sense, that is, if one assumed that the bargaining power of all contracting parties was equal, and this was an assumption which the classical law very largely accepted. There were, of course, the obvious cases, such as persons below the age of capacity, lunatics, and so on, for whom special provision had to be made, but by and large the law assumed that each person could fend for himself, and if he entered into a harsh or burdensome contract he had only himself to blame because there was freedom of contract and he could have gone elsewhere. Manifestly, this assumption was false, even in the nineteenth century. The bargaining strength of the employer, for instance, was usually far greater than that of his employees at a time when trade unions were prohibited altogether or were still in their infancy. The small businessman, again, was no match for the large railway company, and so on and so forth.

Once the agreement was reached, the parties were bound to the terms and the courts would act to enforce such contracts. This approach took no account of the situation in which the contract was made or if some form of leverage was exerted against the other 'weaker' party to sign the contract. The chief question is whether and if so how far the law should assume those parties are free to exercise discretion in considering contractual activity.[6] In fact, this rigid policy of non-interference was not absolute and the courts consistently developed ways of dealing with situations where some element of 'unconscionability' was involved. For example, in *Allcard* (1887) the Court applied the doctrine of undue influence over gifts made to a religious order whilst, in *Evans* (1787, p.1194) the court spoke of undue advantage; 'However, here, I say the party was taken by *surprise*; he had not sufficient time to act with caution; and therefore though there was no actual fraud, it is something like fraud, for an undue advantage was taken of his situation'.

Both of these early cases also mention the absence of independent advice as an important factor. This issue appears in some of the later cases where contracts have been made between parties with a marked difference in bargaining expertise and is a theme to which we return in the final chapter. Gradually different categories have evolved where the courts were prepared to intervene to overturn agreements, even in the absence of fraud. Lord Denning in *Bundy* famously (yet ultimately unsuccessfully) attempted to draw these diverse themes into a more coherent principle arguing that a number of common threads ran through what might be termed the 'categories of unconscionability' and that a general principle could be identified that connected these seemingly disparate instances.[7] Alongside this was the parallel development of restraint of trade and whether attempts to exert control over the liberty of individuals to trade, through contractual relations, was permissible. The original view was that all attempts to restrict the right to trade were contrary to public policy and, therefore void, although gradually courts began to distinguish between general and partial restraints:

> First, all contracts for restraint of trade over all England are void, whether by bond, covenant, or promise; whether of that trade a man is brought up to, or any other trade he afterwards falls into. Secondly, contracts to restrain trade in a particular place are void, if not done upon a fair, just and good consideration (*Mitchell*, 1711, p.661).

An interesting point in respect to this specific case is the notion that any consideration to justify a partial restraint would need to be 'fair and just'. This clearly suggests that the court ought to inquire as to the money paid to buy the restraint, a fairly radical view given the longstanding principles concerning the adequacy of consideration.[8] The doctrine became well entrenched within English law on the basis of this distinction between general and partial restraints, but was also confined, until the latter half of the century, to a limited number of situations. The two areas where the doctrine could be applied were restrictions on former employees and restrictive covenants relating to the sale of businesses. In other areas the doctrine had no effect and, contracts which sought to impose restrictions, did not fall for consideration. Courts would only act to strike out contractual agreements in these two specific areas and on the basis that a partial restraint could be effective. Exclusivity is at the heart of the issue and a contract in restraint of trade has been described as one that involves an element of derogation from the common law right to ply any trade a person may choose:

> ...all contracts in restraint of trade involve such a derogation but not all contracts involving such a derogation are contracts in restraint of trade. Whenever a man agrees to do something over a period he thereby puts it wholly or partly out of his power to 'exercise any trade or business he pleases' during that period. He may enter into a contract of service or may agree to give his exclusive services to another: then during the period of the contract he is not entitled to engage in other business activities (Lord Reid in *Esso*, 1968, p.294).

The longstanding distinction between general and partial restraints was eventually removed in the landmark case of *Nordenfelt*. Thorsten Nordenfelt had previously obtained patents for improvements in quick firing guns and had for a considerable period of time carried out the manufacture of guns and ammunition. In March 1886 an agreement was made between Thorsten Nordenfelt and the Nordenfelt Company for the latter to purchase the goodwill of the appellant's business for a fee of £237,000 in cash and a further £50,000 in paid up shares of the company. As part of this agreement Nordenfelt entered into a restrictive covenant to protect the goodwill. The business was clearly valuable for, as Lord Macnaghten noted, 'His customers were comparatively few in number, but his trade was world-wide in extent. He had upon his books almost every monarch and almost every State of any note in the habitable globe' (*Nordenfelt*, 1894, p.559). In July 1888 negotiations began for the amalgamation of the Nordenfelt Company and the Maxim Gun Company and for the transfer of their business and assets to a new company, 'The Maxim-Nordenfelt Guns and Ammunition Company'. When the amalgamation was finalised it was agreed that the Nordenfelt Company would ensure that the following restrictive covenant, replacing the earlier version, would be made:

> The said Thorsten Nordenfelt shall not, during the term of twenty-five years from the date of the incorporation of the company if the company shall so long continue to carry on business, engage except on behalf of the company either directly or indirectly in the trade or business of a manufacturer of guns gun mountings or carriages, gunpowder explosives or ammunition, or in any business competing or liable to compete in any way with that for the time being carried on by the company...(*Nordenfelt*, 1894, p.536).

As Lord Watson noted, the prohibition placed upon Nordenfelt was far reaching '...it extends to every part of the surface of the globe available for the purpose of carrying on the process of manufacture' (*Nordenfelt*, 1894, p.550). At first instance Romer J had held that the covenant was void as it went beyond what was reasonable in order to protect the company. The Court of Appeal dismissed this view determining that, although the restriction might well be unreasonable if it applied to any business that Nordenfelt might wish to undertake, insofar as it applied to the manufacture of guns and ammunition, the covenant would be valid. This decision was upheld by the House of Lords. Interestingly, Lord Ashbourne almost foreseeing later developments, illustrated the advances that had occurred and observed that the law must not remain static but must be responsive to change:

> The cases that have been referred to are interesting and important as shewing the history, growth, and development of an important branch of our law. In considering them it is necessary to bear in mind the vast advances that have since the reign of Queen Elizabeth taken place in science, inventions, political institutions, commerce, and the intercourse of nations. Telegraphs, postal systems,

railways, steam, have brought all parts of the world into touch. Communication has become easy, rapid, and cheap. Commerce has grown with our growth, and trade is ever finding new outlets and methods that cannot be circumscribed by areas or narrowed by the municipal laws of any country. It is not surprising to note that our laws have been also expanded, and that legal principles have been applied and developed so as to suit the exigencies of the age in which we live (*Nordenfelt*, 1894, p.556).

Lord Macnaghten also challenged the distinction between partial and general restraints and argued forcefully that the issue was solely concerned with the reasonableness of the restriction in any particular case. Thus all restraints, general or partial, were *prima facie* void but could be justified by 'the special circumstances of a particular case'. Therefore in some circumstances (such as *Nordenfelt*) a general restraint could be justified if it was reasonable in the interests of the parties and the wider interests of the public at large. Lord Macnaghten similarly dismissed the view that the amount of consideration should be subject to direct judicial scrutiny though it could affect the reasonableness of the contract, an important factor recognised in *Mitchell*.

The principles of *Nordenfelt* became the touchstone for developments in restraint of trade and its echoes can be heard in the later cases of both *Mason* and *Saxelby*, both of which concerned the category of post contractual constraints being placed upon employees. In *Mason* the issue related to a clothing company who operated what was known as a 'check and credit system' where persons applied to become members of the company by paying for a 'check' or 'share' by instalments. Local shopkeepers would then supply goods to these shareholders on presentation of their 'check'. This business was developed by the use of canvassers who collected the checks and who were each assigned to individual areas or districts. Within the contract of employment between the employer and the employee was the following clause '[the employee] hereby agrees that he shall not within three years after the termination of his engagement and services with the company be in employ of, or be engaged in any manner whatsoever whether on his own account, or as partner with, or agent, or manager, or assistant, for any person or persons, firm or firms, company or companies, carrying on or engaged in the same or a similar business to that of [the employer]...within twenty five miles of London aforesaid where the company carry on business'. Viscount Haldane made the point that such clauses were not uncommon but that their ambit should only be the reasonable protection of the rights of the employer:

Such agreements are frequently insisted on, but they are invalid if they go beyond what is necessary for the protection of the rights of the employer. Whether there are such rights must depend on the character of the business. Now, the character of the respondents' business does not appear to me to be such as to entitle them to say that they had any right which justified them in excluding the appellant from exercising his talents, such as they were, altogether or within a wide area (*Mason*, 1913, p.731).

Accordingly, the company was unable to show that the restriction went no further than reasonably necessary to protect their business, a position that was supported by Lords Dunedin, Moulton and Shaw. Interestingly, Lord Shaw made the point that a separate clause of the agreement also allowed the employers to assign their rights and powers, under the agreement, to a separate unrelated party who might be able to enforce the terms against the employee. This issue of assignability becomes even more important in the later chapters where we examine issues of control within the particular confines of what are often very close (at least initially) relationships. *Saxelby* was similar to *Mason* in that it concerned the attempt by a previous employer to prevent a former employee from being involved in a similar pursuit after the contractual relationship had been terminated, in this case for a period of seven years after the end of the employment. Again, the House of Lords were of the opinion that the restraint was wider than necessary to preserve the business interests of the employer and that the clause was therefore unenforceable. In coming to this decision and upholding the decision of the Court of Appeal, Lord Atkinson identified the dilemma that the area embodied:

> The principle is this: Public policy requires that every man shall be at liberty to work for himself, and shall not be at liberty to deprive himself or the State of his labour, skill, or talent, by any contract that he enters into. On the other hand, public policy requires that when a man has by skill or by any other means obtained something which he wants to sell, he should be at liberty to sell it in the most advantageous way in the market; and in order to enable him to sell it advantageously in the market it is necessary that he should be able to preclude himself from entering into competition with the purchaser (*Saxelby*, 1916, p.701).

The real watershed for the doctrine of restraint of trade, however, arrived with the case of *Esso*. The case concerned 'solus' agreements, which related to the sale of motor fuels to dealers by Esso. Esso supplied garages and filling stations with fuel for sale to the public - this was a reflection of the ongoing practice in Britain where large numbers of stations tied themselves to one of the big oil companies with an undertaking that they would not sell petrol supplied by any other party. At the time around 35,000 of the 36,000 garages in the country had contracted in such a way. The argument centred upon two particular agreements signed between Esso and the respondent, the owner of two garages, one in Stourport-on-Severn, the other in Kidderminster. One of the agreements, signed on 5 July 1962, was to remain in force for twenty one years and the other, signed on 27 June 1963, was to remain in force for four years and five months. Both of the agreements contained clauses relating to the exclusive supply and sale of Esso's fuels. The agreements caused no major problems until the onset of cheaper 'cut price' petrol in 1964 whereupon the owner of the garages began buying from this alternative source and was no longer selling Esso fuel, as provided for in the contracts. Esso sought injunctions preventing the garages from selling petrol not supplied by them during the subsistence of their 'solus' agreements. At first instance, Mocatta J allowed the injunction and dismissed the counter claim of the defendants, however, the Court of Appeal comprising Lord Denning MR, Harman LJ and Diplock LJ allowed the appeal and Esso appealed to the House of Lords.

The question for the House contained a number of elements, the first of which was whether the agreements could be regarded as being in restraint of trade. Lord Reid undertook a thorough excavation of the existing case law, noting that whilst the doctrine was of ancient origin there were surprisingly few examples and that; '...the old cases lie within a narrow compass. It seems to have been common for an apprentice or a craftsman to agree with his master that he would not compete with him after leaving his service, and also for a trader who sold his business to agree that he would not thereafter compete with the purchaser of his business' (*Esso*, 1968, p.293). There was, however, a dearth of cases that did not come within these narrow confines and this provided something of a stumbling block in evaluating how far the principles of the doctrine could be extended. This had certainly been an issue in both *Bette Davis* and *Page One* where both Branson J and Stamp J felt that restraint of trade could not apply to such personal service contracts. Having reviewed all the cases and the developments that had been made, Lord Reid argued that it was too late to say that restraint of trade should be confined to the original areas of sale of businesses and post contractual employment and that as a creature of public policy; '...its application ought to depend less on legal niceties or theoretical possibilities than on the practical effect of a restraint in hampering that freedom which it is the policy of the law to protect' (*Esso*, 1968, p.298). This case thus proved crucial in allowing the doctrine to extend into previously uncharted areas. The questions to be considered in attempting to establish that an agreement was illegal in these situations were first, was the contract one to which the doctrine of restraint of trade could apply? Secondly, if so, did the restriction extend further than to afford adequate protection to the party relying upon the restraint? Finally, is the restraint in itself contrary to the public interest? In simple terms, this translates, as, if the contract is one in restraint of trade; is it *reasonable*?

Star or slave? Enforcing personal service contracts

As we have noted above, the concept of restraint of trade was, until the landmark judgement in *Esso*, only applicable in two areas, competition with ex-employers and vendors of businesses. It had no application outside of these limits and courts would not consider that a contract could be challenged through this route. However, in the field of personal service contracts, developments emerged which had clear links with the principles on which restraint of trade is based. The central issue is similarly that of exclusivity, the purchasing of personal services for a period of time which excludes the right to sell such services elsewhere. An interesting example within the context of entertainment is the Hollywood film industry. Schatz (1988, p.74) has suggested that the very nature of the industry produced disputes:

> The classical Hollywood cinema, by its very nature as a commercial art form, was rife with conflict and contradiction, and the production system it developed in the 1920s and 1930s contained but scarcely subdued its essential discord. It's worth suggesting in fact that the Hollywood studio system, with its factory-based mode of production and division of labor and its distinctive relations of power, not only permitted but virtually demanded a degree of struggle and negotiation in the filmmaking process.

Whilst the studio system was dominated by financial backers rather than creative personnel (Giannetti & Eyman, 1986) a chief resource was still the 'star'. The position of the star varied according to the company, but under the studio system the stars were often heavily typecast and tied into the 'house style' of the studio concerned. This form of commodification had the added negative effect for the star of further embedding the public perception of the artist and this element of control caused great friction between both sides of the industry. Charlie Chaplin, Mary Pickford and Douglas Fairbanks felt aggrieved enough to set up their own company, United Artists, to try and combat the effects of such a system. Notwithstanding this, the amount of control that could be exercised by the studios over most actors was considerable. Bette Davis was one actress, tied in by the constraints of the system, who attempted to break free from her relationship with Warner Brothers in the 1930s. After the stock market crash Warner Brothers (Warners), at the time headed by Harry Warner,[9] adopted a policy of consolidation and efficiency, a strategy that was reflected in the films that the company sought to produce:

> Warner's emergent style shunned the high-gloss, well-lit worlds so often displayed

by MGM and Paramount, as well as the cozy Americana of so many Fox features. Warners opted instead for a bleaker - and a more cost-efficient - worldview, even in its musicals. Its Depression era pictures were fast-paced, fast-talking, socially sensitive (if not down-right exploitive) treatments of contemporary life (Schatz, 1988, p.76).

While some of Warners' stars were prepared to let the studio shape their careers initially, as they became more successful they were keen to enter into contractual negotiations to improve their position. Cagney and Robinson both renegotiated their deals after the successes of 'The Public Enemy' and 'Little Caesar' respectively, although they found that higher wages were not without cost - usually a more narrowly defined screen persona, as the company were reluctant to allow any deviation from the type of roles that the company felt suited them best. Bette Davis had perhaps, an even tougher time dealing with the studio bosses and attempted to exercise some control over her career direction and development. Bette Davis signed for Warners in 1931 for $300 per week and an option was exercised in December 1932 extending the agreement and increasing her wage to $550 per week, this was exercised again the following year increasing her wage to $750. However, whilst her wages had doubled over those two years, Davis was increasingly worried about the type and extent of her workload and had made her unhappiness known to Warners. Because of this, Warners loaned her to RKO to make 'Of Human Bondage' but, on her return she found, much to her disquiet, that she was still being asked to perform the same type of roles as before. She refused to report for 'The Case of the Howling Dog' and was promptly suspended.[10]

Under the studio contracts, the star was usually bound for a period of seven years; in this way the companies were able to have a pool of actors at their disposal and the ability to cast such actors in films as it felt fit. This was considered a successful way of managing the workforce, if someone was difficult they could be 'miscast' in an unsuitable picture with little redress available to them. If they refused to appear or otherwise attempted to obtain redress, the studio was free to exercise the contractual provisions regarding 'suspensions'. These suspension clauses allowed the studios to pause the contractual clock, thus adding extra time to the contractual term. Gaines (1992, p.152) notes that Jack Warner was particularly good at utilising the powers available in this way; 'Warner would assign a high-salaried actor an unsuitable role, and when the actor refused it, the producer would suspend the actor without pay, thus cutting his own costs...Actors who wanted to be free to work for other studios on scripts of their own choice felt trapped by the compulsory extension of their contracts'.[11] This was effectively the position that Davis found herself in - trapped in roles she no longer wanted to take and with the studio merely extending her 'sentence' with them if she refused to comply with their requests. However, just after this dispute, 'Of Human Bondage' hit the screens and Davis's star was certainly on the upturn. Warners welcomed her back to the fold with the promise of better roles, the first of which was in 'Bordertown' with Paul Muni. Muni, by this time, was an established star who maintained some degree of artistic control. After the success of 'Scarface', he was offered the following terms for 'I am a Fugitive from a Chaingang':

> ...a two-year, eight-picture deal paying him $50,000 per picture and allowing him concessions that were given to no other star on the lot. Those included approval of story, role and script; billing as sole star both on-screen and in all advertising; loanouts only on consent, with story and role approval, and at a 50-50 split with Warners on any salary overage; definition of a 'year' as twenty-one weeks, with Muni allowed 'to render his services as he sees fit upon the stage' between film projects (Schatz, 1988, p.79).

Muni's contractual terms were certainly impressive compared to those of Davis. His was an excellent early example of how a bargaining position, or leverage, can help artists to exact terms from the traditionally 'stronger' party. Davis once again put in a good performance in the film but was 'rewarded' with more roles that she deemed unacceptable. The dispute lingered on until in 1936 Warners vetoed her loan to RKO to play the lead in John Ford's 'Mary of Scotland', a part that she desperately wanted. She left Hollywood to attend the Democratic convention in New York and her agent sent Warners a demand for a new contract that included salaries escalating from $100,000 to $200,000 over five years and a greater degree of control over her workload. She refused to start her next assignment without this agreement and Warners placed her on indefinite suspension. Much of the summer was taken up with negotiations but unsatisfied, Davis set sail for England, in August, to discuss a potential agreement with an independent production company. The result of her seeking to sign such an agreement was Warners suing Davis in an attempt to prevent her from doing so. A dispute that began in Hollywood and was exacerbated in New York[12] thus found itself falling to be considered in the High Court of England.

Warner Brothers claimed an injunction to restrain Davis, during the currency of her contract, 'from rendering without the written consent of the plaintiffs...any services for or in any motion picture or stage production or productions of any person, firm or corporation other than the plaintiffs' (*Bette Davis*, 1937, p.209). Under the contract she had signed with Warners, Davis had agreed to render her exclusive services to them, if she wished to work for any other party in any capacity during the contract, she was required, under her contract, to seek written permission from Warners. Interestingly, a further clause provided that, if she refused or failed to perform her contract, the plaintiffs were able to extend the term of the contract for a period equivalent to the period during which Davis refused to perform. Effectively, this could extend the contract far beyond the specified term. A crucial facet of contracts of this type is that performance of a contract for personal services cannot be directly enforced. The prime reason for this, is that to allow a mandatory injunction to be applied in such a situation would be tantamount to legalising a form of contractual slavery, aside from the problems of ensuring such an order was carried out. This principle is enshrined in both English law[13] and in the United States; '...the performer is *not* a product. He or she cannot legally be forced to work, since to force an employee to work is a violation of the involuntary servitude clause of the Thirteenth Amendment to the U.S. Constitution' (Gaines, 1992, p.153).

The format of the injunction sought by Warners was negative, ie rather than compelling Davis to perform her contract it was a preventative measure, to stop her plying her trade with anyone else in breach of the express term of her contract. Branson J noted that Davis initially contracted with Warners in 1931 and this was subsequently renegotiated. The agreement that was the subject of the action was for fifty two weeks and contained options that allowed Warners to extend the agreement with the operation of concomitant rises in salary. The judge was aware that it was a stringent contract but also noted that the amounts of money that she was to receive were 'considerable'. In particular he noted that clause 23 allowed the plaintiffs to extend the term of the agreement in the event that the defendant failed to perform her obligations under the contract - the contentious 'suspension clauses' noted above. Branson J was clear that the Court was able to enforce negative covenants:

> ...where a contract of personal service contains negative covenants the enforcement of which will not amount either to a decree of specific performance of the positive covenants of the contract or to the giving of a decree under which the defendant must either remain idle or perform those positive covenants, the Court will enforce those negative covenants... (*Bette Davis*, 1937, p.217).

It is however important to note that injunctions are an equitable, discretionary remedy and they will only be granted if the potential damages that could be awarded would not be a sufficient remedy for the plaintiffs. Here, the judge felt that with the admitted breach of contract it was a proper case to exercise the court's discretion given that the contract itself placed great store in the fact that her services were 'of a special, unique, extraordinary and intellectual character'. He was, therefore, able to grant an injunction in so far as it did not enforce a positive obligation to fulfil the agreement. The next question was one of extent - how far should the injunction extend? The argument was firmly made for Davis that, because of her position and earning potential and the disparity between other professions, she would effectively be forced to perform her contract by an injunction even if it were framed in the negative. This view was rejected by the judge on the grounds that it was not in accord with the previous cases and that 'the defendant is stated to be a person of intelligence, capacity and means, and no evidence was adduced to show that, if enjoined from doing the specified acts otherwise than for the plaintiffs, she will not be able to employ herself both usefully and remuneratively in other spheres of activity, though not as remuneratively as in her special line' (*Bette Davis*, 1937, p.219). The injunction was therefore granted on the limited basis of the above. Whilst Davis never really achieved all she wanted to with Warners, she did in fact make only one film with an outside party between 1934 and 1949 almost as if; '...despite her struggles with the studio powers - and in some ways because of them - her personality and the Warners style were inexorably bound together, fused in that peculiar symbiosis of star and studio style that was so essential to the new Hollywood cinema' (Schatz, 1988, p.89).

The question of enforceability of personal services contracts, and the applicability of the *Bette Davis* decision came under judicial scrutiny again in *Page One* where a more artist friendly and fair approach was taken by the Court.[14] The case concerned the pop group The Troggs, a band that had success throughout the sixties with hits such as 'With a Girl Like You' (1966) and 'Love is All Around' (1967), the latter re-entering the public psyche as a result of the Wet Wet Wet cover version used in the unlikely hit film 'Four Weddings and a Funeral'.[15] The case echoed *Bette Davis* in that it again centred upon an attempt to secure an injunction preventing breach of contract on the following terms:

> (i) an injunction that The Troggs and each of them be restrained until trial from engaging as their managers or agents or personal representatives in the branches of the entertainment industry referred to in cl. 1 of the agreement of Feb. 1, 1966, or from engaging as their managers conducting all their affairs relating to their professional careers in any medium of professional entertainment, every person, firm or corporation other than the first plaintiff; (ii) an injunction restraining each of The Troggs acting as a group from publishing or causing to be published any music performed by them otherwise than through the medium of the first or second plaintiffs; and (iii) an order that the defendant company be restrained until trial from inducing or procuring any breach or further breach by The Troggs as a group or otherwise of agreements between the plaintiffs and The Troggs for the management of The Troggs by the first plaintiff or the publication by either plaintiff of the music of The Troggs ...' (*Page One*, 1967, p.823).

Again, the terms of the injunction were framed so as to prevent the defendants from working for anyone apart from the parties they were contracted to. Here however, the Court found that to grant an injunction in this case would have the effect of compelling the group to employ the plaintiffs and, therefore, effectively forcing them to perform their contract. Counsel for The Troggs went on to argue that in addition to the fact that specific performance cannot be granted for personal service contracts, an injunction should also not be granted which would have the effect of; 'preventing an employer [in this case The Troggs] discharging an agent who is in a fiduciary position vis-a-vis the employer' (*Page One*, 1967, p.826). Effectively, the argument was that The Troggs could not operate as a group without the services of a manager. The point was made that, as persons of little business experience, they would be unable to perform the role of a manager for themselves and that it is essential, in the music business, to have a manager to stand any chance of success. On this basis, Stamp J felt it was apparent that, if the injunction were granted, the upshot would be that The Troggs would be forced to continue to employ the first plaintiff as their manager and agent and the judge was not prepared to grant the injunction. As a result this case had a crucial distinction from cases such as *Bette Davis* that preceded it:

> ...it would be a bad thing to put pressure on The Troggs to continue to employ as a manager and agent in a fiduciary capacity one, who, unlike the plaintiff in those cases who had merely to pay the defendant money, has duties of a personal and fiduciary nature to perform and in whom The Troggs, for reasons good, bad or indifferent, have lost confidence and who may, for all I know, fail in its duty to them (*Page One*, 1967, p.827).

Whilst both the contracts of The Troggs and Bette Davis were undoubtedly stringent there was no suggestion at this time that either was actually unlawful. Stamp J felt that there was no suggestion that any of the contracts entered into by the members of The Troggs were other than fair and reasonable and there was no evidence that better terms could have been achieved elsewhere. In *Bette Davis* one of the first contentions dealt with by Branson J was that the agreement Davis had was in fact in restraint of trade and unlawful:

> The ground for this contention was that the contract compelled the defendant to serve the plaintiffs exclusively, and might in certain circumstances endure for the whole of her natural life. No authority was cited to me in support of the proposition that such a contract is illegal, and I see no reason for so holding. Where, as in the present contract, the covenants are all concerned with what is to happen whilst the defendant is employed by the plaintiffs and not thereafter, there is no room for the application of the doctrine of restraint of trade (*Bette Davis*,

1937, p.214).

Whilst the judge was of the opinion that the doctrine of restraint of trade could not apply to such contracts, the case of *Esso* some thirty years later made it clear that the doctrine could in fact be extended to embrace new areas. It is to an examination of the ambit of this extension that this book is dedicated, the following chapters analyse the encroachment of restraint of trade into areas of the entertainment industry. Whilst restraint of trade may be the key that 'unlocks' the contracts, the contract may in fact be only an expression of control and that in all of the areas that we deal with, *contractual* control is but one way in which artists may be fettered.

Notes

1. 'Of Human Bondage' was the title of a novel by W. Somerset Maugham, turned into a film by John Cromwell (1934) that starred Bette Davis, an actress whose legal dispute with her film company, Warner Brothers, informs much of this chapter. The film was also remade in 1946 (Goulding) and 1964 (Hughes & Hathaway). This endnote is dedicated to David Fraser.
2. We use the term artist here in a broad sense to denote performers within the field of entertainment. Specifically, for the purposes of this book the artists with whom we deal, are film stars, musicians, boxers, cricketers and association and rugby footballers.
3. We had previously referred to this concept as 'bargaining power' but were introduced to the term 'leverage' by a number of American entertainment lawyers whom we interviewed in June 1993. One such lawyer, Martin E. Silfen, has been a very supportive influence on our work and we would like to extend grateful thanks to him.
4. The High Court is, of course, a court of first instance for civil actions. For further details of the court hierarchy, especially as regards appeals to higher courts see Bailey and Gunn (1996).
5. Atiyah (1995, p.323-4) describes the doctrine of restraint of trade thus; 'Contracts in restraint of trade are one of the most important categories of void contracts at common law. The modern term would be 'restrictive practices' which is, indeed, somewhat wider than 'agreements in restraint of trade', but the economic and legal problems are the same whatever the label. Broadly these are agreements in which one or both parties limit their freedom to work or carry on their profession or business in some way, such as (for instance) by agreeing not to compete with each other in certain places'.
6. Guest (1984, p.4-5) notes the following example of the traditional *laissez faire* approach where, in the 1820s, London Merchants presented Parliament with the following petition; 'That freedom from restraint is calculated to give the utmost extension to foreign trade and the best direction to the capitalised industry of the country' and counters this with the position today where 'Freedom of contract is generally regarded as a reasonable social ideal only to the extent that equality of bargaining power between contracting parties can be assumed, and no injury is done to the economic interests of the community at large'.
7. See for example our previous work, Greenfield & Osborn (1992).
8. Atiyah (1995, p.127) notes 'It was a fundamental part of classical contract law that the *real* value of the consideration was immaterial, or (as it is put by lawyers) that the adequacy of the consideration is immaterial. If a person chose to pay an extravagant price for a promise, or if he

chose to accept a nominal price for his promise, then that was his business and the courts had no right to intervene'.

9. His younger sibling Jack was studio manager and Darryl Zanuck was production chief.

10. For interesting background reading on Davis' life see Higham (1981) and Leaming (1992).

11. See here the later American case of *De Haviland v Warner Bros Pictures* 1944, after which the studios were unable to extend the contract past the 'longstop' contractual term.

12. Bette Davis criticised Warners during her trip to the Democratic Convention; 'Always adept at manipulating the press, she took the opportunity to blast Hollywood's power brokers. The *Evening Journal* ran a story, "Film Bosses 'headache' to Bette Davis", in which she not only criticised the Warners but stated flatly that she would not return to the studio for retakes on "Golden Arrow"' Schatz (1988, p.80).

13. The *Trade Union and Labour Relations (Consolidation) Act 1992* s236 prevents a court granting an order for specific performance with respect to contracts of employment.

14. In this introduction we have examined enforcement of negative covenants via examples in the film industry and music industry. It does of course have implications for all areas of entertainment and we deal with its applicability within boxing in chapter four. For a wider discussion of the enforcement of these covenants in sporting contracts see McCutcheon (1997).

15. Interestingly, The Troggs are the only artists to top the US charts with a song (Wild Thing) simultaneously released on two labels.

Once Luxembourg was a two-bob country known only for its radio station. And the fact it once let in nine goals against England,
Now a judge in the European Court in Luxembourg endangers our national game with his ruling that the transfer system is against European law. This euro madness will drive smaller clubs out of business or force them to merge. It will make football a paradise for players and agents - and hell for the fans.
Who gave Europe the right to take football away from us?
*(**The Sun**, September 21, 1995).*

What is more reasonable than our plea that a footballer with his uncertain career should have the best money he can earn? If I can earn £7 a week, why should I be debarred from receiving it? I have devoted my life to football and I have become a better player than most because I have denied myself much that men prize. A man who takes the care of himself that I have ever done and who fights the temptations of all that can injure the system surely deserves some recognition and reward! (Billy Meredith, quoted in Harding, 1991, p.42).

*Players know that first and last they are the directors' chattels (dictionary definition of which is '**a moveable article of property**'). We are all their stocks and shares, their commodities. Perhaps worst of all, we are their playthings - their Lego blocks. When it suits them, they buy. When your job has been done or you don't perform to expectation or they just get bored with you, they divest. Nothing personal, you understand, business is business. What does it matter whether you're one hell of a nice guy, a complete arsehole or someways in between? You're their puppet and their attitude is that they have paid for the right to pull the strings (Nelson, 1995, p.237).*

2 Selling Soles

Contract and control in football

With the World Cup being held in the United States in 1994, the last bastion of football impenetrability was breached. For the first time, the foremost international football championship was held in a country with no sustained football culture - a requirement that up to that point had been considered crucial to attract the tournament. The importance of staging the competition in the United States cannot be overestimated. Earning the apocalyptic description of 'the last World Cup' (Redhead, 1994), it was certainly the first such occasion that attempted to harness the vast commercial market that had, until this time, been rather sketchily exploited.[1] Amazingly, given the spat that surrounded the English and West German bids to stage the World Cup 2006 (neither of whom has staged the tournament since 1966 and 1974 respectively) FIFA have intimated that the World Cup is likely to return to the United States in the relatively near future. Such is the sway of commerce in football today.

In England both the external and internal construction of professional football has been the subject of enormous change over a relatively short period. This transformation has affected how the game is played, viewed, organised and financed; in short, little is left untouched aside from the basic laws of the game. However, these too have also been subject to some tinkering, avowedly to improve the spectacle of the game although, perhaps fortunately, some of the more radical ideas such as widening the goals to increase the number of scoring possibilities have not yet been adopted.[2] Moreover, the leading players are able to command incredibly high financial rewards, partly as a result of the legal intervention by Jean-Marc Bosman which is discussed in detail later, which would have been unthinkable during the era of the maximum wage.

As part of the financial explosion, clubs are increasingly altering their corporate status from private to public in order to raise funds and this trend seems likely to continue. The commercialisation of football has taken a number of forms, perhaps the most cynical of which is the marketing of products as diverse as branded whisky, chocolate and soft drinks in addition to the more football related kits and videos.[3]

It remains to be seen whether this commercial development of parts of the game will be maintained given the 'boom and bust' cycle that has littered its past.

Consider the following quote from Pawson (1974, pp.180-1):

> Bournemouth's special aim is to be the first League club to run professionally a sports complex based on the football ground. Already their rebuilding programme is advanced and their eager young staff plan to make the stadium an entertainment centre open throughout the week. But everything will hinge on the football success and on overcoming the initial frustrations of promotion missed by a point and transfer payments far exceeding transfer returns despite the £200,000 received for Ted MacDougall. Bournemouth could not aim so high without the backing of a wealthy chairman. It is the same at Brighton and Hove Albion.

A quarter of a century, later such optimism seems wildly unfounded. Brighton and Hove Albion languished for most of the 1996/7 season at the bottom of the English Third Division, only narrowly escaping relegation and with the prospect of no permanent ground in the future, whilst Bournemouth Athletic moved at one stage into the hands of the official receivers. With all the glamour, excitement and, most of all, money that now appears to surround the game at the highest level it is easy to forget that, during the 1980s, professional football was facing a crisis that seemed to threaten its very survival. The 1980s were truly football's 'decadus horibilus'.[4] Whilst Britain languished in the worst recession since the 1930s, football began to feel the effects of the economic and social climate as its own infrastructure began, quite literally, to crumble. Many clubs had decaying grounds left under-maintained and undeveloped for years, the spectre of football hooliganism, squabbles over TV rights and dwindling attendances - all were crucial and depressing issues for football in the 1980s although even these were put into the shade by the tragic events at Bradford, Heysel and Hillsborough.

The Hillsborough Report (Taylor, 1990), the inquiry into the deaths of 95 Liverpool fans at an FA Cup semi final in April 1989, was the culmination of both football's worst decade and the last in a series of reports and inquiries that had examined a number of issues affecting football. Only four years earlier, Mr Justice Popplewell (Popplewell, 1985 & 1986) had been appointed to undertake an inquiry into events at the grounds of Bradford City and Birmingham City on 11 May 1985.[5] After Popplewell had begun his work, football was further shocked by the tragedy during the 1985 European Cup Final between Liverpool and Juventus at the Heysel stadium where thirty nine people died and many more were injured. Although 'Heysel' was not part of Popplewell's original remit, it was decided that he should take account of the events and any lessons that could be learned from that tragedy. Notwithstanding these official reports, Lord Justice Taylor expressed concern that his was the ninth official report covering crowd and ground safety and many of these had contained recommendations not acted upon. Certainly

Hillsborough provided football with one last chance to put its house in order - a chance that in the 1990s appears to have been largely grasped. One of the major problems faced by the football authorities was its somewhat strained relationship with the government of the day. On 13 March 1985 there was widespread crowd disorder at a sixth round FA Cup tie between Luton Town and Millwall played at Luton's Kenilworth Road ground:

> At the end of it, 47 people, including 33 police officers had been injured; 700 seats were ripped out of the Bobbers 'Family' stand by intruding Millwall fans, and damage inside the ground was estimated at £15,000. An estimated £10,000 worth of damage was also caused outside the ground where local residents - many of them of Asian origin - were attacked and their cars, homes and shops bricked. British Rail estimated the cost of damage to trains taking Millwall fans back to London at £45,000 (Williams *et al*. 1989, p.10).

The televised pictures of both this disturbance and of the hooliganism at the Chelsea versus Sunderland match at Stamford Bridge led to the direct intervention by the then Prime Minister, Mrs Thatcher. The Minister responsible, Neil Macfarlane, reported to the Commons on the day after the riot at Luton that Mrs Thatcher had personally requested that he obtain a report from the Football Association, within a week, detailing what action it intended to take against those clubs who had a history of crowd violence. Following this the Prime Minister and other senior Ministers met with representatives of the Football Association and the Football League on 1 April 1985 to discuss steps to counter hooliganism. Neil Macfarlane outlined to the House of Commons those steps that the football authorities would take including: examining the responsibilities of clubs, accelerating the introduction of CCTV, ensuring that perimeter fencing was in place at grounds where 'problem matches' might be played, the possibility of membership cards for certain matches, player behaviour, alcohol consumption at matches and encouraging family enclosures (*Hansard* (HC), 4 April 1985, Col. 752).

These measures reflected the government view that hooliganism was a problem for football rather than society generally, hence the use of CCTV, fencing and a ticketing policy. The emphasis was firmly on the authorities, the clubs and indeed the players to adapt their behaviour. Following the Heysel stadium disaster the Prime Minister had responded to Neil Kinnock's request for an investigation into 'the breakdown of behaviour in society' with a fierce rebuttal:

> The right Hon. Gentleman suggested that there should be an inquiry into crime and hooliganism. That could go on for years and find as many answers as there are

people on such an enquiry. There is violence in human nature. There are only three ways of trying to deal with it - persuasion, prevention or punishment. We shall try to operate all three (*Hansard* (HC), 3 June 1985, Col. 25).

Although primarily considered a problem for football, the Government had indicated that it would be prepared to legislate even without the support of the governing bodies. This is clearly demonstrated over the vexed issue of membership card schemes, investigation of which was in the 'shopping basket' of measures extracted from the authorities at the 1 April meeting. Following Popplewell (1986) the Government introduced the Football Spectators Bill which contained in Part I, Government proposals for a National Membership Scheme to be operated by the 'Football Membership Authority'. This scheme (although still within the *Football Spectators Act 1989*) has never been implemented following the conclusions of Taylor (1990).

Football's rehabilitation was certainly galvanised through the responses to the Hillsborough disaster although some positive steps had already been taken in terms of the creation of fan groups, such as the Football Supporters' Association, and the growth of the fanzine movement (Haynes, 1996). This transformation saw itself translated into new stadiums and a post 'Italia 90' respectability exemplified by Nick Hornby's Fever Pitch (1992):

> One of the by-products of *Fever Pitch* was the rehabilitation of football as a respectable pastime. At the time of its publication, a series of developments had already brought about fundamental changes in the football industry - most notably the Hillsborough disaster, but also the fanzine movement, supporters' associations, academic bodies like the Sir Norman Chester Football Research Centre, as well as an increase in public interest stimulated by England's performance in Italia 90. *Fever Pitch* seemed to crystallise this change of atmosphere, and provide a bridge into the game for a new middle-class audience (Barrett, 1997, p.88).

In tandem with these changes came the most far reaching organisational change - the formation, amongst much angst and debate, of the FA Premier League and the television and merchandising deals that ensued. With the greater financial clout that football now had, the players at the higher echelons of the game began to attract salaries and bonuses that would have been beyond the wildest dreams of players plying their trade even ten years before, let alone at the inception of the professional game, when terms and conditions were poor.[6] Contemporaneously, player contracts have become virtually unenforceable by clubs, with discontented players able to move almost at will irrespective of the remaining term.[7]

This chapter is essentially concerned with this development, of how players have come to enjoy this revolutionary change in terms and conditions, from limitations on wages and the historical restriction on changing clubs even at the end of their contractual period, to the current position. The context for the change in the players' bargaining position is the changing nature of the game itself in terms of organisation, commercialisation and administration.

The administrative structure of the game

> Football has always been characterised by a fascinating set of dynamics: North versus South; working class versus middle class and middle class versus upper class; new money versus old status. Professional players in the hundred years of the League's history have been predominantly working-class; administrators of the League have been predominantly first-generation middle-class; administrators on the level of the Football Association have been more upper-middle and middle-class. This has led to many clashes of values, of a classically patrician-plebian kind, in which the old amateur/professional tensions have been relived (Tomlinson, 1991, p.26).

A brief analysis of the changing nature of football's organisation is important in order to understand some of the contemporary trends within the game and particularly the increasing commercial opportunities for clubs and players. We are acutely aware that when discussing the financial explosion within football there is a tendency to generalise and, it ought to be recalled that, there are large areas of the professional game, which still retain more traditional characteristics.[8] Not all players and grounds have benefited from the increased income as fundamentally as those belonging to the leading clubs. A major historical division has revolved around the relationship between the Football Association and the Football League,[9] whilst at the beginning of the 1990s there were moves to amalgamate the two, the objects of the two bodies are markedly different. The Football Association is the governing body of the entire game, the guardian of the laws and responsible for football at all levels. It sanctions the creation of Leagues, the most important of which, historically, were the four divisions of the Football League which was subject to an annual contractual renewal. The object of the Football League was to run the League Championship, the League Cup[10] and other cup competitions for clubs within its jurisdiction. There is a great contrast between the League Cup, run by the League and confined to League clubs and the Football Association Challenge Cup (the FA Cup) which is open to all affiliated clubs. The latter tournament attracts great prestige partly because there is the opportunity for non league clubs to perform 'giant killing' exploits. In recent years the League Cup has been seen by some of the leading Premier clubs, generally those also engaged in European matches, as an unnecessary additional competition although up until the 1996/7 season it still carried an automatic place in the UEFA Cup for the winners.

The longstanding power struggle between the two bodies reappeared as the game attempted to restore its fortunes, after the disastrous 1980s. There had for some time been discontent inside the Football League itself, as the larger clubs of the first division sought to improve their financial position, even if this was at the expense of the smaller clubs. As Fynn and Guest (1994, p.22) neatly put it, Irving Scholar the Tottenham Hotspur Chairman thought his club had; 'more in common with Milan than Coventry City'. Of the two, the Football League was first out of the blocks with its proposals, launching 'One Game, One Team, One Voice' in October 1990. The essence of the plan was power sharing, a new joint body to run the English game. The Football Association sought to respond with its own vision and during a meeting in January 1991 at the Football Association Fynn (who was present as a consultant) describes what he terms the 'bombshell' dropped by Charles Hughes (Director of Coaching and Education). This bombshell was that the FA were ready to countenance a new Premier League comprising eighteen clubs; a move that would see the FA overseeing the new League and the 'trouble making' Football League marginalised forever (Fynn & Guest, 1994).

In June 1991 the proposals of the Football Association, 'The Blueprint for Football', were published; the Football League document having been rejected by the FA Council in April. At the heart of the proposals was a new structure at the top of the game. The Association strongly argued for a pre-eminent position for the national side at the 'apex of the pyramid of excellence'. It was submitted that the support for the national side had, in the past, conflicted with the Football League who had sought to maintain its own narrower interests. This dispute had, according to the Football Association, undermined the chances of success. The perceived need, therefore, was to create a position where the national side could thrive without conflict. The requirement was for a unified approach that, in essence, meant the domination of the Football Association but, more radically, a reduced number of clubs in the First Division:

> A smaller First Division of 18 Clubs would mean fewer matches and, therefore, more time in which to prepare players correctly for all matches including international matches. It would also mean less wear and tear on the players. This, in turn, would mean that standards of play and standards of fitness would increase. This would provide not only a better chance of success; it would also produce an improved product in commercial terms (FA, 1991, Para 4.3).

The problem, though, was how to manage this change. Given that the Football

League represented all the League clubs, it was unlikely that it would support a reduction in the First Division. It would certainly not be in the interests of many of those clubs already in the top flight who were perennially concerned with relegation, or those in the division below, who wanted to gain promotion. A smaller number of clubs at the top represented fewer opportunities to join this elite group and, with the likely opposition of the Football League to such proposals, the Football Association saw two alternatives; either a break away league or a 'Premier League' within the administration of the Football Association. This was in many ways a revolutionary proposal, that the Football Association ought to run the major professional league in addition to its widespread responsibilities for the game. In support it cited the German example where this structure existed and argued that this was a contributory factor in the German national side's success which in turn had led to Germany's powerful influence within both UEFA and FIFA. The Football Association Council had already supported the principle at its meeting in April 1991 for the league to commence at the start of the 1992-3 season. One of the key arguments advanced by the Football Association, in support of this new structure, were the improved commercial opportunities that it would provide. However, the Football League was not going to surrender without a struggle and the proposals eventually led to litigation.

The legal battle ground was fought over an application for judicial review of the Football Association's decision. In order to join the infant Premier League, clubs would have to give notice to quit the existing League and both the Football Association and the Football League had regulations governing such termination. In 1988 the League had amended its rules to encourage commercial sponsorship so that a club leaving had either to give three season's notice or, indemnify the League. Clearly, such a requirement would act as a serious impediment to the new League and, in 1991, the Association amended its own rules so that any rule of the Football League that required a longer notice period than that required by FA rules was void. The decision of the Football Association to form the Premier League and institute such a rule change led the Football League to seek judicial review. The FA, meanwhile, had already issued its own summons seeking a declaration that it had acted within its powers. Whilst the first two proceedings were expedited and heard together, there was a third action, based in tort and contract, grounded on the same factual issues. Clearly, the outcome of the case was crucial in determining where the real power base of English football would lie in the future. Rose J's decision was unequivocal; 'I have crossed a great deal of ground in order to reach what, on the authorities, is the clear and inescapable conclusion for me that the FA is not a body susceptible to judicial review either in general, or more particularly, at the instigation of the League, with whom it is contractually bound' (*FA v FL*, 1993, p.848).

It was clear that there were no legal impediments to the actions of the Football Association and the new Premier League was duly launched in the 1992/3 season. However, the Football Association was not in total control of the events and, as the old first division clubs sought to join the new League, it became apparent that the new League would have far more autonomy than first envisaged. The commitment to an eighteen club division disappeared and it started with the full complement of twenty two. In many ways the 'new' Premier League carried with it the same contradictions and disputes that had existed in the old first division, the existing grievances had merely been transported into a new structure. The divide between the bigger and smaller clubs was maintained and again brought to a head over the sale of television rights which saw BSkyB win the contract against the wishes of the 'Big Five' clubs (Fynn & Guest, 1994). The major success of the Premier League has been the income it has attracted; these resulting riches of the Premier League clubs have caused some consternation throughout the remainder of the professional league and such concern was firmly repudiated by the Football Association. Despite the fact that the new league has been an undoubted footballing success the original 'dream' has not been completely realised. There are still significant club versus country disputes and, whilst the England side is becoming more successful, it is difficult to attribute this importance directly to the new structure. As Fynn and Guest (1994, p.xi) adroitly note the power battle has only been shifted and not resolved:

> In the culmination of a battle that had raged for most of the 1980s, the Football League was all but destroyed as the first division created their own Premier League. The FA, which initiated the breakaway, was itself sidelined in all the important decisions concerning the new league and within a year played no part whatever in its operation. Instead of creating one all-powerful body, which was the FA's original intention, there were now three completely separate power-centres; the FA, the new Premier League and the rump of the old Football League. Far from the national team being placed at the top, it once again has to exist in a system in which no-one can be sure what the real priorities are.

The shape of football has changed and the increasing income for the top clubs has led to an influx of foreign players. At the highest level, clubs have introduced leading overseas players, such as Asprilla, Gullit, Bergkamp and Zola from both Europe and South America. Part of the European dimension to player movement has been the *Bosman* decision, though, more important is the ability of clubs to offer significant financial incentives to the players. This 'invasion' has brought with it some concerns about the long term effects on the game, in terms of opportunities for young players, and the consequent effect on the national side.

What is clear is that, for those at the top of their profession the status and financial rewards have never been higher. Players 'out of contract' can move freely between clubs and the restrictive effect of the transfer system has been greatly reduced. To achieve this progress for players has however taken some considerable time and required collective organisation, threats of industrial action and legal intervention.

Towards a players' union

The first attempt to form a players' union was that instigated by 'Billy' Rose of Wolverhampton Wanderers, who wrote to all League clubs in 1893, suggesting that leading players should get together to have a voice on the issues that were pertinent to them - his efforts, however, met with little response. After this abortive first venture, it came as something of a surprise when the *Lancashire Daily Post* in 1897, reported that 'Football Professionals Form a Union', a body that, by February 1898, was known as the Association Footballers' Union and was involved in the day to day running of the game. Whilst this inaugural attempt to start a proactive union met with little success, it proved to be the precursor of a stronger movement that drew comfort from what was happening in the Trades Union Movement generally.[11] In December 1907 at the Imperial Hotel in Manchester, the Professional Footballers' Association (PFA) was formed. Chaired by Billy Meredith of Manchester United it was far better organised and supported than the defunct Association Footballers' Union. Shortly after its inception, it claimed to count the majority of players in League football as members. At this point, the union was seen by the governing bodies as a fairly innocuous organisation because of its weak financial position (Harding, 1991). It became apparent very early on that the PFA would only be able to assert itself fully by taking legal action. The case of *Kingaby* proved to be the first test brought to challenge the PFA's chief bone of contention - the transfer system.

Kingaby was bought by Aston Villa in 1906 from Clapton Orient and was paid £4 per week for his services. Soon after he had been signed, however, Aston Villa decided that they no longer required him and offered him back to his former club for half the price they had paid for him. Orient could not afford even the reduced fee and, accordingly, Kingaby was placed upon Aston Villa's retained players list. As he was not receiving any wages, Kingaby moved to Fulham, who at the time were in the Southern League and not covered by the League's regulations (he was prevented from signing for any other club in the League because of the 'retained list' agreement). In 1910, the Football League signed an agreement with the Southern League and Kingaby, by then a player at Leyton Orient, found himself again on Aston Villa's books. However, he now had an increased price tag on his head and was effectively prevented from playing football as Villa refused his request for a free transfer to Croydon Common. Whilst the PFA saw this as a perfect opportunity for them to test the legal water, Kingaby was determined at first, to attempt to win his case without assistance.

Aston Villa eventually offered him the free transfer he requested, at which point Kingaby told the Union he would be prepared to carry on with the case if they 'conceded certain terms to him', terms which Veitch, the PFA Chairman, thought ridiculous. With rumours circulating that the Union had dropped the case, Veitch threatened to reveal the demands that Kingaby had made and Kingaby, in turn, threatened to sue the Union for libel. It was in this confused legal state that Kingaby and the Union joined forces once more and the case of *Kingaby* opened. Harding (1991) contends that counsel for Kingaby made a critical mistake early in the case when he sought to attack the motives of the club rather than the system itself - certainly the case proved a disaster for the Union with the judge holding, within two days, that Aston Villa had no case to answer.

The tension that was evident between the PFA and the Football League was still prevalent in the late 1950s. Hill (1963) complains of the lack of any meaningful negotiations, which he attributed to the attitude of some members of the Football League Management Committee. Whilst the twin elements of the maximum wage and the retain and transfer system were still staunchly supported by the League, Alan Hardaker (League Secretary) maintained that, not only had they withstood the test of time, but that any change would result in the sort of anarchy that existed before the League was formed. Cliff Lloyd for the PFA rebutted this anachronistic assertion; 'This is surely a long time ago and I can hardly feel that those gentlemen who founded the League thought the maximum wage and transfer system would continue to be doggedly insisted upon without any real variation over seventy years afterwards...' (Harding, 1991, p.276). The dispute over terms and conditions continued with little sign of movement and was subsequently brought to a head by the players in 1960:

> At the AGM of the Professional Footballers' Association, the facts previously recorded of the two years' negotiations were put before the delegates of the League clubs. They were so enraged at the irresponsibility of the authorities, and particularly at their refusal to discuss what had been the two main bones of contention since the players' organisation started, that they empowered the Committee to take any steps they thought necessary to bring about the removal of these restrictive and unjust Football League rules (Hill, 1963, p.24).

At the AGM, four fundamental issues were isolated for negotiation; (i) the abolition of the maximum wage provisions, (ii) that a player was to have a right to retain a slice of his transfer fee, (iii) that a new system dealing with player retention was to be developed, and (iv) that a new contract be drawn up that was more in line with the needs of modern players.[12] The League's response was to offer certain concessions such as, a rise in the minimum wage, an increased television fee and a sum to be paid to players on the transfer list. This, however, failed to deal with the roots of the PFA's discontent - the maximum wage and the transfer system. As Hill (1963) observes, whilst agreeing an increase in television fees, the League was also deciding that there would not be any televised matches. The response of the PFA was to organise three players' meetings in London, Birmingham and Manchester that, virtually unanimously, supported taking further action in support of their original demands.[13] Accordingly, the League's offer was rejected and the PFA issued a strike notice that would expire on 21 January 1961. With the threat of a strike causing the League some disquiet, significant concessions were offered; the abolition of the maximum wage and the promise of longer contracts being the centrepiece. The offer still, however, failed to tackle the main bone of contention, the retain and transfer provisions, and the PFA rejected the offer as it stood after having consulted its members. On 18 January, three days before the strike was due to begin, the two sides met with Labour Conciliation Officer, Tom Claro as 'referee', in an attempt to forge a resolution of the dispute:

> After two-and-a-half hours of talks, the PFA men went to an adjoining room to consult with the rest of the Management Committee. At 6.45 the Minister of Labour, Mr Hare, was summoned to make an announcement to a gathering of some sixty press and TV men. Agreement had been reached concerning the retain and transfer system. The battle, it seemed, had been won! (Harding, 1991, p.278).

Whilst the seven point agreement produced euphoria in many quarters, it was soon to emerge that it was not all that it first appeared. The agreement, basically, provided that, if a player refused terms that were offered, he would be put on the transfer list and his availability would be made known to other clubs. If he had not been transferred by 30 June, he would receive a minimum wage and, if still not transferred by 31 July, would be placed on a monthly contract until the League Management Committee could sort out the dispute. Further to this, whilst it had been heralded as a significant shift in the retain and transfer system, many league clubs were hostile to any change in provisions that they felt were crucial to the health of the game. Accordingly, at the Extraordinary General Meeting, the League Management Committee rejected the deal completely. The League's position was that, without the retain and transfer system, there would be chaos with agents entering into the contractual equation and the clubs being forced into extortionate deals. The PFA insistence on a clause that provided for a player who refused terms to be retained and also placed on the transfer list caused problems -

the League eventually compromised, whereby a player could refuse terms and be placed on a weekly wage as long as the Club so wished.

After seventy years, a further year of meetings, strike calls and Ministry of Labour intervention little meaningful change had been produced. The 'new deal' had effectively removed the maximum wage provisions whilst leaving the retain and transfer system largely intact. The militant mood of the players and, in particular, the support of the 'star' players (who as they saw it had won the main victory) began to wilt. Whilst union action seemed unlikely to be the way forward, given the divided nature of the players, the PFA was given the chance to confront the League provisions, through the Courts, rather than by direct action, when George Eastham began his attempt to free himself from his contract with Newcastle United.

Shovelling coal in Newcastle

At the heart of the *Eastham* case was the way in which players could be traded between clubs. The career of a professional footballer is necessarily a perilous one; not only is it the case that few can command the type of wages that stars such as Alan Shearer and Dennis Bergkamp reputedly earn, but their careers may be cut short at any time by injury, loss of form or even by failing to fulfil early potential. At the end of their relatively short career (normally at the age of around 35 if they are able to maintain fitness) few players in the past have been able to amass a sufficient nest egg to allow themselves a reasonable standard of living. Similarly, few players have taken advantage of the opportunities, provided to members of the PFA, to participate in vocational training schemes that might help them find a career after football.[14] Footballers were, whilst the retain and transfer system existed, unable to maximise their potential earnings in the free market. This restriction has been described as a; 'monopsonistic device, [which] together with a system of maximum wages, severely limited the economic freedom and income of players' (Dabscheck, 1986, p.351). It is ironic that, given the difficulties encountered during the fight to remove it, the original perspective (in an 1899 memo) of the Football Association towards the transfer market was:

> the practice of buying and selling players is unsportsmanlike and most objectionable in itself, and ought not to be entertained by those who desire to see the game played under proper conditions...some clubs derived considerable pecuniary advantages from training young players and then selling them to the more prominent clubs. We think the practice in such cases, when applied to human beings, altogether discreditable to any system bearing the name of sport (quoted in Dabscheck, 1991, p.223).

This view was not maintained by the Football Association and the Football League considered that the retain and transfer system continued to occupy a crucial position at the heart of the professional game. The fundamental principle of the retain and transfer system was that a player was bound to the club he originally signed to, for the rest of his playing life, unless the club saw fit to release him. At the end of each season clubs operated two lists, the first containing the players which the club wished to retain, the second, those players the club wanted to transfer. Whilst often the two lists or systems operated in tandem, this was not necessarily the case and each system requires examination.

Players were at the time employed by league clubs on yearly contracts that ran from 1 July to 30 June. The contract contained a specific clause that the player would be bound by the regulations of the governing bodies. Clubs had to register all players with both the FA and the Football League if relevant. No player could be registered for more than one club and any move between clubs involved a transfer of registration with approval required from the relevant governing bodies. It was within the Football Association rules that the following provisions were contained. At the end of the contract period there were four possible outcomes; (i) The player might be *re-registered* for his own club between 1 April and the first Saturday in May; his contract was simply renewed; (ii) The player might be *retained* by the Club serving a notice (between 1 May and the first Saturday in June) detailing the terms that the Club was offering. The wages need not be the same as the previous engagement but must have been the minimum (£418 per year at the time of *Eastham*). If the Football Association considered the offer to be too low it was able to refuse the retention. The consequences of the retention was that the player remained a registered player of the club and was debarred from signing for any other club. A player could be retained by this method indefinitely; (iii) The player might be placed on the transfer list at a fee fixed by the club; or (iv) If none of the preceding options were taken the player would be free to negotiate independently with any club at the end of June.

The power to retain a player was a potent one especially given that the wages offered could be reduced to the bare minimum, subject to Football Association consideration. If the player were retained, he would still need to sign a new agreement in order to be available to play for the club but perhaps more importantly, to be paid. If option (ii) was adopted, the player had two choices; sign the contract at the offered rate or refuse to sign. This option was in essence a 'half way house' between re-registration, which would happen if he re-signed under the terms offered, and transfer listing. The player could seek to appeal to the Football Association that there were special grounds that should allow him to change clubs despite the fact that the original club sought to retain his services.

The transfer system

If a player was moved onto the transfer list, his name and the fee required would appear on the register sent to the League, before the end of the season and after the decisions on player retention had been made. This list would then be circulated to all clubs. The fee was determined by the club and, in order to be transferred successfully, the player and club had to sign the requisite form which would then be approved by the League. No transfer could be registered until the fee had been paid. If a club was prepared to pay the requisite amount, the player could be duly registered with the new club, however, whilst on the transfer list there was no obligation for the original club to pay the player. Indeed, he was in a quasi-contractual position, not entitled to payment but neither free to move, unless the player moved outside of the League.[15] The only alternative for a player in limbo was to appeal to the League Management Committee who had the power to reduce the fee being requested or even to give the player a free transfer. The risk for the club in placing a player on the transfer list, was that they might not get the fee they wanted or indeed any payment at all.[16] Clubs could avoid this by keeping the player on the retained list, so, in essence, although they might be quite content to transfer the player, they would place him on the retained list in order to prevent the possibility of a reduced fee or free transfer being granted.

George Eastham began playing for the Ards club in Northern Ireland in 1952 and, after turning professional in 1956 accepted a transfer to Newcastle United for a fee of £9,000 on the normal annual renewable contract. In December 1959 Eastham asked to be placed on the transfer list, some four months later in April 1960 the club informed him that it had decided to retain him for the 1960/61 season at his current wage and the club gave the Football League notice of his retention on 3 May 1960. Eastham refused to re-sign and, unable to move clubs, sought employment in a business unrelated to football. He wrote, in July 1960, to the League Management Committee to ask their permission for a transfer, as he felt unable to continue playing for Newcastle. Newcastle, for their part, made representations to the Committee stating that they had acted in accordance with the regulations and expressing their hope that; 'the management committee will uphold them in the stand which they had felt bound to take' (*Eastham*, 1963, p.151). On 22 July the appeal was rejected as it was considered to be purely a matter between the player and club. Eastham then appealed to the League Management Committee, under a more general regulation, which required them to adjudicate on disputes between club and player. Unable to cajole Eastham to re-sign, Newcastle instructed the club's manager to effect a transfer. This decision was reported to the League and was sufficient for the League to determine that the problem had been resolved. This was almost two months after his first reference to the Committee and from the manoeuvrings it appeared that the League was backing the club in the dispute with the player.[17] There was clear evidence of the club communicating little to the player whilst informing the League that they would transfer him. In early October Eastham's solicitors wrote to the club requesting that their client be placed on the transfer list at a fee that was 'not prohibitive'. The club failed to reply and accordingly the writ was issued on 13 October.

The PFA saw the case as an opportunity to challenge the lawfulness of the retain and transfer system and, after a consideration of cost and overall chances of success, decided to pursue the action. A prime motivation for using this as a test case was that Eastham was a model professional who had conducted himself with great decorum in this matter. This was in great contrast with some of the comments attributed to Newcastle directors, one of whom allegedly; 'declared that he would see Eastham shovel coal before he left Newcastle' (Harding, 1991, p.283). The writ was served by the union solicitor alleging that the club was depriving him of any opportunity to ply his trade and acting in restraint of trade. The immediate reaction was that during November, Newcastle allowed Eastham to sign for Arsenal for £47,500. Whilst Eastham no longer had any direct interest in pursuing his action, he was persuaded to continue. The case was heard in the High Court in 1963 and the important judgement given by Wilberforce J, who at the outset outlined the issues involved within the context of football and his task:

> The transfer system has been stigmatised by the plaintiff's counsel as a relic from the Middle Ages, involving the buying and selling of human beings as chattels; and, indeed, to anyone not hardened to acceptance of the practice it would seem inhuman, and incongruous to the spirit of a national sport. One must not forget that the consent of a player to the transfer is necessary, but, on the other hand, the player has little security since he cannot get a long term contract and, while he is on the transfer list awaiting an offer, his feelings and anxieties as to who his next employer is to be may not be very pleasant. The defendants and their directors - such of them, at least, who appeared before me - reasonable men whose attitude to their players was as much paternal as proprietary, have evolved a euphemistic description of the transfer fee which apparently satisfies their consciences - they do not 'sell' players, they receive compensation for the transfer of the registration. In this case I am not called on to choose between the descriptions of the practice; all that I have to decide is whether the plaintiff's attack on the system as opposed to a recognised principle of English law can succeed (*Eastham*, 1963, p.145-146).

Eastham claimed that the retention provisions operated in restraint of trade as; 'they restrict[ed] his freedom to seek employment and use his skill after the termination of his engagement' (*Eastham*, 1963, p.146). They had effectively kept him out of professional football for three months before the writ was served. It was argued by the defendants that the retention system was merely an option to extend the contract, however, the player needed to re-sign before any new contract came into being. The player was retained in that he could not move elsewhere but was not actually contractually bound; his previous contract had expired, a new one not yet brought into existence, yet he was not a free agent. Wilberforce J considered that the retention system might be justified if it only operated for a short period (such as whilst the club sought to buy a replacement), however, in its present guise, it could have indefinite effect and was used, in practice, to enhance the power of a club who actually wished to transfer the player. As the two systems (of retain and transfer) operated in tandem, Wilberforce J moved to consider whether or not the combined system was justifiable. The defendants had argued that complete freedom of movement after the end of any contract period would be disastrous for the public, most of the clubs and 'the large majority of professional footballers'. The rationale was that, if the retention system was abolished, the best players would be signed by the wealthier clubs, especially given that the maximum wage provisions had recently been removed (interestingly, a similar argument was to be raised some thirty years later in *Bosman*). The judge rejected this view and, accordingly ruled that the legitimate interests of the Association, the League and the employing club could not justify the system in its present form. With respect to the transfer system he noted the benefits that flowed from it (essentially supporting the necessary circulation of players and financially assisting the poorer clubs at times) and thought that the restraint involved could be legitimate. The problem though was the umbilical relationship between the issues of retention and transfer:

> I conclude that the combined retention and transfer system as existing at the date of the writ is in unjustifiable restraint of trade, but that is as far as I am prepared to go; whether the transfer system could be justified if supported by a modified retention system, one which would let the player free after a short period, or if it were divorced entirely from the retention system, is another matter which is not the subject of dispute in the present action, nor one which I have the material to decide (*Eastham*, 1963, p.150).

Accordingly the declarations sought against the Club, the League and the Association were granted. The challenge now for the football authorities was to devise a system, or adapt the old one to encompass the judge's comments whilst still retaining some lawful control over player movement. The result of the decision was an immediate change in the arrangements for the retention and transfer of professional players. At the end of the playing season each club had to indicate which players it wanted to retain and which were being placed on the transfer list. Any players not on either list were able to obtain free transfers when their contract expired; players placed on the transfer list might also be free transfers or the club could require a fee. If the player was still required by the club, he would be offered terms and would have twenty eight days to accept, and re-sign, or reject them. If the player had not signed by 30 June a dispute was deemed to exist between club and player. It is essentially at this point that the changes, forced by *Eastham*, appeared. The Management Committee of the League could adjudicate, if requested, by either party and this process had to be completed by 31 July. If the player still disputed the principle of his retention or indeed the terms that he was being offered by 31 August, the matter could be heard by a new Independent Tribunal. The Tribunal could hold a personal hearing at the request of either party and had to determine the case by 30 September. Throughout this time the player continued to receive his contractual wages despite the fact that he had not re-signed. The tribunal was also open to those on the transfer list that contested the size of the fee being sought. Thus disputes over the issue of retention, the terms on which it was offered or indeed the nature of the transfer could be subject to independent arbitration.[18]

The post *Eastham* changes to the workings of the transfer market were outlined by the Chester Committee (1968) who argued that the abolition of the maximum wage coupled with the increased freedom to move had reduced the number of retained players, as evidenced in the following table:

June	No. of registered profs	Transfer Fee Required	Percentage of Total	Free Transfers	Percentage of Total
1962	2,640	192	7.3	296	11.2
1963	2,511	179	7.1	317	12.6
1964	2,466	214	8.7	355	14.4
1965	2,415	86	3.6	489	20.2
1966	2,384	70	2.9	480	20.1
1967	2,395	55	2.3	410	17.1

Source: (Chester, 1968, p.77)

It is clear that from the 1965 season there was a large increase in the number of players who obtained a free transfer and a corresponding decrease in the number of players for whom a fee was sought. It was argued that the lessening of the constraints on players that had been imposed by the old retain and transfer system could be viewed as a double edged sword; 'This change has meant greater freedom for the player. But unless another club is prepared to offer him a contract at least as good as that offered by his existing club it is freedom bought at the expense of his pocket' (Chester, 1968, p.77). Chester (1968, p.81) also proposed that the existing contractual arrangements should be further altered particularly with respect to the requirement for option periods in the contracts that were renewable only by the club:

> We can appreciate the value to the club and to the player, and indeed the game as a whole, of having professional players in formal contractual relationship with their clubs. But a contract which is renewable indefinitely on a year to year basis at the option of one of the parties seems to us to go beyond the normal contractual relationship and to be more one-sided than the situation demands. In general we are against one-way options unless freely negotiated. **We recommend** that every contract between club and player should be for a definite period at the end of which either party should be free to renew it.

This was the next stage on from *Eastham*, the movement towards a greater degree of freedom for players at the end of a clearly defined contract period. It would be a significant step, as it would mean that transfer fees would only apply during the duration of the agreement. It was argued that this would provide a more legitimate rationale for the payment of fees, it would relate directly to the 'buying out' of a contracted player rather than appear as 'the buying and selling of men'. If such a system had been adopted, it would, undoubtedly, have led to longer contract periods and more purposeful negotiations, as clubs would no longer have the option period to fall back upon. The Chester recommendations gave further impetus to the PFA in their ongoing negotiations with the League. After several false starts, the new Joint Negotiating Committee, which comprised members from both sides, and an independent chairman, established the basis for eventual agreement. Players out of contract could move freely to another club but a form of compensation would be payable to the former employer. The League rejected using a multiplier based on (amongst other factors) age and wages but the other principles were accepted. Thus by 1978 the League and PFA had negotiated a new system which recognised the right of players to change clubs at the end of their contracts. More than this, a change in leadership at both the PFA and Football League[19] heralded a major shift in the relationship between the parties with daily contact between the two and a common regard that; 'their basic function as finding solutions to the various problems that emerge' (Dabscheck, 1986, p.351). The rationale and operation of the system is neatly outlined by a former player:

> Transfer tribunals were the logical and inevitable consequence of the PFA gaining 'freedom of contract' rights for players. Their coming into being arose from the need for an independent body to reconcile the 'legal rights' of the parties - existing employer club, employee player, would-be employer club - involved in negotiations/dispute as an existing contract comes to its end. A player's current club have two options. They can dispense with a player - i.e., give him a 'free' - or retain him. Crucially, to retain him they must offer him a new contract that is at least as favourable as the one just ending. This does create problems for Boards. With players who are doing the business well enough to justify the original outlay on them and justify their first team selection, the club will not want the contract to expire. Every attempt will usually be made to offer a new one that is sufficiently attractive for the player to want to sign. But he (and certainly where applicable, his agent!) will appreciate that he is negotiating from a position of strength. What he now considers 'attractive' may be a considerable escalation on his previous terms (Nelson, 1995, pp.261-262).

The freedom that the Tribunal system has brought can also provide those players, who have some leverage, with increased bargaining power with the club who wishes to retain the player's services, although, the step from compensation at the end of a contract to complete unrestricted freedom of movement was to be taken outside of the domestic relationship.

Another famous Belgian

> Football was thrown into financial turmoil last night with a European Court ruling that threatens to bankrupt half of England's football clubs (*The Guardian*, front page, 21 September, 1995).

The quote above gives a flavour of the English media's response to the European Court of Justice (ECJ) decision in the *Bosman* case. Jean-Marc Bosman, a Belgian footballer, signed as a professional in 1986 with Standard Liege, a Belgian first division club. He was transferred in 1988 to SA Royal Club Liegeois, on a two year contract, with earnings of approximately BFR 120,000 per month. Immediately prior to the expiry of this contract, he was offered a new one year contract but on the basic minimum wage (BFR 30,000 per month) as provided by the rules of the Belgian Football Association. Bosman refused this offer and was, accordingly, placed on the transfer list which was forwarded to the national association. Throughout May, a player on the list could be compulsorily transferred with the move agreed between the player and the new club, even against the wishes of the old club. To prevent any financial impediments being constructed, the fee was subject to a mathematical calculation, viewed as compensation for the original club. The formula was based upon multiplying the player's gross annual income by a factor between two and fourteen, according to age. Accordingly, Bosman's fee was set at BFR 11,743,000, a fee that did not attract any interest from buyers. He then negotiated a temporary one season transfer to the French second division club, US Dunkerque for a fee of BFR 1,200,000 plus an option for a permanent transfer for an additional BFR 4,800,000. However, the deal had to be completed by 2 August and RC Liege, doubting the ability of US Dunkerque to pay, failed to obtain the requisite clearance certificate from the Belgian Football Association. The contract collapsed and RC Liege suspended Bosman; if they had not done so, under the Association rules, Bosman would have been re-classed as an amateur player. This route would still have been open after two years suspension without a new contract or transfer, though also without playing. Bosman's response was to seek a court order requiring the club, not only to pay him until he changed clubs but also to not claim any fee for him. This was coupled with a request for a referral to the European Court of Justice as to the lawfulness of the transfer restrictions. All three were originally granted although on appeal the court, whilst upholding the first two parts of the claim, overturned the referral to the ECJ.

Bosman was able to obtain a contract with another French second division club, Saint-Quentin, though this was terminated at the end of the first season. After a contract with Saint-Denis de la Reunion, Bosman signed for the Belgian third division club Royal Olympic Club de Charleroi, in May 1993. His main action, which encompassed a claim for damages, against Liege was proceeding and in August 1991 UEFA was joined as a defendant. Prior to this, the Belgian Football Association had sought a declaration that its rules and the relevant UEFA rules were valid. The rationale for this move was, that part of Bosman's claim was based on the assertion that the rules of the transfer system were unlawful. Bosman, simultaneously, brought a claim against UEFA itself, arguing that its transfer system rules amounted to a breach of Articles 48, 85 and 86 of the Treaty of Rome. By April 1992 the claim had been refined to include an order that the transfer rules **and** the rules limiting the number of foreign players did not apply to him. Finally, in June 1992 the court made a reference to the ECJ as to whether the rules of the transfer system were contrary to Articles 48, 85 and 86; this position was upheld by the Court of Appeal, which made its own (and the third) reference to the ECJ. The two questions referred from the Court of Appeal to the ECJ for a preliminary ruling were whether Articles 48, 85 and 86 of the Treaty of Rome of 25 March 1957 were to be interpreted as:

(i) prohibiting a football club from requiring and receiving payment of a sum of money upon the engagement of one of its players who has come to the end of his contract by a new employing club;

(ii) prohibiting the national and international sporting associations or federations from including in their respective regulations provisions restricting access of foreign players from the European Community to the competitions which they organize? (*Bosman*, 1996, p.152)

It is apparent that there were two very different, but clearly important issues at stake; the validity of a transfer fee at the end of the contract period, but also the lawfulness of the UEFA imposed restrictions on 'foreign players'. This latter issue had been the subject of considerable negotiation between UEFA and the Commission over a long period and had, more recently, in 1989, included an investigation by the European Parliament (Vahrenwald, 1996). Whilst there had been some movement by UEFA, it seemed clear that, eventually, the matter would have to be finally determined as there was a strong argument that the restrictions could be considered incompatible with aspects of Community law relating to free movement and anti-competitive practices. Weatherill (1989, p.87) suggests that the 'national' dimension of football created a potential source of conflict:

> The organization of football appears to be on a collision course with more than one area of the Treaty of Rome. This should not occasion surprise. The industry is one which retains strong national identities, while at the same time operating, as it has for many years, internationally. European attitudes are beneficial to football, in that the sphere of attractive and lucrative competition is widened, but also constitute a threat to the game in the light of the fact that a continuing national identity within a national League remains a strong motive for continued spectator/customer support.

This, in many ways, is the crux of the issue, the fitting of the individual national football associations and leagues into a European Community framework that demands standardisation of economic elements such as free movement of players. This conflict is also apparent at a lower level. Within the English national game, there has been a continual simmering dispute between club and country over the availability of players.[20] A parallel of which has recently emerged in the newly professionalised rugby union. As discussed earlier, one of the major reasons for the formation of the break away Premier League was to create a structure which placed the English national side at the top of the pyramid. The Football Association may seek to speak on behalf of English football but, because of the internal contradictions inside the professional game, it cannot always provide a consensus view. The English game is not homogenous but, combinations of self interest that sometimes concur; certainly, an analysis of a number of areas demonstrate this point, not least a perusal of responses to the negotiations over the television deal in 1992.[21] Some of the leading clubs have come into conflict with the governing bodies over issues such as participation in the League Cup and fixture congestion.[22] A possible, or indeed probable development, which would indicate the ability of clubs to transcend national issues, is the formation of a European 'Super League', an idea which is periodically mooted. Whilst this would undoubtedly be beneficial to the elite clubs involved, it would, as with the Football League Cup issue, leave the domestic leagues poorer. It would also weaken the power of the national associations who would see the leading competition move out of their control. In essence, this move has started with the change in 1997/8 to the European Champions League structure and the additional admittance of sides who had obtained second place in their national leagues. With the league structure of the competition it is possible to see how the transition to a European league might easily be organised; 'the Champions League is all-important. It is turning into a European League and over the next three or four years I think that will become more and more clear' (Arsene Wenger, Arsenal manager reported in *The Guardian,* 21 October, 1997).

Whatever the long term future for the organisation of administration of football the ECJ had to determine issues pertinent to the immediate structure. Both questions to the ECJ were limited to their operation in the professional game only. The question of the applicability of European law to the sphere of sport had been previously dealt with by the court and it was returned to by Advocate General Lenz in his opinion. Reviewing the cases of *Walrave* and *Dona* Lenz drew the following conclusions:

> ...(1) The rules of private sports associations are also subject to Community law. (2)The field of sport is subject to Community law in so far as it constitutes an economic activity. (3) The activities of professional football players are in the nature of gainful employment and are therefore subject to Community law. (4) Either art 48 or art 59 applies to those activities, with no differences arising therefrom. (5) The court allows certain exceptions to the prohibitions contained in those provisions (*Bosman*, 1996, p.104).

Whilst *Dona* had demonstrated that professional (and indeed semi-professional) football constituted an economic activity and was therefore subject to community law, UEFA and the Belgian Football Association argued that the provisions of Articles 48, 85 and 86 should not apply to situations such as those in the present case. One of their more implausible arguments centred upon an idea that, only the biggest clubs in Europe constituted an economic activity, and that many clubs, including those concerned in the *Bosman* action, did not have this crucial characteristic. This was given short shrift by Lenz who held that, if professional football had been held to be an economic activity, then it mattered little whether the club concerned was large or small or whether their profits were astronomic or not. In a similar vein, UEFA argued that, if the provisions of Article 48 were to apply to transfers then, as the purpose of these rules was, avowedly, to subsidise smaller clubs, the court's decision would necessarily impact upon all of football and not just the professional game. Lenz felt here that, whilst the effect of the decision would undoubtedly have to be taken into account, the question that they in fact were considering at this stage was one of the applicability of European law and that UEFA's submission on this point was somewhat misplaced. A further argument raised by the Belgian Football Association was that, as most of the football clubs under its jurisdiction were non-profit making, the rules on transfers had no relevance between club and player and that, therefore, Article 48 would not be applicable, another point that Lenz could not accept:

> The distinction suggested by URBSFA is of an artificial character and does not correspond to reality. The rules on transfers...are of direct and central importance for a player who wishes to change club. *That is shown precisely by the present case: if it had not been for the transfer rules, nothing would have hindered Mr Bosman's transfer to US Dunkerque (Bosman, 1996, p.105).*

UEFA outlined two further arguments in favour of exempting sport from Article 48 on the basis that, firstly this provision was not appropriate to deal with the peculiar problems of sport, and also a tenuous line of argument, that the situation was purely an internal one and not within the ambit of Community law. Lenz dismissed both arguments. He then considered the applicability of Article 48 to the system of transfers and the rules on foreign players. Article 48 provides that freedom of movement for workers is a prime facet of Community law and further that 'such freedom of movement shall entail the abolition of any discrimination based on nationality between workers of the member states as regards employment, remuneration and other conditions of work and employment'. This freedom of movement is only qualified by certain limitations on the basis of public policy, public security and public health.

The regulations on foreign players concerned limitations that were in place in various member states, limiting the number of non-home players who could be fielded at any one time by a team. This also applied to competitions run under the auspices of UEFA, and hampered a number of English clubs engaged in European competitions, notably Manchester United who had the thorny problem of who to leave out amongst Schmeichel, Kanchelskis, Cantona, Irwin and Keane in the

1994 Champions' League campaign. By the time Bosman brought his action the limitation imposed by UEFA under a 'Gentleman's agreement' with the Commission was a '3+2' (three foreign players plus two assimilates).[23] The Advocate General conceded that it was less obvious why Bosman was fighting this aspect of discrimination, though the player had argued that he might well wish to seek employment outside of Belgium (which he had actually done in moving to France) and that his efforts to do so could be hindered by the 'foreign player restriction'. The Advocate General also conceded that the ECJ, on the basis of its own decisions, could choose not to consider the second question but, urged it to do so, in order that this controversial issue could be determined. As Lenz observed, the foreign player restriction had been the subject of considerable negotiation between the football authorities and the Commission, since the decision in *Dona*. Given that the Commission had not used its own powers to challenge the rule, he could not see how, aside from in the present action, the Court would have the opportunity to determine the compatibility of the foreign player rule with Article 48. There is some considerable strength in this strand of argument; the rules of football associations actively discourage attempts to use the courts to resolve disputes. For example, the FA Premier League regulations provide that; 'Any dispute or difference not otherwise expressly provided for in these Rules between a Club or Clubs and any Player shall be referred in writing to the Board for consideration and adjudication' (FA, 1996, p.44). In addition, a further regulation provides a right of appeal to the Football League Appeals Committee; the emphasis is firmly on internal settlement.

Lenz noted at the outset that; 'No deep cogitation is required to reach the conclusion that the rules on foreign players are of a discriminatory nature. They represent an absolutely classic case of discrimination on the ground of nationality' (*Bosman*, 1996, p.106). UEFA's original response was that the rules, as they stood, were not in breach of Article 48 as they only related to the number of players that a club could field in a given match and not on the number a club could, theoretically, have on its books. Lenz felt this had little impact given that only the very richest clubs would be able to contract more players than it could actually play in such circumstances (Barcelona was a good example of this where at one time choices had to be made between players such as Stoichkov and Hagi!) and that this still, fundamentally, affected freedom of movement. The next question to consider was whether the rules could be justified on the basis of previous case law. *Walrave* and *Dona* had made it plain that Article 48 would not affect the composition of teams, selected on the basis of matches not primarily of an economic nature such as a national sport team. However, in *Dona*, the court expressly limited the exclusion of foreign players to *specified* matches, distinguished by a *special* character and context, and, moreover, stated that the limitation had to remain restricted to its proper objective (*Bosman*, 1996, p.108). Whilst *Dona* and *Walrave* only gave national teams as examples of where such an exception might apply, Lenz was of the opinion that it could not be deduced from this that the court would find that the restriction on foreign players was acceptable for national leagues. Three further arguments were put forward attempting to justify the rules:

> First, it is emphasised that the national aspect plays an important part in football; the identification of the spectators with the various teams is guaranteed only if those teams consist, at least as regards a majority of the players, of nationals of the relevant member state; moreover, the teams which are successful in the national leagues represent their country in international competitions. Second, it is argued that the rules are necessary to ensure that enough players are available for the relevant national team; without the rules on foreigners, the development of young players would be affected. Third and finally, it is asserted that the rules on foreigners serve the purpose of ensuring a certain balance between the clubs, since otherwise the big clubs would be able to attract the best players (*Bosman*, 1996, p.109).

The first element of this was countered by the fact that many teams used foreign players in some capacity, and that, in terms of identification, players such as Eric Cantona and David Ginola had developed a phenomenal degree of fan rapport. Further to this, club and national sides were often managed by foreigners and this helped emphasise that such a 'national character' as outlined by UEFA was somewhat misplaced. The second was rebutted by an analysis of the way in which young players are traditionally developed - as they usually graduate upwards via a series of clubs, to which many of these rules do not apply, this attempted justification failed, as did the argument on the affect on future national teams.[24] This final argument was given some support although, it was considered that the objective of maintaining this balance could, and should, be achieved without placing restrictions upon freedom of movement of players.

Having considered the '3+2 rule' and, given that Article 48 concerned the abolition of discrimination on grounds of nationality, it had to be established whether the transfer rules, at issue, caused nationals of any member state to be discriminated against. This was refuted by the Belgian Association on the basis that the regulations were applied irrespective of the nationality of the player concerned, a perspective shared by UEFA. The Advocate General however considered that in his opinion '...there can be no doubt that the application of the transfer rules in the Community may *in principle* lead to discrimination' (*Bosman*, 1996, p.114). The Court followed this reasoning and stated that the transfer rules could obstruct trade contrary to Article 48 and then went on to consider whether, in Weatherill's words 'the football industry was able to show sufficiently compelling reasons for maintaining its transfer system despite its apparent incompatibility with Article 48' (Weatherill, 1996, p.1004). One of the 'football industry' claims was that the transfer rules were necessary to preserve the financial balance between clubs and to support and nurture young players; justifications on grounds of 'dynamic equilibrium' and the future playing generations that the Court held to be legitimate (*Bosman,* 1996, p.160). The problem for UEFA and the rest of football was that whilst such endpoints might be justified, in EC law the means of achieving those ends must also be justified and the transfer system was not deemed a suitable method of achieving such aims:

> The rules neither precluded richer clubs buying the best players nor prevented the 'availability of financial resources from being a decisive factor in competitive sport thus considerably altering the balance between clubs'. The Court agreed that a transfer fee system might act as an incentive to clubs to recruit and train new and young players, but it observed that because only a handful of young players will repay the investment by making the professional grade, it is impossible to predict the fees that will be obtained. In any event such fees will be unrelated to the actual cost of training all players (Weatherill, 1996, p.1005).

As these objectives could be achieved by other means that did not impede freedom of movement for workers, the Court was loath to adopt any of the justifications put forward. Consequently, the transfer system was held to be in contravention of Article 48, and the court referred to Lenz's suggestions as to other permissible means of achieving their aims without contravening Community law. Lenz indicated that these could be achieved, either by a policy of collective wage capping, or a distribution of funds on a more equitable basis, as, without other clubs, an individual club would wither. A further point that remained unexplored by the court was the applicability of Articles 85 and 86. In his opinion the Advocate General took the view that Article 85 had the same effect on the issue as Article 48; 'Article 85 of the Treaty is to be interpreted as precluding agreements between clubs and decisions of sports associations whose content is as described at 1(a) or 1(b) above' (*Bosman,* 1996, p.146). The points he referred to as 1(a) and (b) were the ability of a football club to demand payment for a player whose contract had expired and the issue of controlling players through nationality. The court decided that it was not necessary to rule on the question of Articles 85 & 86 given the decision in respect to Article 48. Given the application of Article 48, it could be considered that the Article 85 issue might be purely academic, such a response would, however, be somewhat premature. Whilst an initial view of *Bosman* was that it might not apply to purely internal transfers, Weatherill makes the point that Article 85 could be used in this situation:

> The juxtaposition of a domestic system requiring the payment of transfer fees and an absence of fees payable on cross-border deals affects inter-state trade patterns. The distortive effect on the wider market of a horizontal agreement between clubs relating to player acquisition brings it within Article 85(1) (1996, p.1021).

Thus, whilst the ECJ felt it unnecessary to determine the point, Lenz's opinion on the issue could have been of great importance had the football authorities sought to interpret the case in a 'limited' fashion. Whilst the *Bosman* decision drew a strong response from parties concerned with the business of football, there were limits to the judgement, or at least some confusion concerning its eventual scope.

Beyond Bosman

> The pink forms arrived this morning along with all the explanatory information which any player whose contract is up at the end of the season needs to know. This form is to an unsettled player what an UCCA form is to a would-be student. Sent out by the PFA, duly completed and returned to them, it lists the complete career details of every player being given a free transfer or opting for freedom of contract status...A player failing to complete his form in time is held to be guilty of one of the biggest own goals it is possible to score - as bad as not fully understanding his contractual rights (Nelson, 1995, p.328).

The reaction following *Bosman* was, unsurprisingly, one of horror followed by a stark realisation that the business and culture of football was to be fundamentally changed forever. The UEFA president Lenart Johansson for example, commented that it 'had created a mess for football' whilst Rick Parry, Chief Executive of the Premier League, felt that *Bosman* could be the catalyst for 'constructive and positive dialogue' (*Independent on Sunday*, 17 December, 1995). For agents at least the judgement appeared to be unequivocal good news, Eric Hall noting 'I now believe in Father Christmas. I really do. I owe [Bosman] a monster Christmas present. I'm going to get his name and address and send him presents' (Hodgson, 1995). The immediate extent and effect of the judgement was somewhat unclear however, and there was some confusion between the various bodies on a number of relevant points. Whilst UEFA attempted to hold out against the ruling that clubs should be free to field as many European nationals as they wished, the Premier League abolished the 'foreigner rule' (Duxbury, 1995). UEFA also battled hard to avoid the changes regarding transfer dealings post *Bosman* but backed down faced with the possibility of fines being levied by the EC; 'UEFA have finally accepted changes demanded in December [by *Bosman*]. They have notified the European Commission that the transfer-fee system for players moving between European Union countries at the end of their contracts will be scrapped' (Cranford & Johnson, 1996). For the domestic football authorities the major point was whether the system, that had been subject to adaption following *Eastham* and ongoing negotiations between the parties, would need further alteration. Rick Parry was adamant that English football would fight to protect its own system (Thomas, 1996).

The domestic (pre-*Bosman*) transfer provisions were not provided directly in the contract but found in the rules of the relevant League (Premier or Football League). However, the Code of Practice set out the timetable of events for players whose contract was about to expire (all contracts of whatever duration, except monthly contracts, must expire on 30 June in the relevant year). By the third Saturday in May, the club had to make its offer to the player who then had the minimum of a month to consider it. If the club did not want to retain the player, it could allow him to leave on a free transfer, not make him an offer or make an offer below his previous terms. If any of these circumstances occurred, the player was free to look for another club and no fee would have been involved. If a comparable offer was made to the player, he could still choose to reject it, in which case he was able to approach other clubs interested in signing him. If a new club was found, the size of the fee was for the clubs to determine through negotiation. If this process failed the issue could be referred, by either the clubs or the player, to the Football League Appeals Committee (FLAC) for determination. The rules, despite the existence of independent arbitration, still permitted a fee at the end of the contractual period. Free movement by players at the end of their contracts could not, however, be resisted by the clubs. The argument would be over the size of the fee paid and if not agreed by the clubs settled independently. The issue, post *Bosman,* was whether these rules could survive and the applicability of the decision to intra state transfers. It was reported that Newcastle were to be the first club to test the veracity of this when contesting whether a fee had to be paid to Blackburn Rovers for the transfer of goalkeeper Shay Given when out of contract. When the two clubs failed to agree a fee for Given, the matter was referred to FLAC with Newcastle warning 'Following the European Court of Justice ruling in the *Bosman* case the requirement for the payment of a compensation fee at the end of a player's contract may be unlawful where the player moves between two English clubs' (Thorpe & Ross, 1997). This was certainly the view taken by Jonathan Ebsworth from the Players out of Contract Association (POCA), the Association itself was; 'set up [in January 1996] in the aftermath of the *Bosman* Judgement in December to pursue total free agency on behalf of players' (Ebsworth, 1996, p.1). There has also been a further debate on whether the *Bosman* ruling only applies to players at the end of their contract or can also apply to players wishing to leave during the currency of their contract. UEFA, for example made their initial position clear in the immediate aftermath of *Bosman*; '...the ruling only affects the transfer of players no longer under contract. It is therefore still possible to obtain a transfer fee for a player under contract, irrespective of where the player is transferred to' (*The Independent*, 18 December 1995 'Football: UEFA clarifies *Bosman* ruling'). It is extremely unlikely that purely domestic fees could survive though the issue of compensation for the transfer of in contract players is more problematic.

The contractual playing field

In order to see the effects and potentialities of the *Bosman* judgement upon English footballers it is useful to give the context of the contract footballers sign when playing in the FA Premier League or Football League. This also gives a flavour of the other areas of potential control that can be exerted upon players by the operation of both contractual provisions and governing body regulations. The standard form contract for Premier and Football League players is drawn up under the auspices of the Professional Football Negotiating and Consultation Committee (PFNCC)[25] which has the following functions:

> (a) to consider questions concerning players' remuneration and other terms and conditions of employment, including contractual obligations, minimum pay, bonuses governed by League rules, pensions, fringe benefits, holidays, standard working conditions and insurance, as well as procedural matters involving the negotiating machinery, and the contract appeals machinery. This should not be regarded as an exhaustive list. No major changes in the regulations of the Leagues affecting a player's terms and conditions of employment shall take place without full discussion and agreement in the PFNCC; and
>
> (b) to facilitate consultation between the parties on any matter relating to professional Association Football upon which any of the parties considers that the view of the PFNCC would be desirable to help further the best interests of the game (FA, 1996, Misc Provisions, p.6).

The PFNCC is the chief vehicle for consideration of the club/player contract, and the terms of the contract are drawn up by PFNCC. On the face of it, it is a remarkably straightforward and simple document consisting of twenty-eight clauses plus an additional Schedule that contains remuneration details. Given the value of the players involved and the level of payments, such simplicity is surprising, though refreshing, and perhaps lies testament to the hope expressed in the FA/FL notes on contracts that the player/club relationship needs to be a strong and open one:

> What is special about the relationship is its closeness. There is a need for total commitment to the interests of the Club and for an atmosphere of mutual trust. In this way the footballer's occupation can be said to be truly professional, involving the continuous development of personal skills and the ability to meet the pressures that arise in a highly competitive sport. A Club is built upon success on the field of play, on commercial prosperity and upon the maintenance of a close relationship with its supporters in particular and its local community in general. It is impossible to depict in a legal document the range of responsibilities invariably accepted by the good Club and Player. It is obviously impossible to create by legal rules the essential unity of purpose (FA/FL, undated a, p.1).

In addition to the contract itself, there are a number of different sources that will affect contractual terms; the Code of Practice (produced jointly by the Football Association, the FA Premier League, the Football League, the Professional Footballers Association and the Footballers' Education and Vocational Training Society), the rules of the Football Association and the Football League as well as any individual club rules. These regulations are incorporated by virtue of clause 5 of the contract.[26] The contract contains a number of provisions that, as would be expected, restrict the ability of a professional footballer to play for clubs other than the club that holds his registration - this is secured by the operation of clause 4. In addition, this exclusivity is compounded by the combined effects of clause 2; 'The Player agrees to play to the best of his ability in all football matches in which he is selected to play for the Club and to attend at any reasonable place for the purpose of training in accordance with instructions given by any duly authorised official of the Club'. Further to this clause 3 gives the club the right to direct attendance at matches even if the player has not been selected to play. These clauses are fairly standard in any personal service contracts of this nature and it is unlikely that these would cause any problem in a legal sense. By the same token clauses requiring players to reside in a geographical location that the club deems appropriate for the performance of his duties and to seek consent of the club before embarking upon any other business or occupation should be straightforward.[27] In addition, clause 7a would seem similarly unproblematic even though it directs what the player is able to do in his free time:

> The Player shall not without the written consent of the Club participate professionally in any other sporting or athletic activity. The Player shall at all times have due regard for the necessity of his maintaining a high standard of physical fitness and agrees not to indulge in any sport, activity or practice that might endanger such fitness.

Perhaps of more interest are the provisions regarding disciplinary measures (clause 16) and contacts with the media. This latter issue has also proved controversial with respect to cricketers and their employers. The media is obviously of prime importance to football, both in terms of promoting, reporting and, crucially, financing the game. The relationship is, therefore, a close one and one that football needs to nurture to a large degree, and it is largely expected that players will 'perform' for the media as part of their job. Indeed, clause 13 of the agreement provides that the player will contribute to the media in a 'responsible manner' and where possible to inform the club of his intention to contribute to the media so that the club could make representations to the player if they deemed it necessary. This is further amplified by the Notes on Contract (FA/FL, undated a, p.4):

> 1. The Player should remember at all times his overriding duty to the good name of his Club in particular and the game of football in general. Indeed all concerned with playing or running football at all levels are bound by this provision of Football Association Rules. Breach of these Rules could lead to discipline by the Football Association, The League or by the Club concerned. This is an obligation that is not just confined to Players.
> 2. The Player should whenever possible inform the Club of his intention to write or broadcast and give the Club an opportunity to discuss the matter with him should they so wish. It is always wise for those whose views are to be given wide coverage to seek advice so that misjudgements are not the cause for later regret. There will of course be occasions when it is not possible or reasonable to expect prior notice to be given.

If the player were to breach this provision, he would in theory be subject to the disciplinary provisions outlined in clause 5, compounded by the operation of the FA Premier League Rules or the Football League Regulations. These provisions would also cover any other misconduct or breach of the rules and embrace areas as diverse as breaches of the contractual agreement (for example failure to turn up for pre-season training) and breaches of regulations on proscribed drugs etc.

The task for football

> I walked into his office and found myself facing two men: Morris [then Southend manager] and...Anton Johnson, chairman of Rotherham United. It became immediately evident that he was in *de facto* control at Southend too. He gave me an ultimatum. Politely expressed it went: sign this contract or piss off (Nelson, 1995, p.263).

The struggle between professional footballers, their employers, the clubs whose business is football and the governing bodies to change basic terms and conditions, has been a tortuous one. The important milestones are the two cases of *Eastham* and *Bosman* and it required such legal action for players to achieve fairly modest aims. The other major issue, the removal of the maximum wage provision, was won through a more traditional workplace method, collective solidarity and threatened industrial action. Clearly the PFA played a crucial role during this turbulent period and its achievements ought to be recognised alongside the two court victories. It should also be emphasised that the basic principles at stake were simple but vital. Firstly, the right to move freely in the marketplace and not to be bound outside of agreed contracts; this required the abolition of the iniquitous retention system. Once this was achieved, via *Eastham*, the focus shifted to the right to move after the expiry of the contract without the imposition of a transfer fee. In many ways this would always be more problematic; despite the recommendations of the Chester Report (1968) in the negotiations that followed both sides agreed that some compensation should be paid.

Given the relative unenforceability of football contracts, or at least the unwillingness to enforce them, it now seems a little odd that this was such a crucial issue. Certainly in the English game the leading players may move relatively freely providing that buyers for their services exist. The sanctity of contractual relations has been destroyed by the willingness of clubs to tempt 'in contract' players to sign for them and the understandable collusion of the players with this. Following the *Bosman* decision clubs may move to longer contracts for their best players despite the danger that this may bring in terms of (de)motivation. Clubs will need to sell during the contract term to recover any fee and, accordingly, clubs will either be looking to extend contracts as they near completion or sell prior to expiry. Buying clubs may then develop a waiting strategy until the player is contractually and financially 'free'. For players the bargaining strength will increase at the point where they are moving into free agency, with respect to the original club, and this will increase further with regard to other clubs at the point when they are no longer contractually bound. Essentially, of course, the key issue is the marketability of the player concerned and the state of the game's finances. It may now, given the phenomenal rewards available to the leading players, seem strange to view the retain and transfer system as anything other than an historical antiquity.

Notes

1. The heyday for United States 'soccer' was undoubtedly the 1970s when under the auspices of the North American Soccer League (NASL), New York Cosmos persuaded Pele to sign a four year deal - a move that was swiftly followed by the capture of other eminent players such as

Beckenbauer and Neeskens.

2. These have included in recent times outlawing the 'back pass rule'. Perhaps the most contentious attempted changes have been at the behest of the United States market and have involved proposals to alter the size of the goals (to increase the number of goals scored) and increase the frequency of breaks (to increase advertising penetration and income). Both have so far been repelled but the economic pressures should not be underestimated in this regard. Note also that association football is termed 'soccer', a bastardisation of association football, in the United States to distinguish it from their own peculiar brand of football.

3. A perusal of Manchester United's merchandise catalogue for autumn 1996/7 includes eight different types of branded footballs, 'Ryan Giggs' duvets, assorted clocks along with two different types of particularly unpleasant wallpaper (green stripe borders also available). This marketing strategy is replicated, although not always at such a high level of intensity at other Premier League clubs. Tottenham Hotspur for example also offer a range of duvets and wallpaper that have recently been seen in Martin Fowler's bedroom in 'Eastenders'.

4. Our phrase is an allusion to that of the Queen and her 'annus horribilus'.

5. At Bradford City's ground 'The Valley' fifty six people died after a fire in the stand, at Birmingham City's St Andrews ground there was serious crowd disorder and a fifteen year old boy died after a match against Leeds United.

6. The 1996/7 season saw a number of distinguished 'foreign' players move into the English (and Scottish) Premier League with corresponding superstar wages. Middlesborough for example signed two Brazilians, Emerson and Juninho in addition to the Italian striker Ravanelli from European Champions Juventus. Newspaper reports estimated the latter player's wages to be in the region of £42,000 per week. Ironically the club lost two cup finals and was relegated.

7. During the 1996/7 season Middlesborough indicated that they would not allow their Brazilian player Emerson to leave, despite his protestations that he no longer wished to play for the club, and eventually he returned, albeit temporarily. In February 1997 we interviewed a Vice President of Barcelona who explained that although their star player, Brazilian Ronaldo, was contracted for ten years if he no longer wished to play for the club he would be allowed to leave. Ronaldo was subsequently transferred to Inter Milan in the process rendering our own souvenir no. 9 shirts obsolete.

8. In response to claims that pricing policies were driving fans away from Premiership matches Derek Snowden wrote to a leading football magazine noting the following points; 'At my club, Plymouth Argyle, it's still possible to: 1) get myself and my two sons into the game for less than £10; 2) stand on dearly loved, but dilapidated terraces; 3) stand in your own and everybody else's urine in sub-standard toilet facilities; 4) 'enjoy' being owned by a chairman who appears to have fewer brain cells than people in the crowd; 5) have the pleasure of eating cold pasties and drinking thoroughly disgusting coffee; 6) get into the ground and stand in your normal spot even though you only arrived at 2.59pm' (*Four Four Two*, November 1997, p.32).

9. For an excellent analysis of this historical antipathy see Tomlinson (1991).

10. Originally titled the League Cup, in recent years the name of the competition has been determined by the name of the sponsor.

11. See Harding, 1991, chapters 2 and 3 for a detailed history of these events.

12. For greater detail and analysis of this from the perspective of one of the main 'players', see Hill (1963).

13. The resolution passed at the players' meetings read: 'This meeting, having considered the report it has received on negotiations, and the letter received from the Football League, gives one

month's notice of strike action, and appeals to all its members to support the decision taken' (Hill, 1963, p.39). The figures with respect to the voting at the three meetings were London 250 for none against, Manchester 254 for 6 against and Birmingham 186 for 12 against (Hill, 1963).
14. An attitude neatly exemplified by Alan Smith, the ex Arsenal and England striker; 'To a man footballers are loath to prepare for life after 35. The PFA does its bit. It regularly sends circulars to every club informing the lads about vocational courses. The costs of these are even subsidised by the players union. But its easy to have a manana attitude to these courses and I must admit I was as guilty of this as the next person'.
15. This potential route of escape could be blocked by the club paying the player the minimum wage.
16. In the *Eastham* judgement Wilberforce J noted that; 'over the seven years between 1956 and 1963 out of 2232 players on the transfer list at a fee there were appeals in 499 cases, of these 259 - that is over 50 per cent - got free transfers, and 123 - about 25 per cent - got the transfer fee reduced' (*Eastham*, 1963, p.148).
17. 'On Oct 6 the League secretary wrote to the secretary of Newcastle United saying that if Newcastle United sent a circular to other clubs saying that they would consider offers, this would not release the plaintiff "so long as that offer of retention is alive and you are prepared to sign him, he cannot sign for anyone else either inside the League or outside". So the League is here supporting Newcastle United's attitude in retaining the plaintiff' (*Eastham*, 1963, p.152).
18. The constitution of the panel was an independent chairman, and the Secretaries of the League and the Professional Footballers' Association.
19. Gordon Taylor succeeded Cliff Lloyd at the PFA and Graham Kelly succeeded Alan Hardaker at the Football League.
20. In football, an example is provided by the withdrawal from the England squad in June 1997 of Steve Macmanaman and Robbie Fowler, with their club, Liverpool, indicating that neither was fully fit. Glenn Hoddle, the England coach intimated that this action might jeopardise the future chances of the players as others will be given an opportunity to impress. Both have since been restored to the international squad.
21. 'Ken Bates was delirious with pleasure. "I'm delighted I smashed ITV's monopoly", he said. "Whereas in the previous four years David Dein (that is, Arsenal) was making a million pounds plus out of television, I was banking £100 to £150,000 year."...Bates then revealed the secret agenda behind the television vote. Support for Sky was not entirely dependent on the merits of its case. "The clubs did the Sky deal," said Bates, "because we were determined to smash the Big Five dominance and we were determined to get a fair share of the money..."' (Fynn & Guest, 1994, p.78).
22. At the end of the 1996/7 season the eventual Champions, Manchester United, complained of fixture congestion at the end of the season and asked for an extension. This was refused and led to some bitter exchanges with rival clubs.
23. An assimilated player was one who had played for an uninterrupted period of at least five years, including three years as a junior, in the relevant country.
24. Players are usually released by foreign clubs for international matches and this appears to have caused no particular disadvantages. Lenz himself noted the Danish national team who won the European championships in 1992 and the German side who won the World Cup in 1990 as good examples of the inapplicability of such a justification.
25. The PFNCC comprises (a) four representatives from PFA, (b) two representatives from FL, (c) two representatives from FA Premier League, (d) one representative from FA and the chief

executive officers of (a)-(d).

26. FA/FL (undated b) clause 5 provides that; 'The player agrees to observe the Rules of the Club at all times. The Club and the Player shall observe and be subject to the Rules of the Football Association and either the Rules of the FA Premier League or the Regulations of the Football League as appropriate. In case of conflict such Rules and Regulations shall take precedence over this Agreement and the Rules of the Club'.

27. However, Stan Collymore's failure to move closer to Liverpool was allegedly a cause of dispute between the player and club during his rather brief stay.

I am shocked and extremely disappointed at the Judgment of Mr Justice Parker. Having received this judgment, I would like to reiterate the reasons why I embarked upon these proceedings:-

1. Firstly, when I was 18 years old I entered into a recording contract with CBS Records. My contract still has 10 years to run.

2. Secondly, even though I both created and paid for my work, I will never own it or have any rights over it. I have no control or say in the way that my work is exploited. In fact I have no guarantee that my work will be released at all. If Sony reject my work it will never see the light of day.

3. Thirdly and perhaps most importantly, I have no right to resign. In fact there is no such thing as resignation for an artist in the music industry. Effectively, you sign a piece of paper at the beginning of your career and you are expected to live with that decision, good or bad, for the rest of your professional life. (Press Statement of George Michael, 21 June 1994, after the High Court dismissal of his action against his record company).

...there is some essential human activity, music making, which has been colonised by commerce. Pop is a classic case of what Marx called alienation: something human is taken from us and returned in the form of a commodity. Songs and singers are fetishised, made magical, and we can only reclaim them through possession, via a cash transaction in the marketplace (Frith, 1987).

3 Rough Trade[1]

Contract and control in the music industry

The music industry has prospered since a number of technological developments provided it with the potential to expand. Historically, music publishing was the bedrock of the industry with the major income generated through the sale of sheet music which was vigorously marketed by the publishers; 'They hired "song pluggers" (such as the young Irving Berlin and George Gershwin) to play their numbers on pianos set up in music stores to encourage the purchase of printed music. The song pluggers also auditioned numbers for theatrical, vaudeville, and cabaret performers in the hope of achieving exposure for the catalogs of their employers' (Biederman *et al.* 1992, p.384). At this stage, income could also be generated from the performances of the musical works, an area protected by copyright. Copyright occupies a central role for the music industry being the vehicle by which artistic creativity can be commercially exploited.[2] The ownership of songs and the ability to assign the copyright, or parts of the copyright, in such songs is the *raison d'etre* of music publishers. Historically 'pure' songwriters would write a song that would, hopefully, be recorded by a famous star, become a hit and bring in money via mechanical royalties. Similarly record companies could exploit their ownership of the copyright in the sound recording brought into existence when the original composition was recorded. In order to collect the royalties payable, when such works are utilised in their numerous forms, licences or assignments are given to agencies that collect and distribute the royalties.[3] A number of important changes have occurred within the music industry that have altered not only the relationship between songwriter and song, but have provided increased technological ability to enable new forms of music utilisation and creation.

At the same time, the (economically) successful popular music phenomenon consists of more than the mere music produced by the artists. Whilst the sale of recordings is undoubtedly crucial and a substantial part of the industry, it is becoming more and more prevalent for other marketing and merchandising devices to be utilised both to sell the 'product' and fully 'exploit' the artist.[4] Indeed, what is now required is a marketable package that can be adapted to appear in a variety of multi-media forms; an idea that was not lost upon The Beatles, early pioneers of the music/film crossover, and can be seen in the 'construction' of The Monkees.[5] This widespread use of the 'commodity' of music is one of the two interdependent parts to the transformation of the music business. This ubiquity of product would not be available without the changing technology that has revolutionised the process of creating music and is increasingly affecting its distribution. In short, music is being made differently and used in many more diverse ways than would have been envisaged even twenty years ago and traditional notions of creation, dissemination and exploitation are being rapidly re-evaluated.

In terms of software development, apart from the advent of the compact disc, the industry has seen the emergence of Digital Audio Tape (DAT), the (Sony) Mini Disc and the (Philips) Digital Compact Cassette. The introduction of compact discs had provided the industry with a huge boost as many consumers have not only purchased the format for new releases but also renewed parts of their existing vinyl collection. The most significant change in hardware, which has yet to be fully realised, is the use of multimedia computers to access music from the Internet. Similarly changes in broadcasting technology with the switch to digital output will revolutionise the quality of material received. Contemporaneously, the development of the cable network will permit audio and audio-visual works to be rapidly transmitted and downloaded without consequent loss of quality. We are beginning to witness the merging of previously distinct media; television, radio, film, music and computer generated works can all be available 'downline'. These changes will affect the music industry from creation through to the point of (re)sale and will undoubtedly lead to the further restructuring of companies - a process that is already underway. Companies that have in the past, concentrated on the provision of hardware, have steadily moved into the software market; 'Technological innovations require software as well as distribution outlets, which, in turn, motivates knowledgeable participants in the entertainment industry to control programming and distribution' (Biederman *et al*, 1992, p.xiv).

This, in essence, is the 'legal' challenge - to apply existing established concepts such as copyright protection and contractual provisions in a legally unidentified environment (Greenfield and Osborn, 1997). Effectively, it is the struggle of the law to colonise music. In simple terms, historically the (ab)use of copyright material was protected via the field of intellectual property. However once material can be taken, adapted and reworked using new technology, the old 'principles' concerning such use cannot apply without raising critical questions as to ownership and authorship. By strictly applying the dictum 'what is worth copying is worth protecting'; sound sampling, itself a creative process, may be effectively prohibited. Similarly, the co-existence of both hardware and software within companies has led to difficulties, not so much in terms of legal conflicts, but more with regard to business practices; George Michael, for example, complained that Sony treated him as is he were a piece of 'software'. Litigation of disputes on the scale of *George Michael* will probably only involve a highly successful performer, but it illustrates the value of such an artist and the limits that the 'owners' of such talent will go to retain such a benefit.

In economic terms and as a career move, the record industry does not provide stability, cast iron guarantees or even the prospect of a return on investment. Indeed, the requirements of the market dictate that someone's success is at someone else's expense; that the industry is a frail one and subject to the whims both of the market and the public is neatly outlined by Hirsch (1972, p.136):

> Most cultural items are allocated minimal amounts for promotion and are 'expected' to fail. Such long shots constitute a pool of 'understudies', from which substitutes may be drawn in the event that either mass media gatekeepers or consumers reject more heavily plugged items. I see the strategy of differential promotion as an attempt by cultural organizations to 'buffer' their technical core from demand uncertainties by smoothing out output transactions.

In contractual terms, this translates itself into a series of terms, often in standard form, that are heavily weighted in favour of the party with the most leverage or bargaining power - almost inevitably the recording or publishing company.[6] However, whilst the contractual relationships dictate to a large degree the extent to which artists are harnessed or constrained in terms of their own expression, it is important to place this relationship within the wider context of an industry that has a number of further constraints that fetter the artists' ability to express themselves. This chapter firstly considers the restraints that may be placed upon artists in terms of the nature of the material produced, and subsequent conflicts with the 'employer' and possibly the criminal law. It then examines the changing nature of the music business and the process of creation, and the problems faced when trying to apply traditional legal concepts to them. Whilst contractual terms will form a central part of this chapter, there are a number of other potential restrictions placed upon the artist outside of these paper terms, although, these too, may also be translated into contractual terms as they become contentious issues for the industry. One aspect of this has been alluded to above, the process of 'sampling', the highest level of musical copyright infringement, that also may have implications for artistic control. Also of importance, especially in the United States, is the notion of censorship as this is another area that may fundamentally affect an artist's ability to ply his trade and for the public to hear the fruits of his labour. The issue of control via censorship will be analysed after the control of compositions has been outlined.

Copyright, collage & censorship

> Culture is more than commerce. The law should begin to acknowledge the artistic domain of various creative techniques which may actually conflict with what others claim to be their economic domain. Art needs to acquire an equal footing with marketers in court. The question that must rise to the surface of legal consciousness now is: At what point in the process of sound fragment appropriation does the new creation possess its own unique identity, which supersedes the sum of its parts, thus gaining its own right to legally exist? (Negativland, undated).

The relationship between art and commerce has proved difficult to reconcile in jurisdictions such as North America and the United Kingdom, although some civil law systems have adopted a more art/artist centred approach to some copyright provisions. For example, countries such as France and Germany have long recognised the moral rights (*droit moral*) of creators, a right that has the capacity to conflict with the economic element of copyright, which may be freely bought and sold. The attempts by the United Kingdom to incorporate moral rights have indicated this uneasy relationship between art and economics. This tension can also be seen with respect to the application of traditional copyright protection where ownership of works may affect their later incorporation in the creative process of artists. This is further exacerbated as the methods of producing 'art' evolve and adapt to shifts within the social/technological/legal terrain. The contentious issue of the extent to which previous (copyright) work can be 'used' in order to create new work must be viewed within the context of the new technologies that have permitted such use to become far easier. The whole nature of (sound) sampling reflects the uneasy relationship between law, new technology and the creative artist. As Negativland note, it is important to make the point that 'appropriation' is a deep rooted and historically accepted part of creativity:

> Any serious observer of modern music can cite a multitude of examples - from Buchanan and Goodman's humorous collages of song fragments in the fifties to today's canonization of James Brown samples - wherein artists have incorporated the actual property of others into their own unique creations. The whole histories of folk music and the blues are typified by creative theft. Jazz and rock are full of this, too. In the visual arts, there is a long-standing tradition of found image collage, from Schwitters and Braque to Rauschenberg and Warhol. This is a twentieth century mode of artistic operation that is now nothing short of dramatic in its proliferation, in spite of all the marketplace laws designed to prohibit it (Negativland, undated).

The notion of appropriation has, indeed, become more pronounced as, both the means to create and use such work, has become cheaper and easier and the proliferation of the raw product in the form of the increased mediatisation of society. Whilst historically appropriation would have taken the form of the use of a melody or a lyric, appropriation now is perhaps more likely to involve the utilisation of a sound recording taken from a variety of media. That is not to say that issues of copying in terms of traditional work may not still be at issue and permission still needs to be sought for the use of a musical work or a literary work under the provisions of the *Copyright Designs and Patents Act 1988*. Such issues have plagued the Mancunian artists Oasis, who have been accused of borrowing riffs from a number of sources as eclectic as The Beatles, The New Seekers and T Rex amongst others. Indeed, whilst their multi-platinum 'What's the Story (Morning Glory)' album does credit Gary Glitter and Mike Leander on its opening track 'Hello' (for the refrain from 'Hello, Hello I'm back again', MCA Music Ltd), a further song, 'Step Out', which was originally intended for the album, had to be removed at the last minute as such permission had not been given. The track eventually appeared, with the requisite Wonder/Cosby/Moy credit, on the flip side of their 1996 single 'Don't Look Back in Anger'.[7] A number of other bands such as Elastica and The Verve have also found their royalty levels reduced due to the use of material from other artists. However, both were still able to release the tracks, notwithstanding that they were saddled with a reduced royalty rate. Even more contentiously, the owners of work that has been later utilised can effectively veto the production and, more likely, distribution, of 'new' work. This situation has become more pronounced as the technological means for re-using sound has become more refined.

The arrival of digital music technology has manifestly altered the way in which music is produced for consumption; with the advent of digital samplers and sequencers we have seen the dawning of a new culture that is able to appropriate sound recordings and utilise them in fresh 'creative' ways as part of new compositions. These new technologies have heralded a distinct type of music culture, a culture that charts changing relationships between performers, audiences and the forms of representation. Technological change has always, of course, had implications for music making and consumption; throughout history, all forms of music making have been dependent upon '...some kind of deliberately designed and specialised equipment or technology' (Durant, undated, p.178) and just as this is true for instruments, so it is true for amplification, recording, transmission and reproduction. The difference is, however, that this second type of technological change has implications for the working relationship within the studio as the engineering of raw material becomes more fundamental and pronounced. The prime change in music technology has been one of encoding - that musical signals can be stored in digital form rather than analogue. These digital forms can then be manipulated and edited in the studio; a technique that has become more prevalent as manufacturers agreed upon a standard interface (Musical Instrument Digital Interface) and the hardware has consequently become much cheaper:

> What followed this standardisation of the musical-digital interface was then the design and production of a wide range of relatively cheap, digitally-based musical 'instruments'...Many different types of instrument have been devised; a new generation of drum machines, which store pre-defined drum sounds that can be triggered in pre-programmed patterns; samplers - in effect, combinations of a keyboard with a (technically very simple) tape recorder - which record and replay excerpts of sound and then allow manipulation of sounds which have been stored...(Durant, undated, p.182).

These developments have permitted a number of new composition possibilities. In terms of music composition, it allows a layering and texturing of sounds and the creation of entire musical pieces effectively fashioned as a collage of previous works. There are myriad examples of the use of sound sampling. For example American artist Vanilla Ice had a massive hit in 1990 with the song 'Ice Ice Baby'; the song contained a melody clearly recognisable as originating in the David Bowie and Queen collaboration 'Under Pressure'.[8] Similarly, MC Hammer acknowledged the debt he owed Rick James for 'U Can't Touch This'.[9] Perhaps the most prominent example of this process occurred with the JAMM's '1987: What the Fuck is Going on?' album. The LP was well received in the main by the music press, but some of the artists 'used' were not so ecstatic. Whilst the album incorporated samples from Sam Fox, Top of the Pops (TOTP) broadcasts, Petula Clark and the Sex Pistols amongst others, one track in particular proved problematic. 'The Queen and I' was based upon Abba's 'Dancing Queen' and the writers objected vehemently to its use. The JAMMs reacted to this by attempting to justify their use of the song and their interpretation of it:

> I sat down and started writing this whole thesis on the defence of what we were doing, artistically, and creatively, saying that if machines were going to be invented like samplers, you can't stop them....So our whole idea was to go over, meet up with Benny and Bjorn, sit down with them, artist to artist, and sort of go through it. They were singing in English for a start, which was taking our language, they were taking a form that was American popular music, and making it into something their own, and selling it back to the world. I just thought that there was no difference in what they were doing, to what we were doing (Robinson, undated, p.7).

In the event, the MCPS wrote to the JAMMs in August 1987 notifying them that Abba were not prepared to grant a licence for the track and ordering them to; '(i) cease all manufacture and distribution, (ii) take all possible steps to recover copies of the album which are then to be delivered to MCPS or destroyed under the supervision of MCPS, and (iii) deliver up the master tape, mothers, stampers and any other parts commensurate with manufacture of the record' (Letter from MCPS to JAMMs, cited in Robinson, undated, p.8). All masters were surrendered[10] and the LP was re-released in 'sample free' format later in the year, resplendent with long gaps of silence and details of how to recreate the original LP:

> If you follow the instructions below you will, after some practice, be able to simulate the sound of our original record. To do this you will need three wind-up record decks, a pile of selected discs, one t.v. set and a video machine loaded with a cassette of edited highlights of last week's *Top of the Pops*...(noted in Frith, 1993, p.5).

Whilst the ownership of copyright material and the ability to prevent its use is one manifestation of control, perhaps of a higher profile is the control that can be exercised in terms of the dissemination of material that is deemed to be in some way 'unsuitable' or worthy of regulation. The censorship of artistic material has a long and chequered history and two distinct approaches have emerged to deal with material that falls under this umbrella. One approach is to prevent the distribution of 'obscene' material and the other is to outlaw indecent 'exhibitions'[11] and the law in England has developed in such a way that there are now both common law and statutory provisions that may be applied to controversial output.[12] There are a number of notable examples of attempts at censorship that illustrate the difficulties in making judgements concerning what amounts to 'obscenity' or 'indecency'. For example, the common law offence of outraging public decency has been used to objectively judge the quality of articles regardless of whether any 'damage' has been caused (Feldman, 1993). This provision was controversially applied to the 'artistic' display of earrings manufactured from human foetuses ('Human Earrings') in the case of *Gibson*. Both the artist (Richard Gibson) and the gallery owner (Peter Sylveire) were convicted at the Central Criminal Court in February 1989 of outraging public decency and fined £500 and £350 respectively and their subsequent appeal to the Court of Appeal was unsuccessful. The use of the common law offence attracted much critical comment as its use avoided any defence available under the *Obscene Publications Act 1959* but also because it carried unlimited penalties rather than those laid down under the statute. The *OPA 1959* makes it an offence to publish any obscene article[13] and the definition of 'article' includes sound recordings and therefore encompasses records, cassettes and compact discs in addition to audio-visual material. There is however a limited defence under s4:

> ...a person shall not be convicted of an offence against section two of this Act, and an order for forfeiture shall not be made under the foregoing section, if it is proved that publication of the article in question is justified as being for the public good on the ground that it is in the interests of science, literature, art or learning, or of other objects of general concern.

The *OPA 1959* has been applied against the publishers of books such as 'Lady Chatterley's Lover', 'Fanny Hill', 'Inside Linda Lovelace' and 'Last Exit to Brooklyn' and an interesting analogy to the debates concerning rap music in the 1980s and 1990s is that it was not so much a matter of the material itself but accessibility to it that caused most disquiet. There has historically been some limited activity in the United Kingdom with respect to controversial sound recordings, certain types of music may be 'policed' by both the music industry themselves and pressure groups. Bands such as Crass and Flux of Pink Indians had their records boycotted by several retailers in the late 1970s and early 1980s, and were the subject of attempts to ban their recordings under the *OPA 1959*. The owner of a shop in Nottingham was found guilty at Northwich Magistrates Court in 1984, fined and a seizure order made against stock such as Crass' 'Sheep Farming in the Falklands' (Cloonan, 1996) although the judgement was overturned in the Crown Court on the basis that whilst the material might be vulgar and crude, it did not fall within the ambit of 'obscene' under the statute. Similarly, major record shops refused to stock Flux of Pink Indians' 'The Fucking Cunts treat us like Pricks' LP upon its release in 1984 and three years later a Manchester independent record shop was raided and copies of the album seized. Holden (1993) attributes this intervention to the controversial then Chief Constable of Greater Manchester, James Anderton. The Director of Public Prosecutions advised against a prosecution under the *OPA 1959* (presumably on the same basis as the Crass ruling), but a prosecution was begun against the owner of the shop under the 'obscene display' legislation although this too was later dropped.[14] A different angle to censorship emerged (though previous censorship existed in other areas) in relation to the political situation in Ireland after the enactment of the 1988 Broadcasting Ban. A Pogues song, 'Streets of Sorrow', was deemed by the Independent Broadcasting Authority to be within the terms of the ban as it was sympathetic to the plight of the 'Birmingham Six'.

More recently copies of NWA's 'Efil4zaggin'[15] was subject to police intervention. The day after its release in June 1991, the Metropolitan Police raided the distributors and seized the offending item. Section 3 of the *OPA 1959* contains an alternative to pursuing the publishers of material through a jury trial which given changing attitudes may well be unsuccessful. A magistrate may issue a warrant to allow a constable to enter premises and seize and remove articles which the officer reasonably believes are obscene and kept for publication for gain. The articles will then be brought back before the Magistrates Court for a determination as to their 'obscene' status. If the articles fall within the Act the court will order that they be forfeited. Evidence was presented to the Williams Committee that this procedure was being increasingly used though it is effectively a short term measure:

> The procedure has little deterrent effect: the case is brought against the material, rather than its publishers, and has no criminal consequence whatsoever. Section 3 seizures occupy a great deal of court and police time, but judgments in these cases do not serve as precedents and the only object of the exercise is to diminish the profits of soft-core pornographers by destroying some part of their stock (Robertson and Nicol, 1992, p.134).

'Efil4zaggin' was brought back to Redbridge Magistrates Court and played to the justices who determined that the album was not obscene and the police returned the 30,000 recordings. In recent years rap music has indeed become the prime folk devil with variants such as 'gangsta rap'[16] evincing moral outrage in some quarters, especially in the United States although this has also been seen in the UK to a lesser degree.[17] A forerunner of the action against NWA/Efil4zaggin in England was the long running dispute in the USA between rap artists and politicians, evangelists, the police and the Parents Music Resource Centre (PMRC). Rap music in particular has been specifically singled out for action and regulation. For example, Ice T's track 'Cop Killer' from the album 'Body Count' created a furore in the early 1990s. The complaints against the track were based around the lyrics, which the critics argued, glorified and encouraged the killing of police officers. The record had been released by Sire Records, a subsidiary of the multi media giant Time Warner, and pressure was applied by politicians and associations of police officers with a list of Time Warner products becoming the subject of a boycott. Some chains of record stores withdrew the album from the shelves. This pressure firstly led to the withdrawal of the track from the album by Ice T, ironically the furore led to an increase in sales and the withdrawal of the album made it a collectors item. The relationship between the artist and company further deteriorated and in January 1993 Ice T left by 'mutual agreement'. In the light of the controversy other rap artists found their work subject to close scrutiny by record company executives.

The original impetus for the formation of PMRC was a complaint in 1983 to the

Parent Teacher Association (PTA) by an Ohio father over the Prince track 'Let's Pretend We're Married'. This led to the involvement of the PTA to campaign against offensive recordings (Holden, 1993). This in turn led to the formation of the PMRC in May 1985, by a group of American women, who felt that the lyrics their children were subject to required regulation. This pressure group contained a number of prominent figures such as Susan Baker (wife of former Treasury Secretary and White House Chief of Staff James Baker), Sally Nevius (wife of former Washington DC Council Chairman, John Nevius) and Tipper Gore (wife of Albert Gore, then Senator of Tennessee). Indeed the Gores were said to have become involved after their eight-year old daughter bought a copy of Prince's 'Purple Rain' that contained a song that included references to masturbation. The aims of the organisation were to make parents more aware of the nature of the music that their children were listening to and campaign for voluntary restraint by the industry itself. The self regulation was to include a standard system of labelling for records that dealt with issues such as drugs and alcohol (D/A), violence (V), the occult (O) and vulgar and/or sexually explicit matter (X) (Deflem 1993).

The PMRC proved remarkably successful; the campaign for voluntary self restraint following Senate hearings in 1985 led to the Recording Industry Association of America (RIAA) agreeing to place labels on albums warning of explicit lyrics.[18] The RIAA has a parental advisory programme that aims to 'help parents set and enforce standards for their children, without imposing their standards on others'. Originally the RIAA had rejected the proposals arguing that there was the overriding protection of the First Amendment. Holden (1993) claimed that the quid pro quo for stickering was legislative provisions in Congress to outlaw parallel imports that were causing problems for the industry and that once stickering took place a marketing advantage materialised. However, the decision to place warnings on the covers also led to a number of artists arguing that such restraints were infringements of the right to freedom of speech. Foremost amongst the critics was Frank Zappa who amusingly placed the following sticker on his LP 'Frank Zappa Meets the Mothers of Invention':

WARNING GUARANTEE: This album contains material which a truly free society would neither fear nor suppress. In some socially retarded areas, religious fanatics and ultra-conservative political organizations violate your First Amendment Rights by attempting to censor rock and roll albums...The language and concepts contained herein are GUARANTEED NOT TO CAUSE ETERNAL TORMENT IN THE PLACE WHERE THE GUY WITH THE HORNS AND THE POINTED STICK CONDUCTS HIS BUSINESS (noted in Denselow, 1990, p.268).

The RIAA refused some of the other demands made by the PMRC which included re-assessment of the contracts of artists who engaged in violence or explicit sexual behaviour and the relocation of 'obscene' records under the counter of stores. One fear was that censorship might extend to other material such as that of a more 'purely' political nature. Labelling has not ended the campaign to ban music, indeed the system has been used to identify those sound recordings that could be banned.[19] It seems likely that the issue of censorship generally will continually resurface, particularly when controversial material is released, though the larger and more vulnerable companies may now be more sensitive to the nature of the work of their contracted artists. As the 'Cop Killer' dispute demonstrates, record companies may find themselves subject to pressure from outside groups who object to an artist's material. Clearly, as the industry's structure alters such boycotts may have greater effect as the number of potential targets increases. The outcome will inevitably be a greater degree of self-censorship so that potentially costly consumer disputes can be avoided. This fear of the more controversial groups has allowed some smaller labels into this lucrative market. Priority Records signed Ice T after the split with Sire, after all he had previously enjoyed a very successful career in terms of sales. Additionally the 'bad' publicity may well stimulate sales; following protests about the 1991 album 'Death Certificate' by Ice Cube it sold one million copies within ten days of its release. Whilst these issues of ownership and control may be subject to state and private regulation, both of these areas may also be dealt with inside the paper terms of a contractual agreement.

Made of stone?[20] The challenge to music contracts

After the decision in *Esso*[21] it was clear that the doctrine of restraint of trade was not confined to its traditional areas of post contract employment and the sale of businesses. It was however not definitively clear how this impacted upon the music industry until Tony Macaulay, a songwriter who had written for Elvis Presley, The Fifth Dimension and The Hollies, and who counted 'Baby, now that I've found you' and 'Love grows where my Rosemary goes' amongst his credits, brought an action against his music publisher. This was the first case that challenged the enforceability of an established music contract. Macaulay was a young unknown songwriter who signed an exclusive song writing contract with 'A Schroeder Music Publishing Co Ltd' in 1966. The contract, signed without legal advice, was the company's standard form agreement with a few alterations. In 1969 Macaulay had negotiated a production deal with Pye Records but the large publishing royalties he had anticipated from his publishing contract with

Schroeder had not realised the anticipated income. He asked Laurence Myers, a specialist industry accountant, to look at the situation and the results proved startling:

> The New York audit [arranged by Myers] had exposed a well-honed system of overseas rake-offs that left the writer with a fraction of his expected earnings. Instead of a 50:50 split, the worldwide Schroeder organization could at times have enjoyed an 82.5:17.5 cut, and possibly more (Garfield, 1986, p.72).

Counsel's advice was sought and Macaulay was told that whilst the contract was undoubtedly unfair he stood little chance of overturning it in court as there was no precedent upon which he could rely. Notwithstanding this Macaulay brought an action to determine the validity of the contract which was first heard in the High Court in July 1972. Macaulay was successful at first instance before Plowman J (26 July, 1972) and the defendants appealed unsuccessfully to the Court of Appeal.[22] The case came before the House of Lords in July 1974 with judgement handed down on 16 October 1974. Lord Reid considered that there were two main questions to be asked in a case such as this. Firstly, were the terms so restrictive that they could not be justified at all? Secondly, if there was room for justification, has the party relying upon such restrictions *proved* justification? Lord Reid analysed the terms of the publishing agreement, many of which are reproduced. The citation of these terms within the contract serves a number of purposes. Firstly, it shows the typical length and coverage of a music contract in the 1970s. As will become apparent, contracts have developed significantly in the intervening period and, may now involve, according to John Kennedy (Sony's expert witness in *George Michael*), a checklist of some seventy points. Secondly, this provides an opportunity to analyse the constituent terms of the contract to identify the crucial aspects that still form the bedrock of music contracts.

A primary issue is the length of the agreement and any ability to terminate it:

> Clause 1. Subject as hereinafter mentioned this agreement shall remain in force for a period of FIVE (5) years from the date hereof (hereinafter called 'the said term'). Clause 9. (a) If during the said term the total of the composer's royalties hereunder and all advances thereon (if any) shall equal or exceed £5,000 then this agreement shall automatically be extended for a further period of FIVE (5) years and for the purpose of this agreement the said period of FIVE (5) years shall be deemed to be included in and be part of the said term. (b) The publisher may at any time during the said term terminate this agreement by giving to the composer one month's written notice to that effect. Such termination shall be without prejudice to the rights of the parties in respect of any antecedent breach of this agreement and the publisher's obligations to pay royalties hereinbefore provided for.

Clause 16 (a) The publisher shall have the right to assign this agreement and all rights and obligations hereunder to any person firm or corporation and shall also have the right to assign any or all rights in a particular work. (b) The composer will not assign his rights under this agreement without the publisher's prior written consent (*Schroeder*, 1974, p.618-620).

These first two clauses determined the overall length of the agreement, an aspect that is crucial given the potentially truncated nature of a career in the music industry. Although there are examples of durable artists whose popularity has been maintained such as The Rolling Stones and Elton John, these are in the minority and there are many more whose moment of fame has been very brief such as Sigue Sigue Sputnik and Martha and the Muffins. In this case the duration outlined in Clause 1 was for an initial five year period. However, by the operation of Clause 9(a) if the composer had been paid at least £5,000 in royalties or advances during that period then the agreement was to be automatically extended for a further five years. Given the method of calculation of the sum (royalty or advance) that triggered the extension, it would have been possible to extend the agreement through an additional advance towards the end of the first term and the effective contract period was ten years. Clause 16 dealt with the right to assign the agreement to a third party. This may be of particular importance where the songwriter signs an agreement with a certain publisher for whatever reason and later finds that the publisher assigns the rights under the contract to a different publisher who may not meet with the composer's approval. The publisher does not need to obtain the consent of the composer in order to do this. Under 16(b) the composer would be unable to assign his rights without written consent of the publisher. There is of course no compulsion upon the publisher to act reasonably when exercising the rights available under this section:

Clause 2. (a) The publisher engages the exclusive services of the composer and the composer will render the same to the publisher during the said term. (b) The composer shall obey and comply with all lawful orders and directions in relation to his services hereunder given to him by the publisher and shall use his best endeavours to promote the interests of the publisher. (c) The composer will not during the said term directly or indirectly work for render services or be affiliated to or be interested in or connected with any person firm or corporation engaged in the music publishing business other than the publisher nor will he during the said term carry on or be concerned in whether alone or in partnership any music publishing business. (d) The composer will not divulge to any person except as may be required by the publisher any confidential information relating to the business of the publisher (*Schroeder*, 1974, p.618).

This clause delivers *exclusivity*. The composer is tied exclusively to the publisher in that he is not permitted to deliver compositions to, or work directly or indirectly, for any other music publisher during the term of the agreement. This is an essential point for the 'employer' as throughout the entertainment industry, the output of the creative artist has greater value if its production may be controlled within the marketplace. However this limitation does not extend to the publisher who is not bound only to the one composer and is of course at liberty to contract with other writers. Indeed the employing company may have any number of composers contracted to it, who may be in competition with one another, potentially to the detriment of each individual composer. In addition there is no positive obligation upon the publisher to do anything with the work so delivered; 'No doubt the expectation was that if the songs were of value they would be published to the advantage of both parties. But if for any reason the appellants chose not to publish them the respondent would get no remuneration and he could not do anything. Inevitably the respondent must take the risk of misjudgment of the merits of his work by the appellants. But that is not the only reason which might cause the appellants not to publish' (Lord Reid in *Schroeder*, 1974, p.622). Whilst duration and exclusivity are undoubtedly key areas in any such agreement, the following four clauses are in many ways just as significant:

> Clause 3. (a) The composer HEREBY ASSIGNS to the publisher the full copyright for the whole world in each and every original musical composition and/or lyric including but without prejudice to the generality of the foregoing the title words and music thereof written/or composed created or conceived by the composer alone or in collaboration with any other person or persons and whether in his own name or under a nom-de-plume at any time during the said term or at any time prior to the date hereof insofar as such latter compositions and/or lyrics are still owned or controlled by the composer directly or indirectly...
> (b) In this agreement references to musical works and/or lyrics shall include the part or parts thereof (if separate and divisible) written composed created or conceived by the composer....
> Clause 4. Where a musical composition and/or lyric to which this agreement applies is a 'work of joint authorship' as defined by Section 11 of the Copyright Act 1956, the composer will procure that his co-author or co-authors as the case may be will join with him in doing such acts and things and executing such deeds and documents as may be necessary to vest the copyright in the said work in the publisher.
> Clause 10. (a) The composer will forthwith submit to the publisher every composition and/or lyric written and/or composed created or conceived by him alone or in collaboration. The composer warrants to the publisher that the copyright in all such works will pass to the publisher free from any adverse claims

or rights from any third party and that all such works submitted to the publisher will be the original work of the composer and his collaborators (if any). (b) The composer will indemnify the publisher against all claims damages and demands and against all costs incurred in the institution or defence of any actions or proceedings relating to the said works submitted to the publisher....

Clause 15. For the avoidance of any possible doubt and without in any way limiting the assignment hereinbefore contained it is hereby declared that the copyright hereby assigned includes: (a) the right to renew and extend the copyright and the ownership of such renewed and extended copyright. (b) the right to make and publish new adaptations and arrangements and to make such additions adaptations and alterations in and to the words and/or music as the publisher may desire and to provide and translate the lyric thereof in any and all languages of the world (*Schroeder*, 1974, p.618-620).

These clauses provide a number of vital elements. The composer works solely for the company and all the work he produces is owned by the company with the full worldwide copyright assigned to the publisher. However it extends beyond the songs created by him during the duration of the agreement. It encompasses work that is co-written and more significantly works created prior to the agreement over which the composer still maintains direct or indirect control. If there are joint authors the songwriter must obtain the necessary consent of the other author to vest the copyright with the publisher. Clearly if the other party has his own publishing contract then this is not legally possible as his part of the jointly authored work will be subject to his own agreement. Indeed if the joint author had a similar contractual clause both joint authors would be seeking to procure the consent of the other. Clause 10(a) further embeds the point about exclusivity outlined in Clause 1, and forces the composer to warrant that the material delivered is original and not the work of a third party (except in so far as it may be a collaborative work). Clause 10(b) also indemnified the publisher against any claims arising out of any breach of 10(a) or any further action relating to the works that had been submitted. This is a wide ranging provision that extends beyond any alleged breach of copyright scenario to other potential claims such as if the work were claimed to be defamatory. Clause 15 goes on to demonstrate the all encompassing nature of the contract making it clear that if the assignment of full copyright could be doubted, though the language is plain enough, that renewals, adaptions and translations were part of this package. This paragraph is rather unnecessary and it is difficult to see the substantive gain for the publisher but by compounding the weak position of the composer only strengthens the view that the agreement is oppressive. The composer is however entitled to payment:

Clause 5. In respect of each work hereinbefore referred to the copyright in which has been assigned by the composer and his collaborators (if any), the publisher will pay to the composer and his collaborators (if any): (a) on all piano copies sold and paid for (after the first 500 copies) in the United Kingdom of Great Britain and Northern Ireland and Eire a royalty of 10% of the marked selling price; (b) 50% of all net royalties received by the publishers in respect of mechanical reproduction of the said works and of all net synchronisation fees; (c) in the event of the said works being published in any country outside the United Kingdom and Eire, 50% of the net royalties received by the publisher from persons authorised to publish the said works in such foreign territories.

Clause 6. (a) Fees in respect of performing rights shall be divided as to 50% to the composer and his collaborators (if any) (hereinafter referred to as 'the composer's share') and 50% to the publisher...(c) If the composer shall be or become a member of P.R.S. and while he remains such member all performing fees shall be divided between the parties hereto in accordance with P.R.S. rules for the time being in force subject to the agreement of the parties hereinbefore contained varying the divisions as permitted by such rules so that 50% of such fees are for the composer and his collaborators (if any) and 50% for the publisher...

Clause 8. (a) The publisher shall pay the sum of £50 to the composer, which shall be a general advance against royalties payable by the publisher under this agreement and to be recouped therefrom but in no case shall the publisher be entitled to the return of any part of such sums. Upon the recoupment by the publisher of said general advance payment of fifty (£50) pounds, the publisher agrees to pay another fifty (£50) pounds, which is to be treated as a general advance as described herein. This same procedure shall continue throughout the said term hereof; i.e. as each general advance of fifty (£50) pounds is recouped in full by the publisher, the publisher shall pay to the composer the sum of fifty (£50) pounds etc. (b) The publisher will render to the composer semi-annually statements showing the amount of royalties due to the composer as at December 31 and June 30 in each year. Such statements shall be delivered within 60 days of the relevant date and shall be accompanied by a remittance for such sum (if any) as may be shown to be due to the composer.

Clause 13. In the event of any breach of the terms or conditions of this agreement by the composer the publisher shall be entitled to suspend and withhold payment of royalties (including the general advances provided for in paragraph 8 hereinabove) until such breach has been remedied. If the composer shall fail to remedy any such breach within one month of written notice by the publisher requiring him so to do all royalties then or thereafter due under this agreement shall cease to be or shall not become (as the case may be) payable...(Schroeder, 1974, p.618-620).

The method of payment was simple. Macaulay was to receive an advance payment of fifty pounds that would then be recouped by the publisher from any royalties that became due to him. Once his original fifty pounds had been recouped he would then be entitled to a further fifty pound payment. If the royalties failed to cover the payment (and there could only ever be a maximum of fifty pounds outstanding) the composer would not be liable to return any balance. The royalty rate was set at ten per cent for sheet music and fifty per cent for all net income for works that were licensed for transformation into sound recordings (mechanical rights). Similarly the income generated by the performance right assigned to and administered by PRS would be equally divided. Lord Reid made much of the fact that the contract as it stood was oppressive.[23] In particular whilst the composer was bound to deliver all the work he produced during that period to the publisher, there was no obligation upon the publisher to actually do anything with such work. This agreement was effectively to last for a period of ten years, a length of time well in excess of most careers in the music industry and the publishers had reserved the right to terminate and assign as they saw fit. As such the contract was not justifiable and was held to be unenforceable, a view that Lords Simon, Kilbrandon and Viscount Dilhorne concurred with. This was a comprehensive victory and indicated not only the advances of the doctrine of restraint of trade but also the fact that similar standard form music contracts that could potentially sterilise creative output for a relatively long period (due to the limited career duration) could be considered unlawful.

From the factory to the diamond mine[24]

> I enjoy certain things, no one else has to enjoy them, and I see certain things in a certain way, but no one else has to see those things in the same way. And then again, no one has the right to tell me it's immoral or selfish or wrong to do what I do (Holly Johnson, from the sleeve notes of 'Welcome to the Pleasuredome' (ZTT Records, 1985)).

Frankie Goes to Hollywood (FGTH) were in the mid 1980s an extremely popular and successful group. Their first four singles all topped the chart in the UK, a feat only achieved before by Gerry and the Pacemakers. The nation's youth were resplendent in 'Frankie says...' T-shirts and one journalist wrote of them 'They have the wit of the Beatles, the decadence of the Rolling Stones and the wildness of the Sex Pistols'(Mike Andrews of the Daily Express, quoted on book sleeve of Johnson, 1994). Formed in Liverpool in the early 1980s, the band had toured and written solidly and were beginning to believe they would never be offered a record contract and break into the business. They had already written the two songs that were to become their first two number one hits; 'Relax' and 'Two Tribes'. However a Kid Jensen session for Radio One and an infamous appearance on the much maligned, and sorely missed, Channel Four music programme 'The Tube' led to Trevor Horn, former member of Buggles and record producer, expressing an interest in signing the band to his new label Zang Tuum Tumb Records. It was made clear at the outset that the offer of a recording contract was intimately bound up with a publishing deal with a sister company Perfect Songs:

> Bob Johnson introduced us to a solicitor called David Gentle who attempted to negotiate on our behalf, but without much success. Both contracts, we were told, had to be signed - or there was no deal. Many attempts at changing clauses were met with a resounding 'No!' from Jill Sinclair, Trevor Horn's wife, manager and business partner (Johnson, 1994, p.158).

Given Trevor Horn's reputation as a producer the band were anxious to secure his services and both the publishing and recording contracts were duly signed on 1 September 1983. Early in the first recording sessions the seeds of later recriminations were to surface with Horn replicating much of the band's music via studio technology, apparently unimpressed with the musicianship of some of the band. This question of who was the creative force behind FGTH was in many ways the underpinning of the later court case. An example of this is encapsulated by the authorship of the song 'Relax'. Holly Johnson was entitled to sixty six per cent of the performance royalties, as he had written the melody and lyrics of the song, to a harmony that had been created by two others. This did not go down well with other members of the band and according to Johnson, Trevor Horn accused him of being greedy notwithstanding the income that Horn could receive from a variety of sources for his input.[25] Whilst Johnson acknowledged Horn's creative role he still felt that such comments were not conducive to the band as a whole or for him personally; 'Trevor's accusation of greed did nothing for the harmony of the band. It is true that we did have Trevor's expertise as a producer, which was a valuable commodity: but he was certainly being remunerated for it, just as I felt I should be for my songwriting abilities' (Johnson, 1994, p.187). Although the band had achieved notable commercial success with the two singles and album Johnson was concerned over the cost of the recordings. By virtue of the contract such costs would be recouped from the group's royalty payments.[26] At this point in 1985, questions as to the enforceability of both agreements were raised. Whilst bringing up the issue of unreasonable restraint of trade the solicitors for the group also discussed the possibility of further negotiation to avoid litigation. This process occurred at the time the group was starting to record their second album. The relationship between Johnson and the rest of the group had further deteriorated though a decision was made not to attempt litigation before the recording of the second album as this would mean that Trevor Horn would not then produce the work. The band completed the album by April 1986 and after some months reworking by Trevor Horn released in November of that year. The basis of Johnson's complaints had been the excessive recording costs of the earlier work, unfortunately the recording costs for the second album reached a figure in the region of £760,000 of which some £500,000 was attributable to the work carried out by Horn between April and September. This was effectively the end of FGTH, after promoting 'Liverpool' Johnson intimated that he wanted to launch a career as a solo artist away from the rest of the group. However such a move was not easily carried out; 'What had started as a creative and exciting adventure had deteriorated into a cliche-ridden rock- 'n'-roll nightmare. It would take years, and huge legal fees, to extricate myself from that unhappy situation' (Johnson, 1994, p.249).

When Johnson 'left' FGTH asserting that the agreements with ZTT/Perfect were unenforceable, the record/publishing company issued a writ claiming that both the contracts were valid, and that, furthermore Johnson was bound by the 'leaving member' clause to enter into a new recording agreement with the company and could not therefore sign a contract with any other company. At first instance (10 February, 1988) the judge (Whitford J) held that the agreements were unenforceable and ZTT/Perfect appealed. The case came before the Court of Appeal and judgement was handed down on 26 July 1989. An analysis of the decision is illuminating for a number of reasons. Firstly, whilst *Schroeder* had shown that restraint of trade could apply to music publishing contracts, this was the first case where the doctrine had been considered in relation to recording agreements. In addition the Court's analysis of the terms is illuminating in terms of both previous and current practice within the music industry.

Dillon LJ for the Court of Appeal determined that whilst a number of clauses were stringent, three provisions in particular were crucial; those relating to length of term, minimum recording commitment and the leaving member clause.[27] The term, or length of the agreement, was to be calculated on the following basis:

3 TERM

3.1 The term of this Agreement shall commence on the 1st day of May 1983 and shall continue for an initial period ending on the 30th day of November 1983 ('the Initial Period') and for the additional period(s) if any for which such term may be extended consequent upon the Company's exercise of one or more of the options granted to the Company under the provisions of Clause 3.2 below.

3.2 Artist hereby irrevocably grants to Company options to extend the Term of this Agreement for Two (2) separate and successive Option Periods and Five (5) separate and successive Contract Periods...(*Holly Johnson*, 1993, p.69-70).[28]

Each contract period was defined, in other clauses, as being either twelve calendar months or 120 days after the date of delivery of the minimum recording commitment in that period whichever was the longer. The minimum recording commitment for each period was ascertained by Clause 4.1 that started with three singles (in the first three periods) followed by five albums in the next five periods. During this time the option periods were to be exercised solely by the company. Perhaps, in particular it was Clause 14 that provided the most important aspect of the case. It was widely acknowledged that Holly Johnson was the most marketable asset within the group and the one most likely to succeed in the event of the group ceasing to exist in their (then) present form. This view is borne out, after the event, by the fact that Holly Johnson had a number of successful hit singles such as 'Love Train' and 'Americanos' and a well received album in 'Hallelujah!' with the rest of the group fading into obscurity. In this context the provisions relating to the situation if one member of the band were to leave, or conversely the terms upon which a new member of the group was to be contracted take on great significance. Clause 14.1 outlined that if any member of the group were to leave during the term, the recording company could *elect* at its option to terminate the agreement with respect to that individual. This provision was not exercised and the draconian sub clauses of Clause 14 are worth examination in detail:

14.2 IT IS AGREED that:
(a) If during the Term any additional party joins the Group whether or not any of the existing members shall cease to be members such existing members shall procure that the joining party(ies) agrees to be bound by all of the terms and conditions of this Agreement before any further recordings are undertaken.
(b) If any member of the Group whether present or future shall subsequently leave the Group and the Company elects to terminate this Agreement as to such leaving member only then this Agreement will automatically continue in full force and effect as to the remaining members of the Group.
(c) If the Company elects not to terminate this Agreement in so far as it relates to any individual leaving member then this Agreement will automatically remain in full force and effect as to the remaining members of the Group and such individual leaving member will if requested to do so by the Company enter into a separate agreement with the Company on all the same terms and conditions as are set out in this Agreement (*Holly Johnson*, 1993, p.70-71).

This term was the nub of the complaint as ZTT/Perfect wanted to be able to sign him as a solo artist because the group had effectively disintegrated and the companies saw Johnson as the one true star - hence they wanted to retain his services rather than seeing him sign rival deals. The argument was that Johnson was bound to the company, with a new agreement, for the remaining unperformed period. At first instance Whitford J had determined that this part of the clause was void for uncertainty, although it is possible to see the perspective argued by the appellants. Clause 14(a) sought to tie in any new member(s) on the same terms and conditions and imposed on the existing group an obligation to realise this, whilst Clause 14(b) allowed the Company to terminate the agreement with respect to any leaving member whilst retaining the others. Clause 14(c) progressed this point logically, so that if the Company wished to retain the services of the leaving individual it could do so on the existing terms. This could however have the effect of multiplying each remaining commitment by the number in the group. Assuming that the company wished to retain the talents of each leaving member this could spawn five individual deals from the one collective agreement. This clause would, however, stand or fall with the rest of the agreement, if the original contract was unenforceable, as an unreasonable restraint of trade, then a leaving member could not be forced back into an unlawful contract. Dillon LJ did not determine the issue of 'voidness' as he upheld the first instance decision that the recording contract as a whole was grossly one-sided and unfair and therefore unenforceable.

The publishing agreement similarly fell on the basis of the terms being deemed oppressive. The period was for an initial year, with two option periods of two years each, totalling five years in all. The exclusive nature of the contract provided that the entire copyright in the works produced was assigned to the company for the whole copyright period. In favour of the 'composer' was a limited obligation to promote the works (best endeavours so far as reasonably practicable) and reassignment of unexploited material, a clause attributable to the earlier decision on publishing agreements:

> While no music publisher will guarantee a particular level of exploitation and/or success with respect to any specific song, publishers will sometimes agree to relinquish rights with respect to unexploited songs...In some instances, reversion may be deferred until all advances have been recouped,...Such clauses are quite typical in UK agreements, as a result of *Schroeder v Macaulay* (Biederman *et al*, 1992, p.391).

Despite these beneficial points they were insufficient to save the validity of the whole agreement. On a micro level the result of the case, given the consequent status of the group, seems fairly inconsequential. However, in terms of the wider industry, the Court of Appeal had ruled on the enforceability of the two major agreements both of which had developed over a period of time. The essential terms of the two contracts, ruled unenforceable, were likely to be repeated many times over in both longstanding and new agreements and as a consequence the potential repercussions were enormous.

Fool's Gold: 'the unfairest contract I have ever seen'

> The Stone Roses are the latest instalment in the resurrection insurrection. You know the argument by now: 'perfect pop' usually denotes a desperately faint echo of a past that cannot be surpassed, only nodded to with sad-eyed, elegiac deference, but there's a precious few who make the dream of 'perfect pop' blaze true (THE STONE ROSES, Simon Reynolds, Melody Maker, 3 June 1989).

The Stone Roses[29] formed in Manchester in 1985. As with girl duo Strawberry Switchblade the name was intended to highlight a contradiction of 'sweet surface and vicious feelings'; indeed an early mooted name for the group had been 'The Angry Young Teddy Bears'. That said there was little evidence of fresh 'perfect pop' on their first single 'So Young' released on the Thin Line record label. The deal with Thin Line was a one off and was followed by another agreement with Wolverhampton's FM Revolver to release the more favourably received 'Sally Cinnamon'. Around this time the band built up a strong and loyal local following in Manchester and began to receive some interest from record companies such as Rough Trade. Eventually the band signed a recording deal with Silvertone Records (the original agreement was signed with Zomba Productions Limited and assigned to Silvertone) and Zomba Music Publishing in April/May 1988. Their first single for the label, 'Elephant Stone' (produced by New Order's Peter Hook) was released later that year. As with FGTH the recording and publishing agreements was a joint package and it was clear that one could not be signed without the other.

The group now started to receive some critical acclaim playing a number of well-received concerts, including a key date at London's Institute of Contemporary Arts. Their eponymously titled debut LP was released in May 1989. The rise of The Stone Roses coincided with a movement termed by the music press as 'Madchester'; a scene based on the marriage of traditional guitar indie pop and the club oriented house music of Chicago (via Ibiza, Shoom and the Hacienda amongst others) that proved extremely successful commercially.[30] The band consolidated their position, headlining epoch defining concerts at Blackpool Empress Ballroom and Alexandra Palace and both The Stone Roses and Happy Mondays appeared on Top of the Pops as 'Fools Gold' and the 'Madchester Rave On EP' respectively crashed into the charts and the nation's consciousness. Later that year the group was pictured triumphant on the cover of the Christmas NME and it appeared that a prosperous, artistic and commercial, future lay ahead. In fact, nothing could have been further from the truth. Their only single of 1990,

'One Love' received only a lukewarm response and their Spike Island 'event' (the band were keen to stress it was not merely a concert) something of a damp squib. This progress eventually became completely stifled and by the end of the year they were involved in litigation that was to result in no further product being released until December 1994. The litigation, following a period of unsuccessful negotiation, revolved around claims that the publishing and recording contracts signed by the band members were an unreasonable restraint of trade and therefore unenforceable. The companies, Zomba and Silvertone, sought declarations from the court that the contracts were valid and enforceable, with injunctions to uphold the agreements. The case came before Mr Justice Humphries in March and April 1991 and he handed down his judgement on 20 May 1991. An important preliminary point was whether the agreements were caught by the doctrine of restraint of trade, the judge admitted that the investigation and evaluation of contracts could only be undertaken in specific and limited circumstances; '...I accept that the investigation of reasonableness of bargains made by persons not under disability, is only undertaken in a limited number of circumstances, so that in this case if the contract is not properly called a contract in restraint of trade further investigation of the terms does not arise' (*The Stone Roses*, 1993, p.159). Relying on dicta in *Esso,* the judge held as a matter of construction that the contracts were in restraint of trade, primarily as they had the potential to prevent the group from plying their trade for many years. Two particular clauses within the (recording) contract emphasised the position of the parties with respect to the product that the band would produce:

Clause 4.1

Zomba and its licensees shall have the irrevocable sole and exclusive right and license whether now in being or hereinafter arising throughout the Territory to use and exploit the Masters in perpetuity and may exercise such rights or refrain therefrom as Zomba shall deem fit and such rights shall include but not be limited to the following rights:

(a) of production reproduction distribution release... etc

(b) of whether how and when to commence discontinue or recommence the manufacture distribution and sale of records...(*The Stone Roses*, 1993, p.160).

Under Clause 6.2 The Stone Roses undertook that they would not:

(a) for a period of ten (10) years immediately following the expiry of the Term...render any Performances of any musical works embodied on any Master whereby such Performances may be recorded in any form for the purpose of manufacture and release of Records whether for sale or otherwise in any part of the Territory.

(b) render Performances of any nature whether falling under this Agreement or otherwise during the Term with or without others either on their own account or for any person firm or company where such Performances may be recorded in any form for the purpose of manufacture and release of Records whether for sale or otherwise in any part of the Territory (*The Stone Roses*, 1993, p.161).

These terms allowed the company the sole use of all the Masters in perpetuity, and included the right to commence or discontinue production of records. Effectively, by clause 4.2(b), the company did not have any positive obligation to release or distribute any records at all throughout the territory covered by the agreement. This becomes even more austere when it is considered that the contract defined the Territory as encompassing 'the world and its solar system'. In addition to this the re-recording clauses outlined in clause 6.2 also seemed far in excess of what might be reasonable to protect the companies own (economic) interests. Clause 6.2(a) prevented The Stone Roses from not only from re-recording any musical works embodied on Masters owned by the company, but also from performing them live when the performance might be recorded 'in any form'. Unsurprisingly, as the contracts were able to effectively sterilise the output of the group the judge found that the recording contract operated in restraint of trade and would therefore be considered by the court.

The next question to consider was, given that the contract was one that was in restraint of trade, was that restraint *unreasonable*? This returns to the point that not all contracts providing for exclusive performance that act in restraint of trade are inevitably unenforceable. The judge similarly observed that the fact that a position of superior bargaining power exists does not automatically mean that a fair agreement cannot be reached; 'It is however, possible, even if one person has superior knowledge and bargaining power for a fair agreement to be reached. Not everyone who was in a position to do so misuses his power to take advantage of the weaker party' (*The Stone Roses*, 1993, p.163). Having reviewed the clauses outlined above in deciding whether or not the contract could be one in restraint of trade, the judge went on to analyse certain other crucial terms within the agreement to determine the lawfulness of the restraint. The length of the agreement has always figured as a crucial factor, even the most severe restraint may be lawful if it is temporal. Here it was calculated on the basis of an initial period of one year (or otherwise calculated) to be followed by six possible option periods, with these options to be exercised at the whim of the company. These of themselves could have amounted to a minimum of a seven year term for the group, but in addition there was an alternative method of calculating the term on the basis of the release of material in the United States of America. Each period would expire nine months after this release of the minimum commitment, which was under Zomba's control, which effectively meant that the contract could be extended indefinitely. Whichever way the length was determined (the plaintiffs argued that the indefinite element was due to a drafting error) it was clear that the period was, at best, expansive:

> In any event, in as much as acceptance of the minimum commitment and release are both terms in the contract entirely within the control of Zomba, I consider that it would be possible under the contract for Zomba or the assignees to sterilise the Stone Roses for seven years, and that even a seven-year sterilisation would be entirely unreasonable to young artists such as the Stone Roses were in May 1988 (*The Stone Roses*, 1993, p.165).

On this basis the Judge considered the recording agreement to be unenforceable and therefore only briefly analysed some of the more minor terms in the contract though as he pointed out these were equally one-sided; 'Suffice it to say that in almost every clause it is the name of Zomba which is being provided for' (*The Stone Roses*, 1993, p.165). For example, under Clause 9.2 the company were given the right to authorise product endorsement on behalf of the artists irrespective of whether the group wished to endorse such a product which led the judge to observe that 'such a clause should not even appear in a recording contract'. In addition, by virtue of Clause 2.2 Zomba had the right to decide on all aspects of recording matters, something that the judge considered was; '...a remarkable and unfair declaration by the plaintiffs of any right of artistic control which no evidence I have heard or read of has justified' (*The Stone Roses*, 1993, p.166).[31] He went on to outline the potential inequity of terms involving royalty rates and the unlimited right of assignment, before accepting expert evidence that the agreement was entirely one-sided. The publishing agreement also fell as being an unjustifiable restraint of trade even though it did not contain all the flaws of the recording contract. There was, as in the FGTH agreement, a 'reasonable endeavours' provision in terms of the company's obligation to exploit material and a limited reversionary element for unexploited work. Interestingly, the relationship between the two agreements, that one could not be signed without the other, led the judge to conclude that even without any inherent unfairness this direct link to an unjustifiably restrictive recording contract was fatal to the publishing contract. Given this conclusion on both contracts the two companies requested that the unfair elements be severed leaving those parts of the contract that were fair intact. Severing clauses from contracts is an uneasy process for the judiciary although, an entire subsidiary element may be removed, if the main promise remains intact. A more likely course of action is the reduction of a restrictive element, provided that the element of severability has been created by the parties. The traditional view is that courts ought not to objectively create contractual obligations but that they may cut out definable elements. Clearly, in those cases that provide for exclusive services severability is extremely difficult without objective judicial inventiveness. The most obvious area where there were separately defined obligations was in respect to the term of the agreement, and indeed counsel for the plaintiffs suggested that the judge redraw this element by removing the additional option periods that rendered the agreement unfair. Thus, if a three or four year agreement would be justifiable, the additional periods could be severed. The judge found two objections to this; as each of the periods was arguably indefinite because of the provisions for the release of the minimum recording commitment in the United States of America, any severance would make little difference. The first period could still last for such a length as to render the agreement unfair. Secondly the whole process would involve the court in determining a crucial element, the term is naturally a key feature in determining the overall fairness, of the contract:

> It would amount to the Court substituting its own view as to the number of those periods and redrawing the parties' contract. If it were permissible to follow Mr Prescott's suggestion that in any contract where the length of term might offend, the dominant party could describe the term as, for instance, one year plus another year, plus another year, plus another year, etc., and ask the Court to decide how many to strike out in the end and how many to leave in. This would be unfair. It would act *in terrorem* to put fear into the weaker party and would be asking the Court not to determine the enforceability but to create an enforceable contract (*The Stone Roses*, 1993, p.168).

The judge would only consider the contract in its entirety; 'There is no way I am prepared to hack away at parts of the overall obligation so as to carve out a new contract which allows the Stone Roses to appear or record on limited occasions. Nor am I prepared to leave out the definition of term of the contract' (*The Stone Roses*, 1993, p.168). Severance was also rejected as a means to fix the publishing agreement and as both agreements were held to be unenforceable the declarations and injunctions sought by the plaintiffs were refused. The group was now free to sign new contracts and duly did, with Geffen. The case had evidently taken its toll on them artistically, as they were not to release any new material for another three and a half years. This bears out the point as to the short and fickle nature of some pop careers, the moment of inspiration and market worth may quickly disappear. Some material was released, in this intervening period, but this amounted to repackaged old/unreleased product via the Zomba group. The case was a logical application of the principles that had emerged in *Schroeder* and applied to *Holly*

Johnson, the question that remained, was given the trend to invalidate such agreements, whether a major international recording artist of superstar status would seek to challenge existing contractual arrangements. The answer was not long in coming.

Freedom's just a song by Wham! The George Michael decision

> It's a crap deal. But no crappier than any other major artists (Giles Smith, *The Independent* 4 September 1993, quoting an unnamed industry source who had examined George Michael's contract).

When George Michael issued his writ against Sony Entertainment in October 1992, it was heralded in the press as the dispute that was going to fundamentally effect and re-evaluate the relationship between record companies and artists. In the event the case, whilst certainly a cause celebre and subject to an inordinate amount of speculation, was not the ground breaking legal decision some suggested it would be. There were a number of reasons for this, most obviously the fact that the decision is that of a court of first instance. On that basis alone Mr Justice Parker's conclusions have little precedential weight especially since there are a number of Court of Appeal decisions and one House of Lords case that have previously dealt with the general area of music industry contracts. The case was settled before it reached the Court of Appeal with George Michael being released by Sony and allowed to sign elsewhere.[32] There was certainly speculation before the High Court decision that the case might go the whole way to the European Court of Justice with a legal timetable pencilled in for the next millennium. Perhaps, this was always unlikely to happen, given the fundamental effect that a break of this length would have had upon the career of George Michael. That said, the George Michael writ certainly acted as a catalyst within the music industry and caused some companies to at least consider the nature of their contractual and bargaining procedures. One example of this possible galvanising effect will be explored in the concluding section of this chapter that considers the post *George Michael* landscape.

At the beginning of his professional career, George Michael (the stage name of Panayiotou) was a member, along with Andrew Ridgley, of successful pop duo Wham! The two had previously been members of a group called The Executive with other school friends. In March 1982 Wham! signed a recording contract with Inner Vision, a small label, who had a licensing agreement with CBS.[33] The group had a number of hit singles during the period from June 1982 until summer 1983 including 'Wham Rap', 'Young Guns (go for it)', 'Bad Boys', 'Club Tropicana' and an album, 'Fantastic'. However the relationship between the group and the record company deteriorated and eventually led to legal action by Wham! with the aim of extricating themselves from the agreement. However, Inner Vision issued a writ against the group for damages and in November 1983 obtained an interlocutory injunction to prevent the group signing for any other company before the matter reached trial. The action was settled with the group signing a new contract directly with CBS (UK) in March 1984, and CBS reaching a financial accommodation with Inner Vision. The 1984 CBS agreement provided for one album with an additional seven options for the company which would result in Wham! delivering eight albums if CBS were to exercise all their options under the contract. Wham! continued their successful start with both singles and their second album 'Make It Big' which was released in November 1984.[34] Consequently in January 1985 CBS exercised the first contract option for a further album. However in the summer of 1986 Wham! split up, mainly at the instigation of George Michael, who wanted to pursue a solo career. In November 1986 CBS exercised the leaving member clause with respect to both Michael and Ridgley so that the 1984 agreement continued for both as solo artists. Michael had already recorded some solo work whilst with Wham! and it was clear that he should have a prosperous future ahead of him. This led to some initial moves to re-negotiate his contract with CBS whilst working on his first solo album. Part of this process was the concept of 'superstar' comparability, so that Michael's contractual terms would be on par with the major artists who were signed to CBS in the USA. After a series of (re)negotiations it was decided that any change in contractual terms would await the response to the first solo album, 'Faith'. This album was extremely successful selling some four million copies by the end of 1987 and eventually achieving over fourteen million sales. This undoubtedly brought Michael's worth as a solo performer sharply into focus and led to a reopening of the contract re-negotiation and a revamped agreement that Michael signed in early January 1988. At the same time Sony Corporation was successfully negotiating the take over of CBS and Sony Music Entertainment became the new owners of Michael's output. This acquisition was part of a policy of the hardware giants moving into the entertainment field.[35]

The renegotiation brought greater financial remuneration to Michael but also extended his commitment by two albums with a long stop of fifteen years duration of the contract. Sony's commitment was for three albums, of which 'Faith' was the first, with options for a further five. Michael spent 1988 touring abroad and, to minimise tax liability, received accelerated payments from Sony in order to increase income for that year which in total amounted to almost £11.5m. In many ways it was the following year that was to set the scene for the eventual litigation as it became clear that Michael was making important decisions concerning his artistic position with respect to his material and likely audience. Part of this move was essentially concerned with how, he thought, the music should be sold and that to progress into a more 'adult' market he needed to let the music speak for itself and play down his own image:

> ...I was aware that my promotion of 'Faith' (and, in particular, the live performances and the videos) had further established my public image as a young man with a primarily young female audience and that this perception was likely to dissuade a more adult audience from listening to it objectively. Therefore, I decided to remove my physical image from the marketing and promotion of my records, at least for the foreseeable future, hoping that in the long term I could reach an audience with whom I was comfortable (Evidence of George Michael, *George Michael*, 1994, p.276).

The success of 'Faith' led to further talks with the avowed aim of placing Michael into the same superstar bracket as other top Sony artists and these were concluded in July 1990. At the same time Michael was working on his second solo album, 'Listen Without Prejudice Volume 1', which was released in September 1990. It sold well, over 5 million copies, though not as prodigiously as its predecessor did. Despite this the relationship between company and artist deteriorated and on 14 February 1992 Michael was advised that it was open to him to contend that the agreement signed in 1988 was unenforceable as being an unreasonable restraint of trade. However, somewhat bizarrely as it turned out, a week later Michael's accountant wrote to Sony to ask for payment of an advance of $1 million due under the very same agreement, although this was later repaid some two months before proceedings were issued in October 1992. The writ argued, not only, that the agreement was an unreasonable restraint of trade, but also that the agreement was, in the alternative, void as being contrary to Article 85 of the EEC treaty. This latter claim was potentially groundbreaking, as all previous cases had focused solely upon the restraint of trade issue without recourse to potential 'European' remedies. This latter issue also has significance in that if successful the agreements would be void rather than unenforceable under the common law doctrine of restraint of trade.

The case itself was long and tortuous. Beginning in October 1993 and spanning some seventy-four days of factual and expert evidence and argument, the decision was finally handed down on 21 June 1994. Mr Justice Parker was not swayed by any of the arguments put forward by George Michael and dismissed the action on a number of grounds. Firstly, the judge considered whether the doctrine of restraint of trade applied to the agreement. Having reviewed previous case law and antecedents, the judge decided that there were no grounds for excluding the 1988 agreement from the purview of restraint of trade. Although he determined that he should consider the 1984 agreement as enforceable this did not rule out the 1988 agreement from the ambit of the doctrine and that such a contract should rightly be referred to the justification stage. Clearly the fact that *Holly Johnson* had placed recording agreements within the doctrine was influential. At this point it seemed that the case was following both *Holly Johnson* and *The Stone Roses* and the sole issue would be whether the terms could be justified, essentially a re-working of the same arguments concerning exclusivity, duration and sterilisation. However a major problem appeared for the plaintiff in the form of the series of negotiations that had taken place since the first agreement with Inner Vision. The 1984 agreement had been borne out of the compromised legal action that would have tested the validity of the 1983 agreement, whilst the 1988 agreement (the subject of scrutiny) was a renegotiation of the 1984 deal. It needs to be recognised that Michael was negotiating whilst in a position of contractual commitment and this becomes a crucial point, for should he argue that the 1984 contract was itself unenforceable then he would not have been fettered in his 1988 renegotiation (that agreement improved Michael's financial position). As it was the plaintiff's amended statement of claim took no view as to whether the 1984 agreement was enforceable or not but argued that investigation as to the enforceability of this earlier contract was irrelevant. Parker J took this position to mean that the negotiations had proceeded in 1988 on the basis that Michael thought the 1984 agreement to be enforceable, whether it was or not. The crucial point was that the 1988 contract led back to the 1984 deal that compromised the legal proceedings. The defendants argued that there was a public policy argument in preventing this compromise from being challenged, a supposition that garnered judicial support:

1. There is a public policy in favour of settlement of disputes in litigation.
2. There is a public policy in favour of the disposal of disputes whether by way of judicial or arbitral decision or by way of settlement *inter partes* being treated as final.
3. There is a public interest in resisting the re-opening or re-litigating of issues apparently resolved by judgment, award or *inter partes* settlement.
4. As a reformulation of points 1-3, where disputes have arisen and those disputes have been disposed of by means of an *inter partes* settlement, public policy favours giving effect to that settlement and to refusing to allow a party thereto to resurrect issues whether identical or similar to those which the settlement had been intended to lay to rest (*George Michael*, 1994, pp.342-343).

On the basis of the public interest, that compromised litigation be followed without further recourse to 'the law, he concluded that it was not open to George Michael to contend that the agreement was in restraint of trade. This view, supporting settled disputes, was itself based on notions of public policy. This probably accurately reflects the shift towards alternative methods of dispute resolution (ADR), and the fears that such systems may be of little use if the law was still used should the parties be dissatisfied with the outcome:

> ... the overriding consideration, as it seems to me, is that if it be open to a plaintiff to challenge a compromise of a restraint of trade issue by alleging that the compromise is itself in restraint of trade, then it seems to me to follow that a restraint of trade issue could never be compromised by the substitution of a new agreement. Unless the parties are able to compromise the issue in some way which does not involve the substitution of a new agreement, they will have no option but to litigate the issue to judgment, whether they like it or not (*George Michael*, 1994, p.346).

This view, based on the public policy of upholding compromise agreements, is not without problems. Firstly, Parker J had already accepted that a renegotiated agreement (1988) of an enforceable contract (1984) was within the doctrine of restraint of trade, even though the changes were not extensive and generally in favour of the plaintiff. It seems odd that the court would enquire as to whether this altered contract is enforceable but not if it was produced by compromise of legal action. Secondly, he is ignoring the precarious position of pop artists that featured strongly in previous cases, it would clearly be a drastic step to pursue litigation given the fragile nature and limited longevity of most careers. Litigation could have effectively destroyed Wham! by removing them from the market place at the time when they were 'hot', a point noted later in the judgement:

> The demand for pop records is to a high degree fickle and unpredictable, and there is virtually no 'brand loyalty' in the sense that a customer will prefer one label to another. Fashions tend to change with bewildering rapidity, and a product which is in high demand one month may suffer a catastrophic fall in demand the next (*George Michael*, 1994, p.348).

Far from encouraging and supporting compromise agreements the logic of Parker J's view is that a band seeking to challenge an agreement need to seek judicial opinion as to whether their contract is in restraint of trade or not rather than agree any compromise which is then sacrosanct from a later challenge. This ignores, not only the position of artists who will inevitably struggle to impose much in the way of changes from a fairly well established set of standard terms, unless in a bargaining war. Even though Parker J excluded the 1988 agreement from scrutiny, on public policy grounds, he still considered whether the terms of the agreement could be justified; '...in case my conclusion on the public policy argument is wrong' (*George Michael*, 1994, p.347). Referring back to the two stages of the *Nordenfelt* case, Parker J noted that once it was established that the agreement attracted the doctrine you had to consider (i) whether the agreement was reasonable in the interests of the parties themselves and (ii) whether the agreement was justifiable in the public interest. Surprisingly perhaps Parker J also concluded that the agreement could also be justified and also dismissed the claims under Article 85.

It is worth underlining the point that those features of the contracts in the other cases *(Schroeder, Holly Johnson, The Stone Roses)* that the courts had objected to were also largely present in *George Michael*. This is unsurprising given the development of industry norms. Parker J suggested that this similarity of agreements was a product of market forces rather than any lack of competition between the majors. Furthermore the negotiations of deals were handled by a small group who acted on both sides and were thus able to set an industry standard. On the key issue of duration the judge took some surprising views based on the economic dimension to the relationship at the expense of notions of artistic control; 'Thus, it cannot sensibly be suggested that if the 1988 Agreement runs its full course Mr Michael will thereby suffer financial or commercial hardship of any kind: indeed, the opposite is likely to be the case' (*George Michael*, 1994, p.365).

This point, that the effect of such a long deal was likely to be financially beneficial to Michael, was reiterated, as the judge thought that at the expiry of the contract the artist would be in a much stronger bargaining position to 'auction his services'. This ignores the fact that his career might not last eight albums and his entire output would be controlled by one company. Parker J was also prepared to accept the argument dismissed in *Holly Johnson* that the length of the agreement was required by the company to subsidise the failing artists. On the use of option periods the judge considered that the utilisation of these would be a measure of success, at least in commercial terms for Sony. This ignores the valid point that Michael might have non-economic career aspirations. Michael could of course bring forward the end of the deal by producing material more quickly although this too may have implications for artistic integrity and quality of product. When examining the other contentious terms Parker J took a similar view, stressing the commercial nature of the agreement, and concluding that the contract could be justified under the *Nordenfelt* principles. It is this latter area of the judgement that takes a markedly different approach to the previous cases. It appears that Michael's status as an international artist and the subsequent rewards, that he was entitled to under the agreement, altered the perception of the contractual terms with respect to justification.

A new dawn

The range of cases, from *Schroeder* to *George Michael*, illustrate a remarkable number of similarities both with respect to the terms and also the bargaining processes. Whilst there is clearly a vast differential with regard to the remuneration on offer, between, for example, Macaulay and George Michael, many of the basic principles are remarkably similar. Indeed, it is these common terms that form the heart of both publishing and recording agreements, a point that has not been lost on the judges prior to Parker J in *George Michael*. The key elements are; exclusivity, duration and territory, the ownership of the material, the provisions for exploitation, and rights to terminate and assign. What is apparent is that even the most successful artist will have to accept that he has limited ability to alter the basic tenets of the agreement though clearly he will be able to negotiate greater rewards through higher royalty rates and larger advances. What is illuminating about George Michael's position is that there was still a *quid pro quo* required for the improved financial arrangements. A further commitment, in terms of increased output, was used to obtain increased monetary benefits. This appears to be the fundamental nature of the relationship, a strict contractual regime with, if the artist is successful, high rewards according to the level of success. The key points of exclusive performance over a wide geographical area (taken to an absurd degree with respect to *The Stone Roses*) for a potentially long, virtually career length, period of time are seemingly cast in stone. No matter what the status of the artist, the company, on the basis of Sony's approach to George Michael, will not concede much in these areas. Indeed, it would require a serious review of the functioning of the industry to alter the basic approach. As long as the successes are used to pay for the high failure rate of bands the industry will wish to tie in those successes as tightly, and for as long as, possible. This is perhaps why despite the decisions in *Schroeder* and *Holly Johnson*, the very terms that the courts had found so objectionable, when gathered together, re-appeared in the later cases. Despite the observations of Parker J, with respect to competition between the major companies, this standardisation of basic principles is a major problem.

The music industry has taken a number of differing and pragmatic responses to the cases that have dealt with these issues of control. In particular there are a few emerging signs of an increased 'transparency', that whilst acknowledging that the 'employer' holds the upper hand, it makes sound financial sense to keep the artist happy. In certain cases this has seen itself translated into an openness about contractual negotiation and terms that may pay dividends in the long term by fostering a closer and more trusting relationship between the parties. That said, there is still the underlying presumption that while 'artists come and go, the record industry goes on forever' and such approaches may be of little overall significance.

Notes

1. The title of this chapter is taken from the Stiff Little Fingers song 'Rough Trade' from the LP 'Inflammable Material'. The song recounts their alleged treatment at the hands of their Record Company, Rough Trade.

2. The first level of copyright infringement in the music industry, and thus the first potential area where control can be exercised is, in relation to plagiarism. In order to examine issues of plagiarism, it is important to grasp what can actually be copied. Under s3(2) Copyright Designs and Patents Acts 1988 (CDPA) when a songwriter creates a song, as soon as that piece of work is **fixed** in some form (this can be taped or written down) the creator enjoys copyright in that work if it satisfies the test of **originality**. The essential element of originality is not uniqueness in terms of end product but relates to the mode of creation. If it is a product of the author's creative process it is original, if it is 'copied' from another work it is not original, aside from the fact that the act of production will probably infringe the copyright in the original work. An original song itself at this point will enjoy two separate copyrights; under the CDPA copyright subsists in the musical work and literary work (the lyrics of the song). Any problem over the legitimacy of creation and therefore ownership inevitably only arises when the song becomes commercially successful, thereby gaining exposure and earning sufficient revenue to satisfy any claim. The case of *Francis Day Hunter v Bron* [1963] Ch 587 provides a good example of how copying of a copyright work can be either 'conscious' or 'subconscious'. The plaintiffs argued that copyright had been infringed in their musical work 'In a Spanish Town' by the defendants' publication of a composition entitled 'Why?'. The defendants denied that their work was an infringement and argued that no conscious copying had taken place. Wilmer LJ accepted that subconscious copying was a possibility and that, if it occurred, it could amount to a breach of copyright. In this instance, however, the High Court's finding, that there was insufficient material to draw the allusion of subconscious reproduction, was upheld by the Court of Appeal. Proving that songs merely sound similar to copyright works creates more problems, in terms of proving an infringement of copyright, than those which can be identified as an exact appropriation or 'steal'. The issue appears to be one of what is meant by originality and a philosophical debate about cultural reference points and the finite limits of popular music; 'The thing is there are only 8 notes in the scale. It's difficult to prove whether plagiarism is deliberate or unconscious' (Nigel Gibb, quoted in NME, 11 March 1995).

3. In addition to the Mechanical Copyright Protection Society (MCPS), who collect royalties for the mechanical rights there is also Phonograph Performance Limited (PPL) who collect royalties payable on the public performance and broadcast of sound recordings and the Performing Right Society (PRS) who are assigned the performance right in the original composition. There are also similar agencies involved in collecting royalties for audio-visual rights.

4. We are aware that both 'product' and 'exploit' have a myriad of meanings. For example product is the industry slang for the music it owns and arguably the artists themselves (see our discussion of George Michael later in the chapter). Exploitation may be legitimate (as we intend it in this first usage here) or have more sinister undertones as our analysis of the music industry cases will show.

5. This notion of construction is embodied in 'The Spice Girls' who have also attempted to enter the political arena with their pronouncements on 'girl power'.

6. Recording deals, as the name suggests, deal with agreements concerning the ownership of sound recordings of material and are defined in copyright terms in CDPA 1988 s5. Recording contracts are predicated upon published work, which is the domain of publishing agreements. Copyright in published work is dealt with in CDPA 1988 s3.

7. Interestingly, apart from the bastardisation of the title of the John Osborne play, the song itself pays homage to John Lennon, a great influence on the band, from the piano introduction 'nod' to 'Imagine' to the lyrical content of the song 'So I start a revolution from my bed' alluding to the infamous John and Yoko 'sleep ins'.

8. The sample was used without obtaining permission for its use. The success of the song prompted the artists, publishers and record company to seek royalties for such use and the matter was settled for an undisclosed sum (Anon, 1992).

9. The song used Rick James' 'Super Freak'. MC Hammer is reported as saying 'Right after I did the song, I said, 'Hey, I gotta pay Rick [James] for this.' I didn't need a lawyer to tell me that ...I'm borrowing enough of his song that he deserves to be compensated' (Anon, 1992). Additional examples include the use of Spandau Ballet's 'True' on PM Dawn's 'Set Adrift on Memory Bliss'; M/A/R/R/S use of Stock Aitken and Waterman's 'Roadblock' on their No.1 hit 'Pump up the Volume'. Another recent example involved Bjork whose album 'Post' had to be deleted the day after its release after she failed to clear a sample of Scanner's 'Mass Observation' and the album re-pressed with the offending sample removed (NME 24 June 1995, p.7).

10. The JAMMs issued the following advert in the aftermath of the furore:

> WARNING: WE interrupt this page to bring you the following warning. Anyone in possession of the Justified Ancients of Mu Mu album '1987' could be breaking the law. If you own a copy please return it to PO Box 283, HP22 5BW (Sounds, 12 September 1987 cited on sleeve of *Shag Times*).

In fact some copies of the LP were ceremoniously burnt (and the event captured for posterity by the NME) and the rest thrown into the North Sea during their return trip to England. Five copies that the JAMMs later found in a second hand record shop were offered for sale in *The Face* for £1000 each and allegedly three of these were sold.

11. The former is related to 'social harm' whilst the latter operates to protect the public from less offensive acts which may merely outrage or offend (Robertson and Nicol, 1993).

12. There is a distinction between the common law offences of outraging public decency and the statutory offences under the *Obscene Publications Act 1959*, see *Gibson* on this point.

13. 'Article' is defined in *OPA 1959* s1(1); 'For the purposes of this Act an article shall be deemed to be obscene if its effect or (where the article comprises two or more distinct items) the effect of any one of its items is, if taken as a whole, such as to tend to deprave and corrupt persons who are likely, having regard to all relevant circumstances, to read, see or hear the matter contained or embodied in it'.

14. An earlier example was the case brought against Virgin Records in Nottingham concerning the Sex Pistols' notorious album 'Never mind the bollocks...here's the Sex Pistols'.

15. NWA were one of the first West Coast gangsta rap groups to obtain a high profile and international success- the LP title is a 'backward' reading of the phrase Niggaz 4 life.

16. Consider the following definition of gangsta rap by Michael Saunders in the Boston Globe; ''Gangsta rap' songs are street tales told in ragged, unblushing rhymes, where life is often a race to 'get paid' and get laid before a bullet stops the party. Women are usually absent for this

million-record-selling landscape of guns and money, except in their roles as gold digging 'bitches' and sex-dispensing 'hos'. This world is distinguished by its colors, the ones that identify friend or foe, and those cordoned behind yellow crime-scene tape: brown bodies with congealed blood a lifeless maroon, and the red rimmed eyes of a new statistic's mother' Saunders M 'Gangsta Warfare' Boston Globe, 3/10/96 B29; retrieved from Censorship in Music Internet site (http://www.ultranet.com/~crowley/news031096.html).

17. This is perhaps because rap is a far more significant cultural force in the US. However, other areas have been subject to action in the UK and the latest area of conflict concerns a small, though financially viable, self contained part of the industry, which promotes white power. The nature of some of the lyrics on albums such as 'Barbecue in Rostock' by No Remorse could lead to prosecution under the provisions of the *Public Order Act 1986* on the ground of inciting racial hatred. Similarly the distributors or organisers of performances might face a criminal prosecution.

18. The RIAA has specified the correct use of the label; 1" by 5/8", Black and White on the front of the permanent packaging under the shrinkrap (see http://www.riaa.com/pap.htm).

19. In Louisiana, Rep. Ted Haik kept alive his biennial tradition of introducing legislation to criminalise the sale of sound recordings bearing the Parental Advisory logo. In three previous attempts, Rep. Haik's bills have been enacted by the legislature, only to be vetoed by two different Governors (http://www.riaa.com/artistic/artistic.htm 10 July, 1997).

20. 'Made of Stone' was The Stone Roses' fourth single.

21. *Esso* is dealt with in the introductory chapter.

22. The Court of Appeal decision is reported at [1974] 1 All ER 171.

23. For the sake of completeness we have included the remaining two clauses of Macaulay's publishing agreement. Note in particularly clause 17 that enforces the composer to act with good faith towards the publisher in the certain instances:

> Clause 12. (a) The composer will execute a standard song writer's agreement in respect of each and every work the subject of this agreement. Such song writer's agreement shall be in the form annexed hereto and initialled by the parties (hereinafter referred to as 'the song writer's agreement'). (b) For the avoidance of doubt it is agreed that any assignment required under clauses 4 or 12 hereof shall be in the form of the song writer's agreement. Clause 17. The composer will at the publisher's request at any time during the said term or thereafter execute any other document and do all other acts or things which may hereafter be required for vesting in the publisher the rights and benefits hereby expressed to be assigned and conferred (*Schroeder*, 1974, p.620).

24. 'From the Diamond Mine to the Factory' was the title suggested by Holly Johnson for Frankie goes to Hollywood's second album, the follow up to 'Welcome to the Pleasure Dome', our re-working of this is a celebration of a popular music myth of escapism and pop music as a 'way out of the ghetto'. In the event the album was entitled 'Liverpool', a title Johnson found ironic given that none of the band lived there any longer.

25. Johnson (1994, p.186-187) makes the point that Horn stood to obtain royalties from his various roles; '... whose companies were getting 35% of the publishing royalties (for doing nothing) while he personally, as producer, got 4% of recommended retail price on each record from ZTT. Not to mention the profit ZTT were making in their deal with Island Records, or the profits of Sarm Studios (owned by Jill and Trevor and family), where we were obliged to record.

26. Dillon LJ noted that the recording costs of 'Relax' were in the region of £26,000 and 'Welcome to the Pleasure Dome' £394,000 (*Holly Johnson*, 1993, p. 71).

27. Dillon LJ referred to Clause 1 (production and delivery of material), Clause 2 (ownership of the masters), Clauses 5 & 6 (exclusivity) Clauses 8,9,10,12 (payments provisions), Clause 18 (promotion) and Clause 20 (assignability).

28. The inconsistent wording (*option* periods followed by *contract* periods) in the clause is odd though insignificant in the final analysis.

29. The group consisted of Mounfield (spelt incorrectly on the writ and judgement), Brown, Squire and Wren. Evans was the group's manager. After Wren and Squire left the band, the Stones Roses carried on with some new personnel for a short period before finally splitting up soon after their performance at Reading Festival in 1996. Squire formed a new band, The Seahorses whilst Mounfield joined Primal Scream. Brown pursued a successful solo career with his first album, 'Unfinished Monkey Business'. See further on the history of the group, Robb (1997).

30. The scene embraced the heavyweight three of The Stone Roses, Inspiral Carpets (for whom Noel Gallagher was a roadie) and the Happy Mondays. There were a number of other lesser lights such as Northside, Paris Angels and Intastella.

31. In addition, in the publishing agreement under Clause 2.3(e) the publisher had 'the sole exclusive rights to make and publish new adaptations and arrangements and to make additions and alterations in and to the works or part thereof' (*The Stone Roses*, 1993, p.170). Again this is quite an extraordinary limitation on the artistic freedom of the songwriters.

32. Notice to appeal was in fact lodged Coulthard (1995, p.731). For details of the settlement/agreement see *Music Business International*, August 1995, pp.12-13.

33. The Inner Vision contract provided for up to ten albums worth of material with advances on a sliding scale of £2,000.00 for the first to £35,000.00 for the tenth with royalties set at eight per cent for the UK and six per cent for the rest of the world (*George Michael*, 1994, p.254).

34. According to the report in *Music Business International* (August 1995) of the eventual settlement of the litigation between Michael and Sony, Wham! had sold a total of some 100m singles and albums.

35. According to the Corporate report in *Music & Copyright* (1993, p.12-13), Sony paid $2 billion for CBS Records and in 1989 paid $3.6 billion for Columbia Pictures.

There is every indication that eighteenth-century spectators rejoiced in the inherent violence of combat sports. The German visitor Charles Louis von Poellnitz noted that spectators cheered when wounds were inflicted. The same custom was noticed by the French traveler Antoine Prevost when, a few years later, he visited Figg's famous establishment, the boastfully named 'Amphitheatre', opened in 1743. Prevost and a crowd seated in banks that reached to the vaulted roof witnessed cudgeling, fistfighting, wrestling, and - finally - a combat with sabres. When the redoubtable Figg sliced off part of his opponent's calf, the crowd shouted for more of the same, '**bravo, bravo, ancora, ancora**' (Guttmann, 1986, p.71).

Altogether, it was the face of a man to be afraid of in a dark alley or lonely place. And yet Tom King was not a criminal, nor had he ever done anything criminal. Outside of brawls, common to his walk in life, he had harmed no one. Nor had he ever been known to pick a quarrel. He was a professional, and all the fighting brutishness of him was reserved for his professional appearances. Outside the ring he was slow-going, easy-natured, and, in his younger days, when money was flush, too open-handed for his own good. He bore no grudges and had few enemies. Fighting was a business with him. In the ring he struck to hurt, struck to maim, struck to destroy; but there was no animus in it. It was a plain business proposition. Audiences assembled and paid for the spectacle of men knocking each other out. The winner took the big end of the purse (London, 1911, p.17).

There are fine people involved in boxing, but boxing also attracts creatures who crawl out of sewers every morning and back into them when it gets dark. Their only goal is to make a buck. And they'll exploit whomever they have to, to do it (Frank Blackman, sportswriter quoted in Meister, 1996, p.2).

But while the top handful of fighters earn fortunes, there are signs that in Britain at least boxing may be dying a slow death, that it resembles a pyramid with a glittering top and crumbling foundations. There are now 12,000 amateurs, but 15 years ago there were 50,000; and there are now 700 professionals compared to 1,000 then. The British Boxing Board of Control admits poor kids are increasingly turning to athletics and football as a way out of nowhere and the martial arts as a means of discipline (**The Guardian**, 8 July 1994).

4 A Brutal Aesthetic
Contract and control in boxing

The Evander Holyfield/Mike Tyson World Boxing Association (WBA) heavyweight title fight, on 28 June 1997 in Las Vegas, and the subsequent furore, perhaps best sums up the tensions and difficulties that resonate throughout the sport. Tyson's personal and boxing history is well documented; he won his first professional fight in 1985, and a year later, at the age of twenty, became the youngest ever world heavyweight champion when he defeated Trevor Berbick in the second round to win the World Boxing Championship (WBC) title. He added to this with the WBA title, in February 1987 and the International Boxing Federation (IBF) title in August 1987. At this point he was seen as a truly great champion to rank alongside fighters such as Ali, Liston and Marciano. However, whilst his professional career had previously been highly successful, his personal life had been considerably less so.

Sent to a remand home in Brooklyn in 1979, accused of assault by his former wife, his apotheosis came in February 1992 when convicted to six years imprisonment for rape. He won his first fight back after his release but then lost a WBA championship fight to Evander Holyfield in December 1996. The fight of 28 June 1997 was the eagerly awaited rematch of this. The pre-fight build up was a cacophony of hyperbole. Available only on pay per view to maximise profits, Don King, Tyson's promoter, noted before the fight, that the show was to be; 'screened to 159 countries, with eleven languages spoken by ringside commentators - including three dialects of Chinese' (Mullan, 1997). Behind on points after the first two rounds of the bout and, incensed by what he alleged was head butting by Holyfield, Tyson came out at the beginning of the third without a gum shield.[1] With thirty three seconds left in the round, and with signs of Tyson regaining some of the initiative, he hooked an arm round Holyfield's neck, pulled him towards him and bit his right ear. Holyfield's reaction was one of severe pain and astonishment. Mills Lane (the referee) examined Holyfield's ear, docked Tyson two points (one for the bite and one for a shove in the back) and allowed them to continue. Seconds later, Holyfield leapt back in agony again, as Tyson sunk his teeth into his left ear. The referee subsequently disqualified Tyson although Lane was criticised, in some quarters, for allowing the fight to proceed after the first bite, when Tyson spat out the piece of Holyfield's ear that had been bitten off. Bob Mee (1997) writing in *Boxing News* posed the question as to whether boxing could have survived the scandal had Tyson gone on to win the fight after the first bite. The incident would undoubtedly have had a destabilising effect on Holyfield and it would only have taken a good punch or set of punches from Tyson to eventually win the contest. 'Demeaning and disgusting' was how *The Guardian* (Williams, 1997) described the incident with other parties such as Barry McGuigan from the Professional Boxers' Association adding to the opprobrium.

The immediate reaction of the authorities was to withhold Tyson's purse pending a hearing of the Nevada Athletic Commission to consider his long term fate; Tyson's personal apology was accepted by Holyfield before the Commission met.[2] The punishment subsequently meted out was probably the sternest that could have been given when it is taken into account that a permanent life ban would have potentially opened the way for a restraint of trade action. However, whilst Tyson was indeed banned, the well worn cliche of every cloud having a silver lining was once again illustrated:

> It is by far the stiffest financial penalty handed out in the sport, and the maximum the commission could deliver - but the reality is that Tyson retains $27 million and will probably get his license back when first allowed to apply for it, 12 months from now. Commercial imperatives dictate that boxing cannot do without Mike Tyson's phenomenal ability to generate wealth (Mitchell, 1997b).

This is the commercial dimension to professional boxing. Perhaps the most barbaric act ever seen in the modern professional sport, certainly the most barbaric 'sporting' act perpetrated in front of an audience estimated to be nearing two billion people worldwide, arguably increased Tyson's draw at the box office to the extent that promoters were already rubbing their hands gleefully at the prospect of the '$200m bite of the century' (Wiechula, 1997). Such is the contradictory and complex interrelationship between boxing and commerce. Indeed, boxing is a sport full of contradictions; winner/loser, poverty/wealth, brutality/beauty, life/death. Whilst boxing may be viewed as a ritual of savagery, this very savageness can be seen as part of a wider sporting artistry. Oates (1987, p.322) makes the point that while boxing can have the power of great poetry and exhibit many aspects of the human condition, it is in reality far from metaphor; 'To the untrained eye most boxing matches appear not merely savage but mad. As the eye becomes trained, however, the spectator begins to see the complex patterns that underlie the "madness"; what seems to be merely confusing action is understood to be coherent and intelligent, frequently inspired'. Brendan Ingle, owner of St Thomas' Club for Boys and Girls, and trainer of Prince Naseem, emphasises the point when commenting on the Benn/McClellan fight:

> It was boxing at its most sophisticated, crude, barbaric, enchanting, skilful - all at
> the same time. Boxing is a serious business. I teach my lads how to take
> precautions - how to survive in the ring. But I remind them that they're not playing
> marbles in there. That fight was what life is all about - it was Benn coming back
> from the brink of nearly getting killed, and surviving. It was McClellan coming
> back from the brink of nearly getting killed and surviving...Just remember: you
> don't begin to live until you begin to die. That's well worth remembering (Beattie,
> 1996, p.246).

In some ways boxing does appear somewhat anachronistic in modern society, comparable more to the diminishing group of blood sports, than any contemporary sporting culture. Certainly the law's relationship with boxing tends to show that what once may have appeared conventional is increasingly difficult to justify (Gunn and Ormerod, 1994). The courts have found it extremely difficult to reconcile boxing with some fundamental legal principles (Parpworth, 1994 & 1996).[3] Even more fundamental than any socio-legal intervention is the conflict that provides the impetus for boxers to survive the gruelling dimension to the sport and prosper. To be a boxer you *need* struggle; when asked why Puerto Rico had so many champions, Jose Torres answered that it was impossible to have good boxers in a society that is content, that you have to know struggle to be a boxer (Callahan, 1991, p.93). There is undeniably a link here with other parts of the entertainment industry such as music and football, which represent the traditional areas that youth have looked to for glamour and upward mobility.[4] In addition, boxing can also be evocative of something more than the sport itself. In his epic and evocative study of the 'Rumble in the Jungle' between George Foreman and Muhammed Ali, Mailer (1975) makes the point that the tension was palpable before the fight and that the stakes were pitched at something more than merely a boxing match with a lucrative purse. However, Ali shrewdly posited that whilst there was indeed a great deal of money washing around the contest, the eventual destination was somewhat fragmented; 'I'm going home with no more than one million, three hundred thousand. Half of the five million goes to the Government, then half a million for expenses and one-third to my manager. I'm left with one million three. That ain't no money. You give me a hundred million today, I'll be broke tomorrow' (Mailer, 1975, p.77-78).

This chapter examines the relationships between the various parties within amateur and professional boxing and concentrates more specifically on the terms and conditions of boxer/manager agreements. It focuses on the legal attempts to intervene in the profession of boxing with respect to the licensing of the participants, the safety of the participants and the subsequent standard form contractual arrangements that may regulate the various relationships. This entire analysis is necessarily set within the historical development of the sport encompassing its organisation and administration and the division between the recreational and income generating sides.

Figg, Sullivan, the 'Bull's Head Terror' and the development of the 'noble art'

The science of boxing has obvious early historical origins in bare knuckle combat. The narrative of the development of the professional sport is inextricably linked to individual fighters; boxing is essentially the story of boxers and the story particularly concentrates upon the 'heavyweights'. In the mid eighteenth century, many fights were sponsored by the aristocracy,[5] if they did not arrange the fight they often 'honoured' it by their presence at the event; a fashionable patronage that continued into the nineteenth century. The increased popularity of prize fighting coincided with questions being asked about its effects upon social order and moral probity (Sugden, 1996). This lack of 'civility' in the sport led to it being outlawed in 1750, although enforcement of such regulation was piecemeal. The earliest recorded champion was James Figg, the 'Father of Boxing' who advertised the teaching of boxing and other fighting arts and promoted exhibitions (Fleischer & Andre, 1979). When Figg became champion in 1719 there was little in the way of formalised rules, it was not until 1743 that Jack Broughton developed the first set of boxing rules and the glove which was utilised for sparring. These rules were the governing procedure until 1838 when the 'London Prize Ring Rules' code was approved. The Broughton Rules provided some basic guidance on 'etiquette' in that hitting below the belt, or when an opponent was down, was outlawed. The fights were, however, still limitless in duration and usually carried on until one pugilist was knocked out or collapsed from exhaustion. In addition to introducing gloves, Broughton also contributed to the tactics of the game by utilising defence in addition to the more usual offensive hitting.[6] Contiguously, America was also becoming an area where the sport was developing, often under English rules, with boxers who had made their name fighting in England. Historic champions such as John L Sullivan emerged and it was clear that money could be made from not only participation but also the promotion of such fights:

> Sullivan's first important fight around New York State took place on a barge anchored in the Hudson river off Yonkers. John Flood, known as the Bull's Head Terror, was his opponent. Five hundred sports paid ten dollars each to see the battle. Sullivan and Flood fought with skin-tight gloves, under London Prize

Rules, for a stake of $1,000. Of which $750 went to the winner and $250 to the loser (Fleischer & Andre, 1979, p.59).[7]

The end of Sullivan's reign also coincided with further regulation, and his defeat by Jim Corbett in 1892, heralded the domination of a new era of boxing with gloves preferred to bare knuckles. In 1866 the Amateur Athletics Club had asked the eighth Marquis of Queensbury to give his name to new rules for the outdoor boxing contests that they ran - in effect the Queensbury Rules were the first attempts to fully regulate boxing contests.[8] The new regime advocated the use of boxing gloves, fixed rounds of three minutes with a minute's rest in between, and the requirement for a referee to adjudicate upon the proceedings. Whilst arguably this was part of the 'civilising' of boxing, others such as Sugden (1996) have commented that in fact these developments did not make boxing any safer than it had been under the Broughton Rules. The addition of hard boxing gloves extended the reach of boxers and, insofar as they protect the protagonist's hands, it meant that more blows could be struck to the head of the other protagonist. Also, whilst there was some limitation on the number of three minute rounds, boxers were forced to carry on for the whole of each of these three minutes, unlike under the Broughton Rules where a tired boxer was allowed to rest on one knee to catch his breath during the bout. In addition to the professional sport, boxing also gained support from those who wished to practice the art for recreational purposes. The sport still divides on these distinct lines although in order to obtain a professional licence it is almost inevitable that an amateur career will have been pursued in the past. This requires that the recreational game remains healthy and concerns have been expressed as to the financial state of American Amateur Boxing due to lack of Olympic success and subsequent falling television revenue (Armit, 1997).

Recreational boxing

The Amateur Boxing Association (ABA) was set up in 1880 by a group of leading members of amateur clubs, Birley (1993, p.287) notes that; '[t]heir championships were immediately popular and the ABA's influence spread quickly - Dublin BC affiliated in 1884 and Cardiff three years later. They were models of decorum'. At the founding meeting a major issue was 'to take into consideration the necessity of revising the laws which govern Amateur Boxing' (Pontremoli, 1995) and boxing quickly gained recognition and was included as an Olympic sport at the 1908 games in London. In 1993 the ABA altered its legal status to form a limited company, the Amateur Boxing Association of England Ltd whose objectives are to promote the sport and practice of amateur boxing in England. In particular the ABA is concerned with the organisation, supervision and running of national and international amateur boxing events; the arrangement of sponsorship and promotion for such events and the provision of training and education.

The public face of the ABA is the running of the national championships. In order to ensure a close degree of regulation there exist a number of Regional Associations who administer the boxing clubs within the different areas they cover through a divisional structure. The divisions have representation on the appropriate Regional Council, which in turn has representation on the National Council; this latter body has Directors and representatives from other interested groups. In addition to the English Association there are similar bodies in Scotland, Ireland and Wales as well as both a European (EABA) and International Association (AIBA). As professional boxing has been the subject of an increasing level of criticism, usually after a tragic event in the ring, some attempts have been made to draw a distinction between the two wings of the sport:

> The latter [professional boxing] is big business, controlled primarily by, in the main, the cash incentives, and whereas it can be agreed that there is a percentage of professional fights in which the accolade of a title is at stake, it has to be conceded that this represents a very small percentage and, of course, winning a professional title is the road towards much greater increases in the financial rewards for boxer, manager, trainer, etc (Pontremoli, 1995, p.2).

The strict regulation of the safety aspects of the amateur sport is advanced in support of a recreation that provides 'sportsmanship, comradeship, discipline and self-control'. Whilst the professional game attracts sporadic, though often severe, criticism that may eventually seriously threaten its very existence, it is clearly in the interests of the amateur sport to try and emphasise the importance of the divisions between the two. There is the potential for fighters, if able and motivated enough, to move from amateur to professional in order to seek financial rewards. The alternative is a route of 'pure' sporting glory, through domestic amateur championships to international competition. Given the increasing movement of paid sportsmen and women into the arena of Olympic competition, this route cannot be entirely discounted in the future for professional boxers. This change could effect the potential length of an amateur career within the sport. If Olympic glory could be achieved as a professional, the rationale for maintaining unpaid status would diminish.

It's chaos out here: the organisation of the professional sport

A key element in the development of boxing, as with many other sports, has been the emergence of an established administrative authority to direct matters and provide a focal point.[9] At various stages in its history the professional sport had developed greater regulation from an original quasi anarchic state, and eventually an overall controlling body emerged when a number of people involved in boxing asked Lord Lonsdale to attempt to give the sport a firmer footing:

> A Board was formed in 1927 but didn't really get off the ground, this was reconstituted at the specific request of people working in boxing, they went to National Sporting Club (NSC) and Lord Lonsdale and said 'Look, its chaos out here, we need someone to be in charge'...and Lord Lonsdale duly became the first President...One of the principal reasons for the setting up of the Board was to control British Championships, but in those days a good chunk of what went on was not licensed fighting, that the influence of the Board grew was down to Jack Solomons (promoter) who came to prominence. Basically since the war all fighting has been licensed, unlicensed boxing still goes on of course, but this is very much a fringe activity (SB).[10]

Since 1929 professional boxing has been administered by the British Boxing Board of Control (BBBC) which altered its status to become a limited company in 1991. Originally the Board was primarily concerned with the procedural aspects of the sport, such as organising professional championships, in line with the ABA. However in recent times the emphasis has developed to encompass issues such as safety and the medical protection of participants, one illustration of this change has been the decrease in the number of fights that a boxer will engage in during his career.[11] When it was formed, the BBBC was composed of independent stewards, without financial interests, and this principle has been retained. The stewards of the Board are now the Directors of the company and consist under the constitution of sixteen administrative stewards. There are in addition sixteen representative stewards, as the BBBC exists with eight Area Councils, and each Council elects two non-financially interested people. There are, in addition, the stewards of appeal who are totally independent of the main board and largely consist of legally qualified personnel. These stewards hear appeals from parties disputing decisions of the Board and do not play any part in the general administrative work.

The major administrative function of the BBBC is to license boxers, trainers, promoters, managers and the other categories of licence holders whilst other day to day administration is divided into the eight Area Councils.[12] Crucially, the BBBC licences not only the participants, but also the contests themselves. A promoter must lodge details of any promotion at least six days before the mooted promotion and the Board has the power to prohibit any contest that it considers is not 'in the interests of boxing'. At this point the Board may rule out contests that appear to be mismatches, particularly with overseas boxers, whose records may need further authentication. The issue of mismatches is an important one as the risk of injury clearly increases when one boxer is less able than the other. The Board will also liaise closely with promoters 'behind the scenes' to attempt to minimise the likelihood of mismatches occurring. The BBBC is clearly in a powerful position with respect to its licence granting powers:

> Only the Board can grant licences.[13] So an applicant for a licence will make an application to his own Area Council who will look at it as is necessary and he will be interviewed, the Area Council will then make a recommendation to the Board, but it is within the power of the Board either to accept, or not to accept, that recommendation. There have been cases, not many, where an Area Council has not made a recommendation and where the Board has overturned that decision and granted it (SB).

The BBBC rules assert that all licences are issued, varied and withdrawn at the 'absolute discretion of the Board' (1996, Reg. 4.2). However, the legal challenge by Mrs Florence Nagle (*Nagle*) over the refusal of the Jockey Club to grant her a trainer's licence makes it clear that the Courts will, in certain circumstances, intervene when a controlling body has such power. The stewards of the Jockey Club were responsible for licensing both race meetings and the trainers and jockeys. In order to enter and run horses at licensed meetings an annual trainer's licence was required. Mrs Nagle had been training racehorses since 1938 but had always been refused a licence as the Jockey Club had an unwritten practice of not granting licences to women. Mrs Nagle's 'head lad' had been granted such a licence, which enabled her horses to run with him 'officially' recognised as the trainer. Her original claim was struck out as disclosing no cause of action, a decision ratified by the High Court. However, Lord Denning in the Court of Appeal, was prepared to reconsider the position utilising the concept of public policy:

> If she is to carry on her trade without stooping to subterfuge, she has to have a licence. When an association, who have the governance of a trade, take it upon themselves to licence persons to take part in it, then it is at least arguable that they are not at liberty to withdraw a man's licence-and thus put him out of business-without hearing him. Nor can they refuse a man a licence-and thus prevent him from carrying on his business-in their uncontrolled discretion. If they reject him arbitrarily or capriciously, there is ground for thinking that the courts can intervene (*Nagle*, 1966, p.646-647).

This area of public policy, 'the right to work', can be viewed as an element of the broader doctrine of restraint of trade but is limited in application. Unlike restraint of trade there is no set of direct or indirect contractual arrangements to establish a relationship. Accordingly, it depends upon looser notions of deprivation of liberty to work, through the capricious exercise of monopolistic power, in a commercial sphere. Ironically, Salmon LJ considered that the refusal to allow a woman a licence to 'trade' could be appropriate in certain situations; 'no doubt there are occupations, such as boxing, which may reasonably be regarded as inherently unsuitable for women. But evidently training racehorses is not one of them' (*Nagle*, 1966, p.655). Presumably following this line of argument the refusal of a boxer's licence to a woman would not be capricious and therefore not open to review, though judicial views on the suitability of women for this type of career may have altered. There is, however, the distinct possibility that the sex discrimination legislation could be utilised to challenge any potential restrictions placed upon the entry requirements for professional sportswomen.

The BBBC is clearly aware of the possibility of legal challenge if a licence is refused on 'illegitimate' grounds. The situation is different if a licence has been granted and then later suspended or withdrawn, this requires a more positive response by the party exercising the power:

> Area Councils have the right to make decisions on misconduct, to arbitrate disputes, they have the power to take away licences without reference to the Board. But in all those cases of course, the parties concerned have the right to appeal - this goes to the appeal stewards, not to the Board itself... no decision of the appeal stewards has ever been overturned in the courts - they are very, very conscious that they do not want any of their decisions to be overturned (SB).

The sanctions that the BBBC can impose for any misconduct (conduct detrimental to the interests of boxing or the public interest) are widespread. Regulation 25.2 permits the Board or Area Council to 'withdraw a licence, or to suspend the same for such a period or between such dates as they may decide, and/or to impose such other penalty, including a fine as they may decide and/or make such order as to the validity of a contract as they consider fit and/or award compensation'. Suspension or withdrawal of a licence in one category can lead to a similar outcome with respect to other categories of licence.[14] The procedure for such a hearing is finely detailed and there is also procedure for an appeal to the stewards of appeal. However by virtue of Regulation 28.2, this right of appeal does not extend to the granting of licences. It is not clear whether the provision eliminating any right of appeal applies only, to any initial application, or whether it might be extended to a refusal to renew. This point could have important consequences given some of the judicial comments in this area.

There has been an attempt to overturn a Board decision regarding the refusal to grant a manager's licence. On 28 May 1976, Peter McInnes applied to the Western Area Council of the BBBC for a manager's licence. This application was refused by the BBBC on 16 July 1976; no reasons were given by the Board for their decision and his request for a personal oral hearing was refused. By an originating summons dated 29 November 1976, McInnes sought a declaration against the Board, that they had acted in breach of natural justice and/or unfairly in refusing his application for a licence. McInnes had a long and ultimately somewhat chequered career in boxing. Initially he was successful as an amateur boxer, becoming captain of boxing at his school, obtaining a blue at Cambridge and representing both the army and England as an amateur. After working as a freelance journalist and television commentator on boxing, he was granted a promoter's licence by the Board in December 1954. This was withdrawn by the Board, the following year, on the grounds that his conduct at a tournament was not becoming that of a licence holder, although the penalty was reduced to a fine on appeal. When the licence fell for renewal in December 1955 (all licences being granted on a yearly basis), McInnes did not seek renewal of his licence as he felt that the sport was becoming unprofitable. There followed somewhat of a lull in McInnes' association with boxing as he pursued a number of other careers and business interests until he applied for a trainer's licence in May 1971. This was initially made via the Southern Area Council and refused, but the following month was granted on the recommendation of the Midland Area Council. The following year he applied to the Southern Area Council for a manager's licence, after various medical reports had been considered the Council refused his application, but invited him to re-apply in six months time. Early in 1973, McInnes applied for and was granted a Master of Ceremonies licence and the Southern Area Council also recommended that his manager's licence be granted. However, before the Board met to decide whether to grant his application, he acted as Master of Ceremonies at a tournament in Bournemouth and his actions, at that event, elicited the following response, via letter, from the Southern Area Council:

> I have been instructed to request you to attend before the Southern Area Council at their next meeting, in accordance with regulation 15, paragraph 1, in that it is alleged that [at the tournament in Bournemouth] where you were engaged as an MC, you did not carry out your duties in a manner consistent with the dignity required of a licence holder in this category, in that you did not appear to have command of the situation, and that your conduct was detrimental to the interests of boxing and the public (*McInnes*, 1978, p.1523).

A further letter, bearing the same date as the above, but sent by the Board, was also received by McInnes informing him that his application for a manager's licence had been refused. This was the first of a number of attempts to obtain a manager's licence over the next three years before the application that became the subject of litigation in May 1976.[15] Megarry VC was quick to point out that it was only the last application that concerned him for the purposes of the action; 'What I am concerned with is, in essence, the procedural aspects of the 1976 application and refusal' (*McInnes*, 1978, p.1526). The judge observed that there was a sharp distinction between allegations of misconduct, where there was an elaborate system of appeal and the person concerned is given particulars of the nature of the complaint, and the application for, and granting of, licences for which the regulations gave no right to an interview. The regulations made it plain that the issue of a licence was at the discretion of the Board. The plaintiff was relying on notions of natural justice as the Board had neither informed the plaintiff of any 'problems' with his application, nor granted him a hearing where he could address any points. The main hurdle facing the plaintiff was how to ground his application; this was not an issue of expulsion but a refusal to admit. The refusal of applications for membership of private clubs was without direct authority, although all parties conceded that it was of considerable importance. However there is a vast difference between a private club and a private body that exercises monopolistic power over the applicant's ability to practise his trade. Megarry VC was clearly dubious about the content or even existence of any 'right to work' such as Denning had referred to in *Nagle*:

> I pause there to say that there may well be jurisprudential questions about the true nature of such a 'right'. I have no intention of discussing the wide variety of meanings which the protean word 'right' embraces: but if a person has a right in the strict sense of the word, then some other person or persons must be subject to a duty correlative to that right. Yet who is under a duty to provide the work? Who can be sued? The 'right to work' can hardly mean that a man has a 'right' to work at whatever employment he chooses, however unsuitable he is for it: and if his 'right' is merely to have some work provided for him that is within his capabilities, then the difficulty of determining who is under the duty to provide it is increased (*McInnes*, 1978, p.1528).

Megarry VC rather obscures the fundamental issue by musing as to the limitations of a 'right to work'. There was no question in this case of providing work but merely allowing the plaintiff to be licensed to obtain work. The crucial point is that without any licence, which was to be granted at the sole discretion of the BBBC, he was prevented absolutely from working as a manager of boxers. The BBBC has no function or any conceivable duty to provide work, but can debar people from the job market by refusing the relevant licence. The judge's analysis focused on three different scenarios within this general area; firstly, where a right is revoked or a member expelled (described as the 'forfeiture' cases); secondly, where there is an existing relationship which alters, such as the non renewal of a licence (the 'expectation' cases), and finally, where there is merely an originating application for a licence or similar (the 'application' cases). Clearly the difference is a pre-existing association in the first two categories which may extend to a contractual relationship. Megarry VC accordingly viewed the requirements of 'natural justice' as only applying to the 'forfeiture' cases and probably the 'expectation' cases as the latter category raised a change in suitability of the licence holder. However nothing would extend any rights to be heard or advised of the 'charges against him' to the application cases. Despite the fact that McInnes had held licences in several other categories this was considered insufficient to create any level of expectation with respect to his application for a manager's licence. This distinction is also somewhat false in that general problems of suitability are likely to apply across the various categories. The extent of the Board's duty towards the applicant was to act fairly, but this did not extend to providing reasons for the refusal or to offer him an oral hearing. The refusal to grant the licence did not cast any aspersions on the character of the applicant because of the perfectly legitimate reasons for refusal that might have been applied:

> There are many reasons why a licence might be refused to an applicant of complete integrity, high repute and financial stability. Some may be wholly unconnected with the applicant, as where there are already too many licensees for the good of boxing under existing conditions. Others will relate to the applicant. They may be discreditable to him, as where he is dishonest or a drunkard; or they may be free from discredit, as where he suffers from physical or mental ill health, or is too young, or too inexperienced, or too old, or simply lacks the personality or strength of character required for what no doubt may be an exacting occupation. There may be no 'case against him' at all, in the sense of something warranting forfeiture or expulsion; instead, there may simply be the absence of enough in favour of granting the licence. Indeed, in most cases the more demanding and responsible the occupation for which the licence is required, the greater will be the part likely to be played by considerations of the general suitability of the applicant, as distinct from the mere absence of moral or other blemishes. The more important these general considerations are, the less appropriate does it appear to be to require the licensing body to indicate to the applicant the nature of the 'case against him'. I think that this applies in the present case (*McInnes*, 1978, p.1532).

In the absence of any suggestion of dishonesty or bias the Board were fully entitled not to give any reasons for their decision to the plaintiff or otherwise. In addition, Megarry VC pointed out that a non-interventionist policy on the part of the courts was to be much preferred in situations such as this as sporting bodies were far better suited to judge these decisions than the courts. The requirement that all applications must be considered fairly and in fact that all applications will be considered is reiterated by the BBBC today:

> Anybody can apply for a licence in any category. Now my understanding of the law is that we have an obligation to consider fairly every application so in fact either of you [Steve Greenfield and Guy Osborn][16] could apply to become a boxer. It may well be that I might have an idea of how we would view it, but we are obliged to treat your application properly and make a decision properly. The only category to which an ordinary person cannot apply is that of a manager, it is not possible under our rules to become a manager unless you have held a licence in another category for at least three years - that is because it is deemed that a person responsible for managing a boxer's career must have some first hand knowledge of the business of boxing (SB).

It seems apparent that a failure to renew, without any reasons or right of hearing, and possibly subsequent appeal might well, even after Megarry VC's limitations, be open to successful legal challenge. The current regulations demand an original interview prior to any recommendation being made by the relevant Area Council (1996, Regulation 4.2) though it is not clear whether this is designed to be of advantage of the applicant. Having considered the licensing requirements of the participants it is useful to outline what this licence allows the participants to do.

The scope of licensing

Within a sport in which the aim is to render the other party incapable or unconscious there will evidently be a number of concerns about the safety of the boxers involved. Boxing is a dangerous sport and this is reflected in the attempts that have been made to provide for the improved protection of boxers - again this is one of boxing's contradictions in that any attempts to make boxers safer has to confront the problem that the aim of the sport is to injure. The debate about the legitimacy of boxing has a long history and calls are periodically made for its banning, especially following serious injuries or any ring death. It is an issue that the courts have periodically considered though often without consistency or intellectual and principled justification. This relationship between boxing and the criminal law governing assault was revisited in the sado masochist case of *R v Brown*[17] and it is worth examining in some depth part of Lord Mustill's speech which indicates the nature of the problem. He considered why the law had historically tried to draw a line between prize fighting and sparring:

> That the court is in such cases making a value judgement, not dependent upon any general theory of consent is exposed by the failure of any attempt to deduce why professional boxing appears to be immune from prosecution. For money, not recreation or personal improvement, each boxer tries to hurt the opponent more than he is hurt himself, and aims to end the contest prematurely by inflicting a brain injury serious enough to make the opponent unconscious, or temporarily by impairing his central nervous system through a blow to the midriff, or cutting his skin to a degree which would ordinarily be well within the scope of s20 of the 1861 Act. The boxers display skill, strength and courage, but nobody pretends that they do good to themselves or others. The onlookers derive entertainment, but none of the physical and moral benefits which have been seen as the fruits of engagement in manly sports. I intend no disrespect to the valuable judgment of McInerney J in *Pallante v Stadiums Pty Ltd (No1) [1976] VR 331* when I say that the heroic efforts of that learned judge to arrive at an intellectually satisfying account of the apparent immunity of professional boxing from criminal process have convinced me that the task is impossible. It is in my judgment best to regard this as another special situation which for the time being stands outside the ordinary law of violence because society chooses to tolerate it (*R v Brown*, 1993, p.108-109).

Historically sparring and prizefighting have been distinguished, with the latter declared unlawful in *Coney*. Lord Mustill's open appraisal avoids the need for intellectual gymnastics to bring contemporary professional boxing within the category of sparring rather than prizefighting. Those progressive elements of sparring may well be present in the amateur version of the sport when in addition to increasing fitness and discouraging smoking and drinking,[18] it may also teach; 'self-discipline and encourages a community spirit where racism is absent and wherein all are treated as equals; all joining in a common spirit of endeavour, in a one for all and all for one spirit of achievement' (Pontremoli, 1995, p.2). Amateur boxing also seeks to minimise the physical dangers to the participants. The length of each round is limited from one and a half minutes at schoolboy level, to three minutes for senior contests, and the number of rounds restricted to three. In addition to gloves boxers are protected by gum shields, scrotal guards, and head guards.[19] The majority of amateur fights are determined on points rather than any knockout blow. In 1970 the ABA introduced a stringent National Medical Scheme which provides for; (i) an initial medical examination before any competitive boxing, (ii) a re-examination every five years or annually after the boxer reaches thirty years of age, (iii) the compulsory retirement of boxers at thirty five years of age, (iv) full documentation of the boxer's career including injuries and (v) a pre-bout medical. The requirements for the medical examinations are strictly set out (ABA, 1996). Amateur boxing also has the advantage of the absence of prize money in the contests; pride and titles are all that are at stake notwithstanding that, a successful amateur career, can lead to professional status. The lack of any purse, coupled with the safety requirements, place the contemporary amateur boxer as the legitimate heir to the sparrer. It is not surprising that such sports have garnered judicial support and the comments of Pontremoli above are firmly in line with Lord Denning's parochial view of village cricket.[20]

Professional boxing, as Lord Mustill points out, lacks this element of 'recreation or personal improvement' except in an individual economic sense. This latter element is clearly the fundamental point, a boxer wishing purely to box for fitness or sporting considerations can do so through the amateur route. Professional boxing is essentially a commercial concern for all the participants. The rules of professional boxing provide that no contest may exceed twelve rounds or contain less than twelve minutes of boxing. Boxers between the ages of eighteen and nineteen can only participate in a contest limited to a maximum of twenty four minutes boxing whilst those between nineteen and twenty have a long stop of thirty minutes. The duration of each round is normally three minutes although contests of eight rounds or less may be two minutes long. The medical and safety issues are also strictly regulated. The BBBC has a crucial supervisory medical role for the sport, it first established a Medical Committee in 1950, and in many ways this is now a primary function. Each Area has a Medical Officer who recommends whether or not the BBBC should grant or renew a boxer's licence; for example, in 1995 thirty three South African boxers lost their licences when it was revealed that they had tested positive for the HIV virus ('Ban on 33 boxers after Aids tests' *The Guardian*, 18 July 1995). To obtain a boxer's licence, the aspiring pugilist must comply with specific medical requirements. There are a number of medical conditions that preclude the grant of such a licence, these include any neurological abnormality (including epilepsy and severe migraine), any psychological disorder, certain eye problems, high blood pressure, certain chest problems such as asthma, hepatitis B or other infectious or contagious diseases, testing HIV positive, chronic ear infections, diabetes, anaemia and alcohol or drug abuse. The boxer must submit an annual brain scan and must, in certain circumstances, have an angiogram. The promoter of every tournament must ensure that two approved doctors are present with one at ringside throughout. Each boxer must have medical clearance prior to the fight and there must be close liaison with the local hospital.[21] All boxers must wear an approved abdominal protector and appropriate gum shield and a number of acts are not permitted during the fight including hitting below the belt, deliberately striking an opponent when down and other ungentlemanly conduct.[22] The referee has the ultimate power to disqualify a boxer for any proscribed acts covered by this regulation. In addition to the medical requirements, the Board also employs inspectors who are responsible for ensuring that all contests are carried out within the regulations. At the conclusion of the fight both boxers are to be subject to an immediate medical assessment by the doctors in the ring. If a boxer is retired, beaten by a knockout, or the referee stops the contest, the boxer's licence is suspended for a period of at least twenty eight days and up to forty five days at the discretion of the Senior Medical Officer present at the tournament (BBBC, 1996, Reg. 5.9). This suspension continues until a Board appointed doctor certifies him fit to box again. If a boxer loses four consecutive fights the licence is suspended until he appears before his Area Council (BBBC, 1996, Reg. 5.11).

The USA has similar stringent requirements and legislation has been enacted to further embed the protection afforded to boxers via the Professional Boxing Safety Act of 1996 (PBSA). This Act, which is concerned with the safety of 'journeymen boxers', is designed to 'improve and expand the system of safety precautions that protects the welfare of professional boxers; and assist State boxing commissions to provide proper oversight for the professional boxing industry in the United States'. By virtue of PBSA s5 the following safety standards must be met:

> No person may arrange, promote, organize, produce, or fight in a professional boxing match without meeting each of the following requirements or an alternative requirement in effect under regulations of a boxing commission that provides equivalent protection of the health and safety of boxers:
>
> (1) A physical examination of each boxer by a physician certifying whether or not the boxer is physically fit to safely compete, copies of which must be provided to the boxing commission.
>
> (2) Except as otherwise expressly provided under regulation of a boxing commission promulgated subsequent to the enactment of this Act, an ambulance or medical personnel with appropriate resuscitation equipment continuously present on site.
>
> (3) A physician continuously present at ringside.
>
> (4) Health insurance for each boxer to provide medical coverage for any injuries sustained in the match.

In addition to this there is now a requirement that each boxer must register with a State Board and that once registered he be provided with an identification card that must be presented at the weigh in of any professional bout.[23] The Act also provides for stringent penalties and methods of enforcement involving both civil and criminal penalties. These are particularly onerous on managers, promoters, matchmakers and licensees who violate the provisions of the Act, leaving them open to potential fines of $20,000 and/or one year imprisonment (s10 (b)(1)). Finally the PBSA 1996 also sets out details of studies and research that need to be carried out, and empowers the Secretary of Health and Human Services to undertake a study of health, safety and equipment standards for professional boxing matches and the Secretary of Labor to conduct a study of the feasibility of a national pension system for boxers.

Boxing has, historically, been an area where there has been little in the way of union organisation. Given the medical issues that pervade the sport and apocryphal tales of exploitation of boxers it is perhaps surprising that until the 1990s there was no boxing union in either the United States or Great Britain. In the US this was remedied by attempts to form an organised boxing committee with avowed aims to give all professional boxers the opportunity to receive and enjoy the benefits of the collective bargaining process. To achieve this purpose the objectives were outlined:

1. To provide a health insurance plan for current boxers.
2. To provide a pension plan for current boxers.
3. To ensure that proper medical attention is provided at ringside.
4. To provide death benefits for dependants should the unfortunate happen.
5. To encourage and support a national computerized record-keeping system for licensed boxers.
6. To eliminate the confusion and conflict between the various sanctioning/rating organizations such as the WBC, WBA, and IBF.
7. To establish an educational scholarship program, perhaps contractually supported.
8. To review the policy of excessive deductions from the boxer's purse.
9. To eliminate coercion in the signing of multiple-option contracts.
10. To eliminate contractual obligations that are dehumanizing and unfair.
11. To establish standards for the training of judges and referees.
12. To improve gym conditions that appear to be unsanitary and unhealthy.
13. To encourage and support the National Association of Boxing Commissions.
14. To ensure that anti-boxing legislature is opposed in a timely, logical, and factual manner.[24]

The formation of such a union would enable boxers to participate in the business of sport and it is broadly similar to the issues that the British Professional Boxers'

Association (PBA) has deemed important for their members. A significant development, although one that has not as yet perhaps achieved as much as it would have wished, within British boxing was the formation, in February 1993, of the PBA, a members organisation with an annual subscription of £25. Unlike other major sports in Britain such as football, golf and cricket who all had their own trade unions, there did not previously exist a body designed to cater for the needs of professional boxers. The PBA has as its objectives, the promotion and protection of its members' interests (including contractual rights), the provision of a variety of forms of assistance in any matter arising out of a member's involvement in professional boxing and 'to establish and/or administer funds for the benefit of members and former members or for such other purposes as the PBA in its absolute discretion deems appropriate' (Hugman, 1994, p.17). Whilst there had been a perceived recognition that boxers needed protection in a medical sense, the formation of the PBA was a reaction to wider concerns of a fiscal nature. There was also the benefit that the PBA could act efficiently on behalf of the individual boxers within the administrative machinery of professional boxing. The PBA's proactive role in attempting to act as a unified body representing the boxers interests can be seen in tandem with the setting up of a BBBC sub committee which is liaising with managers and boxers to see how the existing standard form contract can be improved in the light of the judgements in *Warren* and *Watson*. Both the British and American unions do note the importance of the business side of the relationship and the protection that is undoubtedly needed in that area - certainly the standard form contracts that are utilised within professional boxing have in the past been considered a priority by the PBA; 'The most important aspect we have focused on so far must be the changes we are proposing to the boxer/manager agreement. We are working closely with the BBBC on this' (Hugman, 1994, p.18).

The unholy trinity and the crucial three:[25] managers, promoters and boxers

Once a boxer is licensed for the first time the BBBC regulations provide that he must have a contract with a BBBC licensed manager for a period of at least one year and his licence is subsequently endorsed with the manager's name. In order to manage boxers the individual must hold a valid BBBC licence and this will only be granted to an individual who has been a licence holder in a different category for a period of at least three years within the last ten years. This is designed to guarantee that managers have existing experience in the world of boxing before they can move into the management sphere. More than this the manager is responsible for the development of the boxer's career and given the wide power that the BBBC has to suspend a boxer's licence it is in both of their interests to ensure that progress is steady. By virtue of Regulation 5.11, if a boxer loses four consecutive fights his licence may be suspended until he appears before his Area Council. However at any time the boxer and/or his manager may be called for interview. Although the regulations require a compulsory period of management it is eventually possible to move to a position of self management. However an unmanaged boxer, who is losing fights, may be advised that he will need a manager so that his career is subject to more objective and detailed planning. The issue could be one of protecting a young, possibly naive (in business terms) fighter at the start of his career:

> There is a common belief that managers exploit boxers and so on. Boxers are young men, young men with lots of vim and vigour, and they are not always equipped to make the best decision in their own interests. If they want to make their own decisions that's fine they can manage themselves, but where they delegate that obligation to a manager he is entitled to take contests for that boxer which he considers in the boxer's interests. There are occasions where a (good) manager will turn down a good purse, if he doesn't think that contest is in the best interests of the boxer and the manager is also responsible to the Board, because if a boxer has a number of substantial defeats not only will the Board want to see that boxer, but will also want to see his manager to say 'What the hell are you getting him these matches for?' It is not a valid excuse to say he's getting well paid for it (SB).

This fairly protective approach is also demonstrated by the fact that a manager will not be permitted to enter into a contract with a boxer who resides more than fifty miles away, unless the Area Council is satisfied that appropriate provisions have been made for supervision and training. The agreement between the two parties is a standard form BBBC specific contract, a copy of which must be lodged with the BBBC. The manager has certain specific responsibilities such as being accountable for gymnasium fees incurred in training; more importantly he must ensure that all the medical and licensing requirements are complied with. The role of the manager is considered vital, given the potentially hazardous nature of the sport; it is important the boxer is focused on his own role in the process rather than becoming enmeshed in the conduct of negotiations:

> Most boxers want to be managed - they're happy to be managed and despite the somewhat unfair image managers have, it is the belief of most of us on this side of the game, that boxers should have managers because boxers do not make good managers of themselves. While they are boxing and while they have obligations to keep themselves fit and prepare themselves for contests, they are not always equipped to be the best judges of what is in their interests. That sounds patronising

but it's not meant to. Managers often have to get themselves in very difficult situations immediately before a fight. Now what you don't want is a boxer doing that for himself the day before or even hours before he's due to take part in a contest, he shouldn't be wrangling with people and shouting and screaming, as sometimes happens. To some extent the boxer does need a shield in order that he can do his job as a boxer. The two jobs are not necessarily compatible, although there are always exceptions (SB).

This position is no different from any other artist/manager or artist/agent situation, although in many ways the boxer's manager is more important than the equivalent role in other spheres. The need to maintain a particular lifestyle regime, particularly in the run up to contests, makes the delegation of responsibility a sensible division. The essence is the personal nature of the relationship and it is apparent that those arguments, alluded to above, that strongly favour the creation of such an association apply equally if the necessary trust and confidence dissipate. Thus if the relationship sours there are strong reasons for the break up to be legitimised. Unfortunately for the sport litigation has been required to determine not just the parameters but also the enforceability of such a contractual relationship.

In *Warren*, the boxing promoter and manager Frank Warren, attempted to prevent one of his boxers, Nigel Benn, from breaching the contract Benn had signed with him. Warren wanted to prevent Benn employing Ambrose Mendy as Benn's 'agent'. Mendy was not licensed by the BBBC, as a manager, and described himself as a 'trade development counsellor'. Warren sought damages from Mendy and injunctions, restraining Mendy from inducing Benn to breach the contract.

Nigel Benn had left school at 16 and joined the army at 17, he boxed consistently during his time in the army and by the time he left, aged 22, he had won six titles. He took on a number of part time jobs, when he left the army, and continued his amateur career, winning the ABA middleweight championship in 1986 and subsequently turning professional shortly afterwards. After turning professional he fought eighteen contests between January 1987 and May 1988 winning all of them,[26] this included topping the bill at the Royal Albert Hall and taking the Commonwealth middleweight title in April 1988. As the judge noted; 'With such a brilliant start, it is hardly surprising that Nigel Benn is everywhere regarded as a very talented boxer with prospects of a highly remunerative career' (*Warren*, 1989, p.106). The action hinged upon the series of manager/boxer agreements Benn had signed. Shortly after his first professional fight, in February 1987, he signed a contract for three years with Burt McCarthy. Mr McCarthy remained his manager until after his twelfth fight in December 1987 when it was agreed that Benn would sign with Frank Warren (on BBBC standard terms) which he did on 27 January 1988.[27] This agreement was due to be for a term of three years but in the event only lasted five months and during that time Benn fought six further contests all of which were also promoted by Warren. By June 1988 Benn had become disillusioned with the plaintiff's management and believed it would be impossible for them to resolve their differences. On 23 June 1988 Benn instructed solicitors to send a letter to Warren stating that the terms of the management agreement were unenforceable, as an unreasonable restraint of trade, and further to this that Warren had committed further breaches of contract and failed to fulfil his duty of good faith. The duties of the manager are set out, within the contract, as follows:

> The Manager agrees and undertakes during the continuance of this Agreement...(iv) to arrange the Boxer's professional affairs with a view to the boxer securing due and proper profit and reward therefrom, to negotiate in every transaction terms and conditions as advantageous as possible to the Boxer, regularly to render to the Boxer a full account of all monies received and all expenses incurred, and promptly to pay to the Boxer the moneys to which he is entitled pursuant to Article 5 of this Agreement in connection with any Event, or which have otherwise been received on the Boxer's behalf (*Warren*, 1989, p.116).

Consequently Benn issued a writ on 4 July 1988 in the Chancery Division. Warren's action, in the Queens Bench Division, was commenced on 20 July 1988. On the same day, Warren applied, *ex parte* to the court, and obtained interlocutory injunctions restraining the defendant (Mendy) from inducing any breach of the management contract by Benn, and from acting as his manager or agent with regard to any boxing activities. At a hearing, before Pill J, on 12 September 1988 the injunctions were discharged and Warren appealed against this decision. The first issue for the court to decide was whether an injunction could be granted in such a situation, this involved a re-evaluation of the personal service cases such as *Bette Davis* and *Page One*. The court's view was that; 'Special considerations apart, we are firmly with Oliver J in preferring the approach of Stamp J [in *Page One*] to that of Branson J [in *Bette Davis*], both on grounds of realism and practicality and because that approach is more consistent with the earlier authorities' (Nourse LJ, *Warren*, 1989, p.112).

It is long established practice that contracts for personal services cannot be directly enforced through an order for specific performance and indeed the old common law rule is now encompassed within section 236 of the *Trade Union and Labour Relations (Consolidation) Act 1992*[28] for employees and provides that:

No court shall, whether by way of-
(a) an order for specific performance or specific implement of a contract of employment, or
(b) an injunction or interdict restraining a breach or threatened breach of such a contract,
compel an employee to do any work or attend any place for the doing of any work.

If a 'positive order' cannot be granted, the issue remains as to whether a court can prevent the 'defendant' (ordinarily this would be a two party situation) from working for another. It is clear that such an injunction cannot be granted if the effect is to force the worker back into the relationship without any alternative. In *Bette Davis* it was acceptable for the actress to find other work outside of the theatre, and indeed the pleadings were altered to limit the relief sought to only competitive work. This issue was raised again in *Warren* when the plaintiff suggested that to restore the injunctions against Mendy need not necessarily force Benn back to Warren since there were other avenues of work open to him such as employment as a security guard. The court was not prepared to take such a narrow definition of compulsion and also supported the judge's view of the nature of the relationship between the parties:

> The question which he asked himself is now shown to have been correct. He said that in reaching his conclusion he bore in mind that the trade of a professional boxer was a very specialist one, requiring dedication, extensive training and expertise and that his professional life was comparatively short. He readily accepted that a high degree of mutual trust and confidence was required between boxer and manager. There were duties of a personal and fiduciary nature to be performed by the manager (*Warren*, 1989, p.115).

The issue of the role played by the manager and the duties owed by him were particularly pertinent given that Warren was also promoting Benn, and that part of his duty as manager, was potentially to negotiate with himself. This raised a possible conflict of interest between the two roles of manager and promoter. The point appeared rather as a side issue, the court determined that there was a prima facie case that, when acting as a promoter, the plaintiff was in a position as a constructive trustee of undisclosed profits. This in itself was a valid reason for not forcing Benn back to Warren, as Benn's trust and confidence in the plaintiff had genuinely disappeared. The court also commented, in passing, on the problems of the dual relationship of managing and promoting the same boxer.[29] Another issue, hinted at in *Warren* but not actually crucial to the case, was the applicability of the restraint of trade doctrine to boxing contracts and, if applicable, whether the standard BBBC agreement might be construed as an unreasonable restraint of trade. This issue was however raised in *Watson*.

In 1984 Michael Watson, a very promising amateur boxer, who was heavily tipped to win in the ABA championships, had a meeting with Micky Duff. At the meeting he discussed turning professional and signed a document recording his agreement to turn professional under Duff's management after competing in the Olympics and having a shot at the ABA championship. The agreement was to commence on 30 September 1984 and Duff agreed to pay him £100 per week for living and training expenses.[30] In fact, Watson was not selected for the Olympic team and was beaten in the ABA semi finals. He duly turned professional in September 1984 and a manager/boxer agreement was signed on 24 September. During the term of this agreement Watson had thirteen fights, winning them all. The purses for these fights were £500 for his first six fights, between £600-£850 for his next five and £1,000 for his twelfth and thirteenth fights. In March 1987 Duff asked Watson to sign a new contract, the original agreement had some six months left to run, and after some discussion and advice from his trainer, Watson signed the new agreement. Interestingly, the central controversial feature of the case, the dual relationship of manager and promoter, was apparently considered an important asset when Watson was mulling over the new agreement:

> A promoter-manager was preferable to a manager with no promotional presence. Such a manager would have difficulty in arranging the fights the plaintiff would need to advance to championship level. He did not want to manage himself and preferred the first defendant as his manager-promoter to others in the field, such as Frank Warren (*Watson*, 1993, p.289).

In 1987 Watson had two fights, for purses of £800 and £1200, and the following year he had an important victory over a highly regarded American, Don Lee for which he received £5000. His career was now blossoming and culminated in a Commonwealth Middleweight title fight in May 1989, coincidentally against Nigel Benn. Watson beat Benn, the favourite, in the sixth round and earned a purse of some £100,000. His next fight was against Mike McCallum for the WBA world middleweight title in April 1990 for which his purse was $87,000. It was following his defeat in this contest that Watson decided to instigate proceedings to free him from his boxer/manager agreement. The agreement contained certain crucial terms:

> 2. Obligations of Manager. The Manager agrees and undertakes during the continuance of this Agreement: (i) to act as Manager for the Boxer; (ii) to arrange and supervise a suitable training programme for the Boxer; (iii) to use his best endeavours to arrange for the Boxer a proper programme of boxing contests,

matches and exhibitions, and other professional engagements and events (hereinafter together called 'the Events') which may include but shall in no way be limited to: (a) engagements as sparring assistants to other boxers in training; (b) music hall, theatrical or cinema film appearances; (c) literary contributions or authorisations for literary contributions to any suitable publications; (d) radio, television or other broadcasting; and (e) suitable product, preparation or commodity recommendations and advertisements, acceptable to and honestly subscribed to by the Boxer, and complying in each jurisdiction in which such recommendation and advertisements are to be used or appear with the relevant laws and standards (whether statutory or not) from time to time applicable thereto; (iv) to arrange the Boxer's professional affairs with a view to the Boxer securing due and proper profit and reward therefrom, to negotiate in every transaction terms and conditions as advantageous as possible to the Boxer, regularly to render to the Boxer a full account of all moneys received and all expenses incurred, and promptly to pay to the Boxer the moneys to which he is entitled pursuant to Article 5 of this Agreement in connection with any Event, or which have otherwise been received on the Boxer's behalf; (v) to take reasonable steps to supervise the health and safety of the Boxer in the pursuance and context of his profession; (vi) not to contract the services of the Boxer for any Event arranged to take place after any date on which this Agreement may reasonably be expected to terminate; and (vii) to observe all regulations and conditions of the BBB of C applicable to Full Professional Boxers.

3. Authorisation of Manager. The Boxer hereby irrevocably authorises the Manager during the continuance of this Agreement to act as the Boxer's Agent for the specific and sole purpose of fulfilling the Manager's obligations set out in Article 2 above.

4. Obligations of Boxer. The Boxer agrees and undertakes; (i) during the continuance of this Agreement to be managed and directed exclusively by the Manager and not to enter into any agreement or arrangement with any other Manager or person for any of the above-mentioned purposes without obtaining the prior written consent of the Manager; (ii) to accept and fulfil to the best of his ability all Events reasonably negotiated on the Boxer's behalf by the Manager; (iii) throughout the continuance of this Agreement to use his best endeavours to keep himself in the fittest possible physical condition for the purposes of his profession; (iv) during the continuance of this Agreement to observe all Regulations of the BBB of C applicable to Full Professional Boxers (*Watson*, 1993, p.290-291).

There is an interesting difference, between the obligations of the boxer and the obligations of the manager. Under clause 2(iii) the manager must use his 'best endeavours' to arrange, for the boxer, a proper programme of boxing contests and other events. Such an obligation is not *absolute*. The boxer on the other hand is absolutely prohibited from making agreements for himself by virtue of paragraph

4(i). In addition to this, Paragraph 2(iv) concerning the achievement of due and proper profit, is fine if seen, *in vacuo*, but when the manager is also the promoter this creates a dichotomy that may be hard to resolve in the boxer's favour.

The period of the agreement was, by virtue of clause 5, to be three years initially. However, if during that three year period the Boxer was to become British, European, Commonwealth or World Champion the manager was entitled to extend the agreement. This was done by giving notice to the boxer and the Board of the manager's wish to exercise the extension notice clause. This clause provided for a further three year period to be available to the manger if any of the events in 5(ii) occurred. Following Watson's success against Nigel Benn, in May 1989, Duff exercised his option to extend. When the case came before the Court, it was argued by the defendant, that the Boxer/Manager agreement was one outside the purview of the doctrine of restraint of trade. This view was based on a series of dicta from *Esso*. Scott J had no truck with such an analysis, on the basis that this was far from an 'ordinary commercial contract', in fact the character of the contract was unique in so far as the agreement was tied into the Regulations of the BBBC:

> I do not doubt the necessity, in the interests of professional boxers, of the Board exercising careful regulatory control over the contents of boxer-manager contracts. Enlightened paternalism, however, may be all very well in its way, but carries undeniable dangers. Omniscience is not an invariable companion of omnipotence, and the Board's opinion as to the scope of the restrictions to be imposed on a boxer in a boxer-manager agreement is not necessarily right (*Watson*, 1993, p.297).

On this basis, Scott J held that such agreements are subject to the restraint of trade doctrine. In addition, as the manager's role may overlap with that of the promoter, the agreements were far from commonplace; 'There is an obvious conflict of interest affecting a manager who contracts for his boxer to fight in a promotion in which he, the manager, has a financial interest. In a case where the manager is to all intents and purposes the same person as the promoter, the boxer may find himself contractually obliged to fight for a purse and on terms which have not been negotiated by his manager with the promoter but have been unilaterally fixed by the manager-promoter' (*Watson*, 1993, p.299).

Given that this could allow for the operation of the contract in an oppressive manner, Scott J also felt the contract was subject to the doctrine. As to its reasonableness, he noted that there were a number of arguments in favour of these onerous contractual terms, and that on the face of the agreement itself there was nothing unreasonable. He did, however, find a problem with the extension option afforded to the manager under the contract, feeling that the period of three years was too long given that large financial rewards would be available after the first championship (the trigger for the extension clause) was won. Scott J's main bone of contention was the conflict of interest issue, when a manager also acted as a promoter. The boxer was exclusively bound to the manager and may not seek fights outside of the manager's control, if the manager also promotes it would be possible that every contest during the life of the contract might have this characteristic. The crucial element was that the promoter and manager could have opposing financial considerations:

> In all these contests, the financial interests of the promoter in the capacity of promoter will be in conflict with the duty of the manager to obtain for the boxer the most advantageous financial terms possible. Given that a manager's duty to the boxer he manages is not only contractual but also, in my opinion, fiduciary, a contract which permits such a conflict of interest is to my mind a very strange animal indeed (*Watson*, 1993, p.299).

Scott J determined that the agreement was subject to the restraint of trade doctrine. Unsurprisingly, he found that the conflict of interest was contrary to public policy and accordingly the agreement was unenforceable. This was a far more serious point than the ruling on the substantive term relating to duration and extension. Scott J was suggesting that this crucial aspect of the contractual organisation of professional boxing was unlawful. The BBBC had never been able to satisfactorily resolve the dilemma of the manager/promoter even though it had long been aware of the potential problems. Prior to the late 1950s dual licensing had not been permitted and individuals were either managers or promoters, but not both. This position altered as professional boxing suffered from the effects of an entertainment tax, although it was once again reversed at the Board's AGM in May 1984. After dissent from regional managers/promoters, a Special General Meeting, convened in August 1984, overturned the decision from May. This permitted a return to dual licensing and this situation continued until after the comments made by the Court of Appeal. In order to avoid the problems of 1984 the Board then permitted dual licensing to be retained but with the proviso that it would not be practised in tandem, managers could promote, but not their own stable of fighters. However protests were once again expressed by regional promoters; more important however was the intervention of the Office of Fair Trading. The OFT was concerned that the effect of the new regulations would be to concentrate power in the hands of a small group of dominant national promoters at the expense of local and regional contests. The result has left the position unresolved without any clear direction as to whether such a position is lawful:

We'll find out when we next go to court! There was a time, certainly prior to 1979 when promoters could not be managers. In more recent times promoters have been managers, and then following the decision in *Watson* the Board determined through their AGM that promoters could no longer be managers. However, our friends at the OFT decided about a year later that it would be a restraint of trade and it would have cost us a fortune to take them to court over it...The Board were faced with a position where a judge in a case says it's a conflict of interest to be a promoter and manager and the OFT says it's a restriction upon trade not to allow promoters to be managers, so we set up a committee and we got a boxer/manager contract clause added and the boxer has to sign that. Every time a manager offers him a job for a tournament where he has a financial interest (he needn't be the promoter) then he is obliged to obtain a separate authorisation from the boxer for that contest (SB).

Boxing clever?

Issues of licensing, safety and the contracts of the boxers are still very much live issues notwithstanding the various debates that have raged regarding the sport. In October 1997, a female boxer, Jane Couch, launched a successful action against the BBBC on account of their refusal to grant her a professional boxer's licence. The basis of the action was not the common law notion of the right to work, but rather the Sex Discrimination Act 1975. At the same time that potential sex discrimination and licensing came under consideration, the role of women generally within the sport was raised by a highly publicised amateur fight between two young girls.[31] This issue is, of course, couched in terms of 'safety', interestingly the ABA booklet on safety (ABA, 1996) contains over sixty pages of details on issues of concern to male boxers and the regulations that appertain to their training, preparation and fights. The page headed 'Female Boxing' merely notes 'At present neither the AIBA nor the EABA Commission on Female Boxing have produced a set of rules to control Female Boxing. When they are produced they will be entered in the ABA of England Handbook' (ABA, 1996, p.68).

Professional boxing has attempted to placate its critics by taking a more proactive line with respect to safety issues. In April 1997 boxing's first world medical congress was convened. The overall aim was to seek to improve the safety of, and protection for, boxers. Prior to the Congress Jose Sulaiman, President of the WBC, wrote:

Many of the top organizations in medicine and boxing will be in attendance. These include the International Olympic Committee, the World Association of National Olympic Committees, the International Association of Amateur Boxing, and the International Association of Sports Medicine. The American Medical Association has also accepted the invitation of the WBC to attend. The AMA has long been a detractor of boxing, and the WBC wants them to see what we are trying to do to improve boxing safety. The World Boxing Association and International Boxing Federation will also be represented (Boxing News, 25 April 1997, www.sportsnetwork.com).

The domestic contractual issues have tried to incorporate the effects of the two major cases though change, especially with respect to the management/promotion issue, has been subject to both internal and external pressures. The current boxer/manager agreement is a relatively simple and straightforward agreement containing some seventeen clauses. It is a conditional agreement, reliant on both parties obtaining the necessary individual licences of boxer and manager (Clause 1). The agreement is an exclusive one and the manager is given the authority to make contracts on the boxer's behalf (Clause 2). The length of the contract is a period of up to three years, though it may be extended for a further eighteen months (from the date of the championship win) if the boxer wins a Championship and the contract has less than two years to run. This clause was amended on the back of the *Watson* decision. Clause 3 outlines the responsibilities of the manager which include arranging a suitable training and boxing programme alongside any other activities such as personal appearances, broadcasting work etc. The boxer has the right to decline, on reasonable grounds, any opponent suggested by the manager. If the Boxer is not satisfied with the quality or number of opponents he is able to refer the matter to the Board in accordance with the disputes and arbitration clause of the contract[32] and the Board has the power to decide to release the Boxer from his contract. The boxer's obligations (Clause 8) are simply to keep himself in the best possible physical condition, comply with the rules of the Board, fulfil engagements to the best of his ability and pay monies due to his manager promptly. The contract also stipulates how the income generated is to be treated, deductions are made for sums due to the Board and legitimate expenses such as travelling and training. The balance is divided, twenty five percent to the manager and seventy five percent to the boxer. The major problem with the whole relationship has occurred when the manager has also been involved with promoting the contest, and this is now dealt with by Clause 6.1 of the Agreement:

The Manager will immediately notify the Boxer in writing on Board Form No. 36A if he is intending to arrange an engagement or engagements on behalf of the Boxer and:
(i) The Manager will himself be the Promoter or other person with whom the Boxer will be entering into a contract; or
(ii) The Manager has any financial or other association with the intended Promoter or other person which affects, or might reasonably be thought to affect, the

Manager's ability to act independently in the best interests of the Boxer.

The manager may not enter into any such agreement unless the terms offered are fair and reasonable and until a written copy of the terms has been given to the Boxer. These must be fully explained to him and a reasonable opportunity provided to reflect upon those terms. They must be accepted (or renegotiated) in writing. This is an attempt to provide a safeguard to the problem seen in the dual role of promoter/manager. Professional boxing has managed to survive despite contradictions with the concept of consent within the criminal law. The fact that boxing is on the edge of legality has acted as an impetus for improvements in safety that have occurred. Similarly internal problems surrounding licensing and contractual relations remain despite attempts to make changes. The cases of *Warren* and *Watson* demonstrate the role of the law in forcing such alterations and it seems apparent that a number of issues remain unresolved. At the heart of all the problems, internal and external, faced by professional boxing is the ultimate vulnerability of the participants:

> Only the most expendable men are boxers. All of the fighters who ever died - nearly five hundred since 1918, when the *Ring* book started to keep tabs - haven't the political constituency of a solitary suburban child who falls off a trampoline. Observers who draw near enough to fights and fighters to think that they see something of value, something pure and honest, are sure to mention the desperate background and paradoxical gentleness, which even Tyson has in some supply (Callahan, 1991, p.84).

Notes

1. It is essential in boxing that a fighter wears a gum shield. For example the British Boxing Board of Control (BBBC) Regulations set out that 'A Boxer is required to wear throughout the Contest a properly fitted gumshield. As a precaution he should bring with him two of these to every Contest in which he has to participate. With this exception no other protection whatsoever must be worn by a Boxer on the body above the waist line' (BBBC, 1996, Regulation 3.20).

2. Tyson's apology extended to; the world, his family, the Nevada State Athletic Commission, Judge Patricia Gifford, MGM, Showtime, Don King, and Las Vegas. Addressing Holyfield directly Tyson started with 'Evander I'm sorry. You're a champion, and I respect that and I am only saddened that the fight did not go on further so that the boxing fans of the world might have seen for themselves who would come out on top' (*Boxing News*, 1997, Vol. 53, p.23).

3. See here also McArdle (1995).

4. On the subject of escapism and what is needed to become a boxer, Beattie (1996, p.19) noted the following; 'It does, of course, take a special sort of place to produce boys and men able to step into a ring and trade punches toe-to-toe with another athlete, let alone fighters who nearly became world champions'.

5. For example, apparently the Duke of Cumberland was Jack Slack's backer for a fight against Bill Stevens, which Stevens won. Interestingly, the Duke considered that the match had been

fixed and subsequently became an opponent of the sport.

6. Further advances in technique were provided by Daniel Mendoza who further developed the art of defence using speed and agility as opposed to brute force (Andre, 1979).

7. Flood was knocked down in every round of the eight round contest which lasted only 16 minutes before Flood's seconds threw in the towel. At over $15 per minute this seems to have been a fair return.

8. McArdle (1995) makes the point that such rules were largely concerned with ensuring equality of opportunity for gambling patrons.

9. Even bare knuckle fighting, an unlicensed and illegal version of boxing the essence of which is captured in the quote below, has an administrative body with its own headed notepaper!

10. As part of the research for this chapter we interviewed Simon Block, Assistant General Secretary of the BBBC at Jack Petersen House on 2 July 1997. References to the transcript of our interview are followed by (SB) in the text. We are indebted to Simon Block for his invaluable help and insight.

11. The BBBC gives the comparative example of Tommy Farr and Henry Cooper who both had an eighteen year career in different eras; the former had some 104 contests whilst the latter only 55.

12. In addition to those categories already mentioned, the BBBC also grants a number of other licences for various boxing functions. The annual costs of these licences are as follows:

Promoter (Full)	£160
Promoter (Charity/Special)	£80
Manager	£100
Boxer	£30
Trainer/Second	£42
Agent	£70
Match Maker	£65
Referee (A Star)	£130
Referee (Class A)	£65
Referee (Class B)	£50
Timekeeper	£45
Second	£25
Ringmaster/Whip	£25
Master of Ceremonies	£45

13. 'It's a licence book that we issue, the licence book in itself doesn't tell you an awful lot and in theory an inspector is supposed to be able to look at that book to determine that the licence is up to date. In practice when boxers renew their licence they often forget to send in their licence books, so they may be up to date but the book doesn't say so, but that is more controlled nationally now from head office because before a tournament the promoter or his matchmaker must submit to the Board a list of the boxers he is intending to use. Those licences are then checked to make sure firstly that the licences are in order, that there are no arrears and that the fees have been collected and secondly that the boxers medical documentation is in order' (SB).

14. All fines are credited to the BBBC Benevolent Fund (BBBC, 1996, Regulation 25.3.1).

15. The plaintiff had applied five times, from 1972 -1975, for a manager's licence prior to the 1976 application.

16. Anyone who knows us will be aware that the chances of either of us actually being eligible for a boxer's licence are somewhat slim and not suitable test cases for litigation.

17. The case is also considered in terms of consent, along with sport, in *Criminal Law: Consent and offences against the person* (1994) Law Commission Consultation Paper No 134.

18. The ABA guide on Medical Aspects of Amateur Boxing makes specific reference to the effects of Smoking and Alcohol on fitness in addition to illegal substances (1996, p.16-17).

19. There is some debate as to the relative advantages and disadvantages of protective head wear. England was one of the last European countries to make the wearing of head guards compulsory in amateur contests.

20. Lord Denning was a stalwart defender of notions of community in so far as they were evidenced in the life of the village and the pastoral. See for example his comments in the case of *Miller* and our subsequent analysis (Greenfield and Osborn 1994 & 1996).

21. In addition there must be a trained ambulance crew on site available solely for the boxers and there must be a telephone link set up to communicate with the local hospital who will have previously been advised of the fact that the contest is taking place.

22. Regulation 3.38 provides that the following other acts are not permitted; (b) using the "pivot blow"; (c) hitting on the back of the head or neck; (d) kidney punching; (e) hitting with the open glove, the inside, or the butt or the back of the hand, or with the wrist or elbow; (f) holding, butting, or careless use of the head, shouldering, wrestling or roughing; (g) not trying; (h) persistently ducking below the waistline; (i) intentional falling without receiving a blow; (j) failing to break when so ordered, or striking or attempting to strike an opponent on the break; (l) hitting an opponent after the termination of the round.

23. Section 6 provides, *inter alia*, that an identification card is required that includes a recent photograph and the social security number (or equivalent) of the holder so as to allow proper identification. This card must be presented to the appropriate boxing commission before the weigh in for a professional boxing match.

24. Some of this material is taken from a boxing website (www.uhu.com/boxing).

25. 'The Crucial Three' was the name given to a project involving Pete Wyllie, Ian McCulloch and Julian Cope, three of the key figures in the late 1970s early 1980s Liverpool music scene. That the project never got off the ground was almost entirely due to the gargantuan size of the egos involved.

26. Fifteen of these fights were won in either the first or second round.

27. Interestingly, Warren had promoted all of the twelve fights during McCarthy's period as Benn's manager and this duality of function was to be of note within the case.

28. Previously contained within s16 of the Trade Union and Labour Relations Act 1974.

29. 'It is of course no answer to a claim in constructive trust to say that the Board's regulations permit a manager to act also as a promoter and that there have been, as we were told, many cases where this dual relationship has existed. It may be that there are many cases in which it works to the boxer's advantage. But the emergence of one where it may well have worked to his disadvantage is something which we would respectfully think ought to cause the board concern. They may well wish to consider whether the regulations ought to be revised in such a way that the relationship can, if it is thought to be desirable, continue to exist, but only with stringent safeguards to protect the boxer' (*Warren*, 1989, p.117).

30. Scott J wryly commented on this arrangement for an 'amateur' boxer 'I have a strong suspicion that the amateur boxing authorities would have regarded this agreement with some disfavour...' (*Watson*, 1993, p.288).

31. *The News of the World* (26 October 1997), a tabloid paper, noted that the Welsh ABA had sanctioned the amateur bout of three one and a half minute rounds between two sixteen year old girls. Frank Moloney, the manager of Lennox Lewis was quoted in the paper as saying 'The idea of two 16 year old girls punching the hell out of each other in a ring is nothing short of appalling. Their mothers should be strung up in the gym and used as punchbags. Let them know what it's like to be hit'.

32. Clause 14 provides that 'Any dispute arising out of or in connection with this Agreement shall be referred to arbitration in accordance with Regulations 24, 26 and 28 of the Board's Rules and Regulations. The procedures set out in those Regulations must be exhausted and an award must be made (including, if appropriate, an award made on appeal pursuant to Regulation 28) before the Boxer or Manager may commence any legal proceedings or make any application to a Court'.

Cricket is too precarious. It is all right, if you can rise to the top and get the plums. Otherwise, it is a bare living for a few years, with nothing at the end; one saves a few pounds in the summer and spends them in the winter (Sir Jack Hobbs in Brookes, 1978, p.153).

If one of their serfs wanted to leave, who cared? (Harold Gimblett commenting on Jack Lee's departure from Somerset in Sissons, 1988, p.236).

The heart of the issue is not only whether I could publish this book. It is whether English cricketers should be forced by the TCCB to sign contracts that turn them into slaves...The TCCB wants to own English cricketers lock, stock and barrel, but I refuse to be owned by anyone (Lamb, 1997, p.290).

Of all the forces that have shaped the New Cricket Culture, the media has been the most powerful. The relationship between cricket and the media grows ever closer and no part of the game is left untouched by its influence. From the money injected into the game to the new fans brought in as a result of increased coverage, television has been the main inspiration behind the modernisation of cricket. The press - both tabloid and broadsheet - has played its part in transforming the public's perception of the game in response to the changing agenda set by television (Melly, 1996, p.146).

5 Circus Games
Contract and control in cricket

Cricket is often portrayed as the quintessential English game, conjuring up powerful images of a cohesive rural society in which different classes join together on the village green for the duration of the match. It has also been viewed as a more reactionary sport that has been historically resistant to change.[1] This is undoubtedly because a central feature of cricket is its heritage and the desire to maintain links to the 'glorious' past. The game now acts, for some, as a reminder of a better, more optimistic day; of merrie England, gentility, fair play, honour; all that is thought to be great about England - a myopic and rose tinted view of the national summer pastime that has been cheerfully embraced by the former Prime Minister, John Major, amongst others.[2] The concept of cricket as a unifying national force has been ironically encapsulated by the historian G.M.Trevelyan and the contribution of cricket towards the creation or emergence of national political identities has been noted by both James (1994) and Marqusee (1994).[3] The sport has an important international dimension linked closely to British overseas expansion during the nineteenth century. The membership of the International Cricket Council (ICC), founded in 1909, as the Imperial Cricket Conference the game's governing body, indicates the role of England as a colonial exporter of the game. The original members were England, Australia and South Africa with membership confined to cricket playing Commonwealth countries though this had to be revised as affiliation to the Commonwealth fluctuated. Originally it had little practical influence, run as it was by the Marylebone Cricket Club (MCC), from its home at Lord's cricket ground. However the wider political landscape and internal economic changes to the game have raised the profile and influence of the ICC. The advent of a limited overs World Cup competition has highlighted the international nature of the sport and more importantly the commercial value of such competition.[4] Contemporaneously the administration and control of the international game has shifted away from England and it seems likely that this process will continue (Wright, 1994).

Whilst England's international role has been declining both on and off the cricket field[5] the relationship between the domestic first class game and the national Test side has also been questioned. This has in turn led to analysis and debate over the role and performance of overseas players (McLellan, 1994) who have been recruited by the majority of the Counties, particularly since the relaxation of the qualification requirements in 1968. The use of non-England qualified players has become increasingly controversial as the performance of the national side has deteriorated and there are signs that the introduction of overseas cricketers is also affecting the game at a recreational level (Greenfield & Osborn, 1996). The legitimate issue concerning national representation within the game became soured with allegations of racism following the publication of an article by Robert Henderson (1995), in the respectable *Wisden Cricket Monthly*, which questioned the commitment of England Test players who had been born outside of the United Kingdom. The allegation was that players such as Devon Malcolm and Philip DeFreitas would not be able to play, wholeheartedly, for England, as they would, subconsciously, want the country of their birth to win. The article, unsurprisingly, resulted in a storm of protest. The end result included settled libel actions and apologies from the magazine. Ironically, a major source of non-England born players for the Test side since it was banished from the international game has been South Africa.[6] During the 'Packer affair' much was made of the fact that the England captain of the time, Tony Greig, who acted as a prominent Packer supporter, was actually born in South Africa and this was offered as a rationale for his 'betrayal' of English cricket (Blofeld, 1978).

The most recent source of such problems of 'dual nationality' has involved a number of Anglo (Australian) cricketers who have elected to play for England, Craig White and Martin McCague being prominent examples of this phenomenon.[7] The issue came to a head over the selection of Andrew Symonds for the Australian A squad for a match against the West Indies in December 1996. Symonds had played for Gloucestershire in the 1996 season as a domestic player as he enjoyed dual qualification for both Australia and England. Gloucestershire had already registered their one permitted overseas player, the West Indian captain Courtney Walsh, and could, therefore, only utilise Symonds as an 'England qualified' player. Gloucestershire were keen to persuade Symonds to reject the invitation to play for Australia A as this could have made him ineligible to play for England and effectively ended his county career. Symonds elected to play for Australia A and nailed his colours firmly to the mast of his country of birth stating; 'I am an Aussie and always have been, I will play my cricket for Australia, so I will play on Friday. I love living in Australia...The decision wasn't very tough for me because I have known in my heart that I've always been an Aussie' ('Symonds opts for Australia' *The Independent* 12 December 1996). This became somewhat ironic when he was then left out of the team to play the West Indies, thus leaving his eligibility still in doubt. This fairly liberal approach to national qualification has a long historical lineage with players such as Billy Midwinter bizarrely representing Australia in 1877/8 against the English tourists, and again on the 1884 tour to England, but who also played for England in 1881/2 against Australia. The 'flags of convenience' approach to player nationality is not confined to cricket, the creative (though perfectly constitutional) recruitment of players for the Eire football team under the English born manager Jack Charlton is often cited as a prominent example. Others include the adoption of the 'Canadian' Greg Rusedski (tennis) and the controversial selection of the 'South African', Zola Budd, for the British Olympic team. Perhaps the most important contemporary feature of the game has not so much be the make up of the national side, but the televising of cricket and the consequent relationship with the broadcasters.

The rise in popularity of the one day game, in tandem with its increased television coverage, has made great alterations to public awareness of the international matches; there is not only more cricket but, importantly, more *televised* cricket. Not only has the game of cricket become internationalised to a greater degree but also the players have become global commodities. During the winter of 1996 there were international matches taking place in Africa, India, Australia, Pakistan and New Zealand with BSkyB offering full coverage of England's tour to Zimbabwe and New Zealand for subscribers. Full coverage of Test match cricket may cause difficulties for single channel terrestrial broadcasters who have scheduling pressures as the sheer length of play (at least six hours play a day for up to five days) requires a significant commitment in terms of broadcast hours.[8] Herein lies the beauty of the one day match, instantaneous action with, barring weather interruptions, a guaranteed result. The slow build up that may take place over five days of Test cricket is replaced by rapid stroke play encouraged by limitations on fielding positions and a maximum number of overs permissible per bowler. The conundrum, for both the cricket authorities and the broadcasters, was to achieve the necessary changes to the game which preserved its traditional basis and values whilst creating a product that was marketable for the armchair viewer. It was essentially this dichotomy that was at the heart of the 'Packer affair'; an episode that rocked cricket in the late 1970s and early 1980s, changing the relationship between the game's administrators, the players and the potential broadcasters. As will be outlined below, the professional cricketer's lot was not a happy one and it took a number of developments to allow cricketers the chance to achieve what they felt was their own professional economic worth:

> The reality of the lives of professional cricketers is that until the 1980s they were not accorded the same rights as employees in any other job. Until the abolition of the residential qualification their ability to sell their cricketing skills in the market place was severely restricted. After more than 100 years the professional cricketer is now able to sell his labour like any other worker, and the onus is on the county

clubs to put together packages covering earnings, bonuses, benefits and pensions which offer reasonable rewards and security (Sissons, 1988, p.290).

This chapter concentrates on charting the developments that allowed the professional cricketer to sell his labour more freely and, in particular, will focus on the legal dispute between World Series Cricket (WSC) and the cricket authorities. The importance of this dispute to cricket's commercial history can be viewed on several levels. It indicated, directly, that cricket, or more particularly one day cricket, could be a very marketable commodity to both the viewing public and more importantly for the broadcasters. It also brought into sharp focus the comparatively poor terms and conditions of international players, and the type of contractual regime that existed. The conservative nature of the game's administration was also exposed to scrutiny, as were divisions between the Test playing nations. In order to understand the developments that have occurred it is necessary to consider the historical position of the cricketer in terms of his role and status in order to unpack some of the baggage that has hindered the professional player in his attempts to obtain due reward for his labour.

The origin and traditions of cricket

The very earliest forms of cricket are not well documented, although it does appear that games of a similar type were common medieval village distractions in parts of Europe. Rather than being bound by a common set of rules the game was passed down from generation to generation by word of mouth. This of course explodes a common myth; that cricket was traditionally a game for 'gentlemen', as, in its earliest forms, the embryonic game of what we know today as 'cricket' was played by ordinary folk drawn from the whole community.[9] By the end of the seventeenth century however, cricket was beginning to merit attention in the (recently established) local press, mainly in terms of advertising forthcoming matches. These provide illuminating evidence of the road that cricket was taking, littered as they are with reference to gambling, wagers and 'gentlemen'. For example, Brookes (1978, p.25) notes a match advertised in *The Postman* in 1705; 'this is to give notice that a match of cricket is to be played between eleven gentlemen of a west part of the county of Kent, against as many of Chatham, for eleven guineas a man, at Moulden in Kent on August 7th next'.

Within a fairly short period of time, cricket had shifted from being a rural village pastime played primarily for enjoyment by all and sundry to a game used by the aristocracy and aspirant gentry to occupy their leisure hours. Cricket's modern evolution was engendered by wealthy Southern landowners although cricket like other folk games such as football had previously been treated disdainfully by the state. In 1733 cricket's position was in some ways legitimised by the Prince of Wales donating a cup to be competed for by a team selected by the Prince and another side selected by a 'Mr Stead'. The development of cricket was profoundly influenced by the patronage of the aristocracy and the interrelationship with gambling was pronounced, for example:

> Between 1772 and 1796, the club known sometimes as Hampshire, more generally as Hambledon, met All England in sixty-six matches and won thirty-eight of them. They played generally for five hundred guineas a side, and it has been estimated that Hambledon won £22,497 10s to £10,030 in match-stakes alone. Worked out in modern values, of course those were fortunes but in the obsessional gambling of the Regency period, many times more money than that depended on side-bets (Allen, 1984, p.70).

Cricket at this time was immensely popular as apart from the gambling opportunities it provided, it was also one of the few examples of organised entertainment. The Hambledon club itself is worthy of further consideration as it provides an early example of a putative administrative structure which included its players being subject to a number of regulations reinforced by the prospect of a fine. Whilst the players were subject to possible financial penalties, they were also able to make some economic gain in terms of payments and expenses and the costs of hats for all members was borne by the club! The influence of Hambledon diminished as both the star local players began to defect and the axis of power shifted towards London. With the advent of the aristocratic involvement and increasing patronage of cricket, the notion of cricket as an occupation began to be considered. Early on, a distinction was made between 'retained' and 'independent' players, with retained players employed by patrons in nominal servient positions and 'independent' players not bound to any one team or patron but able to play in a freelance capacity for any team. Effectively this was a precursor of the amateur and professional bifurcation that was to become of prime importance until well into the twentieth century.

Whilst in its narrow construct the amateur/professional distinction was based upon issues of payment, it did in fact denote a far wider and more class riven cleavage. Sport in its 'unsullied' form was seen as character building and noble and formed part of the nineteenth century public school curriculum as a 'civilising force'. The MCC engaged its first professionals in 1825 and apart from playing in matches the professional would spend the rest of his time bowling at members. Little time was therefore allowed to improve his batting and the pattern of the professional bowler and amateur batsman was borne. The relationship between amateur and professional players was a volatile one, umbrage was taken when a professional was chosen ahead of George Parr for the 1861 tour to Australia, the first tour to visit those shores. The differences grew steadily worse until in 1865, 'open warfare' broke out with Nottinghamshire players refusing to play at the Oval and a number of professionals withdrew from the All England XI and the United XI of England with far reaching consequences. This was seen as a challenge to the status quo and an affront to the MCC and the existing establishment. In 1866 the northern professionals disassociated themselves from all cricket played in the south, an action seen by some members as being comparable to the secession of the confederate States of USA in 1862; 'Northern Players secede from Lord's on the day of the Two Elevens match, played for the benefit of professionals, the ground being given to them for that purpose - Gratitude!' (MCC Minutes 21 May 1866, in Brookes, 1978, p.113).

Indeed, the action of the professionals was widely perceived as being akin to a strike and the professional cricketer acquired the reputation of involvement in working class insurrectionism and the class based gentleman/player distinction was forged. Larwood makes the point that whilst cricket was the professional's livelihood, it was the gentleman's pastime and the class distinction was a strong one exacerbated by the authorities:

> I don't think the amateurs actually looked down on the professionals. If there was any feeling between the two it was caused by cricket administrators. They were the ones who insisted on discrimination such as calling the professionals by their surname. Out in the middle we were all equal. I showed my annoyance with anybody who dropped my catches, pro or amateur (Larwood, 1982, p.39).

What Larwood saw as, on field equality, was strongly divorced from the position off the field. Apart from the two groups using different gates to enter and leave the field, different dressing rooms and differences in status accorded by how the names were recorded on the scorecard, the two normally kept apart in the post match socialising. The amateur/professional distinction became even more important with the advent of the County Championship as the establishment began to fear that the game would be completely awash with a working class presence. By finely honing the divide the authorities could allow cricket to flourish economically whilst allowing the gentleman to retain his rights and privileges. The County Championship is a competition that is somewhat difficult to date accurately. Whilst it is generally accepted that it operated in 1873, cricket had started between the counties much earlier (Webber, 1957). Before such competition could gather any momentum however, the vexed question of eligibility had to be considered in order to allow a county to field a side that was representative of itself and to prevent the practice of strengthening sides by bringing in professional players. The date of 1873 as the 'year zero' for County Championship matches may well be, merely, one of convenience as, it was the year, that rules for county qualification were brought into operation after delegates of first class counties met in London in December 1872 and resolved that, *inter alia*; a) No player could play for more than one county in the same season, b) Every player was free to choose which county to play for at the commencement of each season and had to make public his intention, and c) If a player elected to play for the county of his residence he was disbarred from competing against the county of his birth.

These basic tenets were also adopted by MCC although b) and c) were altered so as to allow a cricketer to play against the county of his birth as long as he was qualified to play for his county of residence. With these rules in place, the County Championship began although Wisden did not publish their first County table until 1888. As the Championship became more competitive, the role of the professionals and their position with cricket's firmament caused further problems. This frisson between 'art' and 'economy' was to create difficulties, not least whether a game such as cricket should be considered a business with monetary considerations undermining its ethical base:

> County cricket has become too much of a business, and too much of a money-making concern. There is, I am afraid, very little real sport in it now as a game, and the feeling of *esprit de corps* which ought to exist in conjunction with real county cricket is fast disappearing (C.E.Green, quoted in Brookes, 1978, p.143).

The professional cricketer's life was still not an easy one, riddled as it was with uncertainty and artisan status. Whilst normally unwilling to voice their disquiet or air their grievances, in 1881 there was a serious protest in the form of the 'Nottinghamshire Schism' when seven members of the Nottinghamshire team refused to play for their county unless certain demands were granted by the County Committee. One of these conditions was the desire of a formal contract of employment that would contain a term guaranteeing an automatic benefit on the completion of a given number of seasons with a county. Nottinghamshire refused to accede to any of the demands and the schism proved to be a rare example of professional cricketers taking collective action in support of a demand. The system of control that had been established was to persist until after the Second World War.

Perhaps one of the prime reasons for the overall lack of action to protest against conditions was that the players themselves were happy to be doing a job that they enjoyed at a far better wage than they might otherwise expect. This perhaps is also part of cricket's enduring myth - a more objective view might suggest an alternative analysis. Fred Root of Worcestershire argued that cricket was in fact very poorly paid as his twenty weeks' cricket (1,500 overs, 150 wickets) brought in under £300; deducted from this sum would be hotel accounts for away matches, taxi fares and equipment, all of which could be legitimately claimed by the amateur as expenses. Even the 'benefit match' was not as lucrative as one might expect. Beneficiaries were expected to pay all the expenses surrounding the game in question and some professionals turned down the opportunity of a benefit on the grounds that they simply could not afford it.[10]

In the early twentieth century, the importance of the amateur rapidly declined. Whilst in 1902 J.T. Tyldesley was the only professional player to play in the first Test match that year, this ratio was never to be repeated. After the First World War the professionals filled nearly all the places although there would always be at least one amateur in the team due to the insistence that England be captained by an amateur player and by implication led by a 'gentleman'. In fact it was not until 1950 that a professional captained the England side and even then this was not well received in all quarters:

> So Hutton was the obvious choice to succeed Brown; but he was a professional, and there was no chance that he would take amateur status as Hammond had in order to captain England. Today it seems ridiculous that anyone should be concerned about the prospect of a professional captaining England, but in the fifties there were still those who felt a gut reaction that this was an undesirable state of affairs, whatever the credentials of the candidate (Marks, 1990, p.134).

Whilst the amateur/professional distinction was not formally abolished until 1962, it had in practice been an artificial division for some time as few players could actually afford to remain truly amateur. Some leading players were classified as 'amateurs' but employed by the clubs in some capacity, for example as Club Secretary. The distinction had come under fire on the pages of Wisden for a number of years, with Robertson-Glasgow, for example, rallying strongly against the facade of amateurism or 'shamateurism' as the similar situation became known in rugby union. At the same time that the amateur/professional distinction was being seriously debated, the level of remuneration for professional cricketers was also developing into a significant issue. As there was still no collective body (unlike within association football that was at the same time debating maximum wage constraints) negotiations took place on a county by county basis. However, in October 1967 the Cricketers' Association was formed in London with Roger Prideaux as chairman, Fred Rumsey as secretary and Jack Bannister as treasurer. The first meeting included speakers from the increasingly influential Professional Footballers' Association. At the first AGM at Edgbaston in March 1968 it could count 135 professionals amongst its number, representing a third of the total cricket workforce. However, within three years it could muster almost one hundred percent membership as cricketers came less to fear a mirroring of football's militancy and began to appreciate the real benefits that membership could bring, a view that began to be shared in addition by the authorities:

> The initial opposition barriers of 'union' and 'brother' images were to be expected. Perhaps less expectedly has been the ease with which these barriers have been removed, and in this respect the most pleasing feature to date has been the reaction of the authorities. The MCC and the Counties have welcomed the formation of the Association, and already have shown full co-operation in preliminary discussions on several important issues...it is obvious even at this early stage that contrary to some freely expressed views, the Association is freely accepted and acknowledged as a responsible and worthwhile body (Bannister, 1968, p.2).

The aims of the Association at this time were fourfold; to represent the collective view of county cricketers, to find ways of improving the standards of living of the county cricketer, to create a better understanding between players and county committees and to offer help, generally, to players and, in particular, with respect to the organisation of benefit years (Edwards, 1971). There is no doubt that the Cricketers' Association has encouraged an improved relationship between the employers and the players and perhaps its very existence has contributed to an understanding that an employment relationship exists. It has sought representation on the appropriate committees and attempted to amend disciplinary regulations with some effect; 'For that reason the Yorkshire committee had, in fact, no redress against Geoffrey Boycott for his protest at their "disloyalty" on the Parkinson programme. That was his right of reply negotiated by the [Cricketers Association]' (Allen, 1984, p.220).

However, even as late as 1995 David Graveney, at the time General Secretary of what had become the Professional Cricketers' Association (PCA) lamented with some embarrassment that the lot of many professional cricketers had changed little, 'An uncapped player earns between £5,500 and £8,500, depending on age, while for a capped player the minimum wage is £14,500' (Baldwin, 1995, p.23). While the creation of a cricket union was a sensible and pragmatic step, of more fundamental economic importance to professional cricketers was the 'Packer revolution'. Although the better players were starting to earn more than their predecessors from the game and enjoy other financial opportunities through sponsorship there was still some discontent. The cricket authorities had failed to realise fully the commercial opportunities that the game and particularly the one day version could provide and, as a consequence, there was a marked disparity between the earning ability of the top professional cricketers when compared to sportsmen in other fields. Martin-Jenkins (1977, p.5) offers the following anecdote with respect to the Australian Test party of the early 1970s:

> Wooldridge told the story of some members of the 1972 touring team to England, whose basic tour salary exclusive of prize money was about £16 a day, chatting to Barry Sheene, the world motor-cycling champion. Sheene's reply, when asked what he earned, was apparently: 'About a hundred'. 'Would that be £100 a week or £100 a ride?' his inquisitors persisted. Sheene enlightened them that it was £100,000 a year.

It was clear that the current situation could not continue and that increased professionalisation and commercialisation of the game was inevitable. The surprise to the authorities was, however, not only the extent and nature of the transformation, but also the direction from where the wind of change would emanate.

Oh what a circus, oh what a show

The Packer 'circus' was fundamentally a simple concept.[11] It had become apparent that there were significant defects in the organisation and administration of the international game and, therefore, a potential gap for a rival promoter. The cricket establishment had never had to contend with any serious competition to its control and it was certainly reluctant to change the relationship of Test match cricket to the emerging one day game. One day cricket was beginning to develop as an important addition to the more traditional five day test match.[12] A clear attraction to some cricket watchers, or indeed fans of other sports, was the change of approach required by the players. Athletic run saving fielding became a necessity as did creative and improvised batting, runs per over became the crucial equation and a number of specialist one day shots were devised that took advantage of restrictions on fielding positions to score runs at a quicker rate.[13] Supporters argued that the one day game could attract a new breed of spectators who might not find the traditional game so engaging with its emphasis on attrition and a gradual build up with the distinct possibility that the match might end without a definite result for either team. The crucial relationship was to be formed between this truncated form of the game and broadcasters, clearly the exciting one day format was an attractive option.

Despite the fact that a gap in the cricket market seemed to exist, it was still an enormous operation to mount an alternative series of matches. Without players, grounds or existing administration any competition was likely to be very expensive and fraught with difficulty. Haigh (1993) has documented the rationale for Packer's move into sports coverage, not least the impressive ratings achieved by the Australian Broadcasting Company (ABC) for the 1975 World Cup Final.[14] Packer was however unable to obtain exclusive access to the rights owned by the Australian Cricket Board (ACB) which had traditionally dealt with the ABC. Haigh (1993) notes that by the time Packer obtained a meeting with the ACB in June 1976 a three year contract had already been agreed with the ABC for A$210,000 although it had not been formally signed. Packer offered to buy the exclusive rights for the next three year contract period starting in 1979 for A$1.5m only to be told that this offer would be considered when the contract was up for renewal. It was this rejection that provided the impetus for the creation of an alternative cricket programme. Throughout February and March 1977 the leading Australian players were contracted along with Tony Greig, the then England captain, who was designated as captain of a Rest of the World side. The recruiting continued with Tony Greig acting as an active agent travelling to the West Indies to offer contracts to Pakistani and West Indian players. The seventeen strong Australian touring side that arrived in England in April 1977 contained thirteen players who had signed contracts that committed them to play for a different promoter from their current employer, the ACB, which clearly created a difficult situation for the tour management in attempts to maintain unity. In addition to those touring there were a further five Australians and the other seventeen players who were to form the Rest of the World side signed to WSC.[15]

The shock and indeed horror in some quarters at the World Series Cricket (WSC) proposals when the story broke in England on 9 May 1977 is difficult to overstate; the newspaper headlines of the time spoke for example of players turning 'pirate'.[16] Blofeld (1978, p.23) summed up one response as; '...a feeling of anger that Packer was almost trying to rob England of a national heritage'. The importance of cricket to English society is reflected in the comments of the Secretary of the MCC at the time, Jack Bailey (1989, p.96):

> Here we were, protecting cricket: part of the English heritage, now the world's heritage. A game in which honour was a byword, which had lent its name to phrases in common usage throughout the English-speaking world...Recognised cricket had been sold down the river by a number of players.

Opinion inside and outside of the game quickly became polarised into pro and anti Packer camps, supporters arguing that this new approach could bring great benefits to players and spectators. That the end result, as argued at the time, has been improved remuneration for the players seems to attract widespread agreement. Benaud (1984) expressed delight that player payment had increased because of WSC, whilst both Martin-Jenkins (1984) and Blofeld (1978) have agreed that some of the players had benefited financially though at the cost of increased commercialisation of the game about which both had doubts. Ironically it seems that if, as suggested, cricketers would benefit financially this didn't alter the view of many of the English professionals who, by and large, adopted an anti-Packer stance. At an Extraordinary General Meeting of the Professional Cricketers' Association on 5 September 1977 the members voted (ninety one to seventy seven) in support of banning those players contracted to WSC from the county game.[17] However the meeting also voted in favour of a resolution urging the Test and County Cricket Board (TCCB) and ICC to reopen negotiations with Packer. The opposition of the county players reflects the view that perhaps the most obvious beneficiaries would be the leading international players who were likely already to be the better paid cricketers.

Standing firm against the new proposals was the traditional and very conservative cricket establishment which wanted to maintain the shape and form of test cricket and perhaps more importantly, retain administrative control over the game.[18] It would also quickly become apparent that the problem would not be confined to Australia (who had lost the greatest number of players) and England (the administrative capital and the country with the only fully professional game) but develop into an international issue, as players from other Test playing nations had signed contracts with WSC. A view expressed by some quarters of the English game was that this was a domestic Australian issue, a spat over television rights between the ACB and a potential broadcaster and that the international authorities should not become embroiled in the problem (Bailey, 1989). Given the nature of the opposition and the little that was known of WSC plans the response from the authorities took two forms. First the United Kingdom Cricket Council acted against Tony Greig and sacked him as England captain, the first holder of the position to be dismissed for disciplinary reasons.[19] The next move, which followed an emergency meeting of the ICC, was to arrange a meeting with Packer, which was set for 14 June. The meeting ended in stalemate apparently unable to avoid the stumbling block of Packer's requirement for the exclusive broadcasting rights to the Australian game at the end of the current ABC contract. Bailey (1989, p.91) records the bewilderment of the delegates after Packer had temporarily left so they could consider the issue:

> Back in the Committee Room, the main discussion centred round Packer's last words. Had he *really* said that? We agreed that he had. The proposition was examined. It was really an Australian problem, but a problem which on the face of it seemed insoluble. How could they give such a guarantee in practical terms even if they had wanted to? And even if they could give a guarantee, would it be

in the best interests of Australian cricket? Only they could judge.

It transpired, immediately after this meeting, that Packer had already recruited a full complement of West Indian players providing him with three complete sides; Australia, the Rest of the World and the West Indies, in total some fifty one players. The failure to broker a compromise was the precursor to the ultimately damaging legal action. Packer had made it clear that he would support his players if restrictive action was taken against them, one of his points at the failed meeting with the ICC in June was that he required an assurance that his players would not be victimised. However the ICC was undeterred and at their annual meeting on 26 July, they took action against the renegade players. The WSC matches would not be granted first class status but more importantly the ICC altered its rules with respect to player eligibility for Test Match cricket.

Prior to the change of 26 July the ICC rule that governed qualification to play in Test Matches contained two main principles, qualification by either birth or residence; a player could automatically play for the country of his birth unless debarred by the ICC. The residency period required for qualification, was basically four years although, the ICC reserved the right to impose a longer period in conjunction with the national governing body. Once a cricketer had played Test cricket for one country he could re-qualify but required permission from his former country to play against it. In England the rules of eligibility were amplified within the TCCB regulations which defined country of birth and residency. Other than the automatic qualification through birthplace, the TCCB required a ten year residency for England qualification or residency from the day before the player's fourteenth birthday. The method adopted by the ICC for penalising the WSC players was simple; to make participation in any 'disapproved' match a cause of disbarment from the international game and then 'disapprove' the WSC matches.

Thus, any player participating, or making himself available to participate, in any of the WSC matches lost his eligibility to play for his country. Furthermore the ICC in its accompanying press statement 'strongly recommended that each member country pursue as soon as possible at first class level and in other domestic cricket activities the implementation of decisions made in regard to Test Matches'. Clearly the intention was to prevent players from playing in Test, first class or possibly even club cricket. In England the TCCB had already decided, at its meeting on 15 July, to act and following the ICC decision the TCCB ratified its earlier position subject to the court action. The change to the TCCB regulations on eligibility for the national side, followed the form of the ICC, but then extended the ineligibility to play into the domestic first class game:

Subject to the overriding discretion of the board, no county shall be entitled to play in any competitive county cricket match: (i) Any cricketer who is and remains precluded from playing in a Test Match on the grounds set out in rule 1(e) (whether or not he is otherwise qualified to play in a Test Match) prior to the expiration of a period of two years immediately following the date of the last match previously disapproved by the [ICC] in which he has played or made himself available to play (*Greig*, 1978, p.331).

Within a week of the ICC meeting Packer announced his intention to mount a legal challenge to the ban. The first stage of this campaign was a writ issued on 5 August against the ICC and TCCB by three Packer contracted players (Tony Greig, Michael Procter and John Snow) alleging that the ICC rule change was unlawful. The TCCB were brought into the action because of the statements of 15 July and 5 August. It had been anticipated for some time before the actual decision on 26 July that the ICC would seek to ban the 'rebel' players and the TCCB had indicated on 15 July that it would seek to introduce a County level ban subject to ICC action and support from the Cricket Council. Contemporaneously, World Series Cricket Pty Ltd also issued a writ adding that the authorities were seeking to unlawfully induce a breach of the contracts between the cricketers and WSC.[20] At the heart of this case was the doctrine of restraint of trade and whether a body that controlled and administered a sport could prevent players from participating in independent competition to obstruct rival matches.

The status of the WSC contracts

A primary issue was whether the agreements between the promoter and the cricketers were themselves unlawful as being in restraint of trade. The consequences of such a finding would have been considerable, there could be no liability in tort for inducing a breach of a void contract, and more importantly, it would signal to any of the cricketers who had developed second thoughts about the alternative programme, that WSC could not enforce the contracts against them. Throughout the early development there were rumours of some signed players reconsidering their position, not least the newest 'glamour' figure of Australian cricket, David Hookes:

> He began to buckle, and in early October flew to see Packer with a financial adviser and resignation speech memorised. 'He just laughed at me', says Hookes. 'Well, perhaps not laughed, but he made it clear that there was absolutely no way I could pull out. And if I did I'd end up paying him 90% of my salary for [the] rest of my life. My name had been used in the advance promo material, so I'd be sued for damages' (Haigh, 1993, p.111-112).

More interestingly, after Jeff Thomson announced his withdrawal on 28 July, Haigh (1993) reports that several of the Australian party, who had signed, contacted a former State teammate lawyer who obtained a specialist view on the enforceability of Doug Walters' contract. Bailey (1989) records that any potential problems of enforceability with the original contracts were ironed out after a hearing on 4 August which had alerted WSC to the possibility of this issue. When informed of the potential problem of enforceability, he immediately sent covering letters correcting the matter. Packer was aware that his contracts were draconian in nature; 'I make no apologies for the fact that the contract is tough. I told every player, "This is a tough contract and you'll do as you're damn well told"' (Frith, 1977, p.5). The upshot of the hearing of 4 August was that no action would be taken by the cricket authorities with respect to bans until the outcome of the full hearing.

In order to consider the validity of the WSC contracts, the judge chose to examine the one signed by Tony Greig. The contracts were generally the same except with respect to length and fee. One contract was for five years duration whilst the others were for between one and three years in length. Similarly the fee varied from approximately A$20,000 to A$35,000 for each tour. Greig's contract was for three years commencing on 1 September 1977 and encompassing three 'seasons' which ran from September to March the following year. Greig (and the other players) were committed to be available to play a 'tour' in each season. The tour would encompass up to fifty five days of cricket broken down into five 'Test matches' each of a five day duration, four two day limited over games and an unspecified number of other matches. The fee for the contract was payable in three parts A$10,000 on signature, A$10,000 after the third 'Test match' or on 5 January whichever the earlier and the final A$10,000 on completion of the tour. If the tour took place outside of Australia the fee was the same unless the number of match days altered in which case there was a formula to increase or decrease payment.[21] The contract contained a number of restrictive clauses:

> Clause 3 (b) he will not: (i) play in any cricket match other than a match of a tour without the consent in writing of the promoter first had and obtained, (ii) appear on radio or television nor grant interviews for nor write nor submit articles for publication in any newspaper magazine or periodical except in each case as first authorised in writing by the promoter, (iii) give endorsements for goods of any nature nor allow his name or photograph to be used for promotional or advertising purposes except as first authorised in writing by the promoter (*Greig*, 1978, p.323).

There had been a great deal of secrecy regarding the content of the agreements during the evolution of the World Series Cricket project, although, eventually a copy of one leaked contract appeared on the front page of the Daily Mail in early August. Once the terms were known the question of enforceability began to be publicly debated, McFarline (1977) and Haigh (1993) both quote anecdotal legal 'advice' that the contracts might be open to challenge. A further point arose over the process involved in the signing of the contracts and the apparent lack of legal advice available to some of the players. Blofeld (1978, p.100) quotes Geoff Boycott directly (he interviewed Boycott, who declined to sign for WSC, in the transit lounge of Colombo airport) on the negotiations that took place for his signature; 'Austin Robertson came to see me at the Melbourne Cricket Ground during the Centenary Test Match. He showed me the official contract, but he would not let me take it away and show it to my solicitor....He said that secrecy was the reason I could not take away a copy of the contract, but said that he was coming to England to sign up players, and was also coming to look for suitable grounds where they could play in the future'. The absence of specialist legal advice has proved a significant factor in some of the music business cases, (as we have outlined in the concluding chapter) and this point was picked up by Justice Slade:

> Of the 50 or so players who had entered into such contracts by the time that proceedings were begun, some (such as Mr Proctor) did not receive legal advice on them and most, if not all, were not immediately supplied with copies for them to retain. It may be-I put it no higher-that, on these or other grounds, some individual players would in the particular circumstances of their respective cases have the right to rescind their contracts as against World Series Cricket. For present purposes it will suffice to say that no attempt was made on behalf of the defendants, either by adduction of evidence or otherwise, to show that the contracts were all voidable by the players on the grounds of misrepresentation, undue influence, unconscionable bargain or similar grounds (*Greig*, 1978, p.327).

The suggestion that some of the contracts might be voidable according to the circumstances of each negotiation might well explain why any players who chose not to fulfil their WSC contracts were not subject to legal action despite alleged warnings to the contrary. Justice Slade referred to three specific potential causes of action to avoid the contracts; misrepresentation, undue influence and the wider umbrella term of 'unconscionable bargains'. The crucial difference as far as the cricketing authorities were concerned was that if indeed the contracts were voidable this would only be at the action of the player concerned. The contract may continue unhindered until the wronged party acts. The fact that the contract is voidable offers no defence to a tortious claim of inducing breach of contract.

The claim that the WSC contracts were void, on the grounds of public policy was based on four grounds; (i) the contract duration, (ii) the promoter's right to assign the agreement, (iii) the absence of any term requiring the promoter to stage a tour and (iv) the absence of any player right to terminate.

The crucial concept at the heart of judicial concern over restrictive contractual arrangements was thus present; the ability of the dominant party to maintain the exclusive right to use the services of the other party but never call upon them, thus with the potential to lead to a sterilisation of the talent of the performer. A major point here was that whilst the contracts were for exclusive services they did not cover the entire year and for the intervening period (the English season) players were free to play elsewhere. Similarly the contract duration was unlikely to be a major persuasive point as the relevant period was limited to three years with one agreement extending to five years. Slade J only considered one point in detail, the lack of any obligation for WSC to provide matches. Indeed if the negotiations with the ICC sub committee on 23 June, where talks between the ICC and Packer broke down when Packer's demand for exclusive television rights in Australia rendered further discussion impossible, had produced an agreed outcome it is possible that the whole concept of WSC might not have proceeded much further. If the contracts, signed by the players, had provided Packer with the necessary leverage to strike a deal over the television rights that he had sought, the next stage of confronting the cricketing authorities head on would have become redundant. The players could have then been used for exhibition games in a far less hostile atmosphere, certainly in terms of WSC access to facilities such as grounds.

The WSC matches attracted interest as 'unofficial' Tests but more importantly, the matches contained the best players, thus in many ways, certainly in terms of personnel, these were the 'real' Tests. The official matches, such as the Australia versus India series, might have had the full trappings of establishment blessing but they lacked the vital ingredient, the majority of the established Australian players. If, however, the WSC cricketers had been playing the 'Supertest' series *in addition* to the traditional fixtures it is difficult to see the public attraction for the 'Supertests' as replacements for the traditional international sporting fixtures. It might, however, have been possible to market them on the basis of the creative features such as clothing, innovative rule change and the whole concept of night cricket as an alternative experience. Within this analysis, the cricketers may be viewed as a commodity in short supply (certainly at the highest level) and having established the exclusive right to their services Packer was able to use this as part of a wider bargaining strategy. The absence of a term obliging the promotion of games, falls in line with this view for it could have been a possibility that there would never have been the need to stage games, if the end result sought and achieved, was the acquisition of television rights.

The lack of any obligation to promote was dealt with succinctly on the basis that the court could either imply an obligation to provide work or, more likely, require remuneration from the employer if the other party was ready and available to work. Thus the right to payment only on execution of service which, in turn, depended on provision of work could be circumvented by the implication of a term to pay reasonable remuneration. Justice Slade applied this principle to the relevant part of Tony Greig's specimen contract:

> Under clause 6(a) of Mr Greig's contract, the player is to be remunerated for his participation in each 'tour' in Australia by way of a fixed stated sum, which is to be paid as to a stated part of the date of the contract, as to a further stated part 'following the completion of the third test match or on January 5 in that season (whichever shall be earlier) and as to $10,000 on completion of the tour'. Clause 6 (a) states the 'day rate' of remuneration, but the sub-clause is so drafted that even if, in the event, a 'tour' in Australia arranged by the promoter is less than 55 days, a player, who has participated in the 'tour' and otherwise performed his part of the contract, is entitled to the total agreed fee in respect of that 'tour' without any pro rata reduction. In these circumstances, in my judgement the clear inference is that if, during the term of such contract, whereby the promoter was expressed to 'engage the player to provide his services', the promoter in any year failed to arrange any 'tour' in Australia, a player, who demonstrated his willingness to play on such a 'tour' if arranged and had otherwise observed his part of the contract, would be entitled to the full 'tour' fee (*Greig*, 1978, p.326).

This implication of a right to payment was said by the judge to be a means of 'giving reasonable effect to the presumed intention of the parties' though this principle did not extend to 'tours' outside of Australia. Accordingly the judge was not prepared to determine that the contracts were void. The irony of this situation was that both the contracting parties appeared content with the terms, despite their restrictive nature, and it was a third party, who only had an indirect interest in the performance of the agreement, who alleged that the contract was in restraint of trade. To tear up such an agreement at the behest of a third party, although the legitimacy of such action would be grounded in public policy, might be viewed as a serious attack on the doctrine of freedom of contract. It is clearly a different matter if one party seeks legal intervention claiming that the terms are oppressive, but, to allow relief where the parties to the agreement deny (or at least accept) such oppression, switches contractual analysis firmly from the subjective to the objective.

The lawfulness of the bans

A crucial point in determining the lawfulness of the proposed restrictions was whether the plaintiffs had *locus standi* to challenge the proposed rule changes of the ICC and TCCB, changes that would effect their ability to practise their professional craft. Drawing upon the *Eastham* case, Slade J held that such a right existed in that an employee may seek a declaratory judgement against, not just his employer, but also any association of employers that sought to restrict access to employment. The issue then switched to whether any interests existed that the ICC and TCCB were entitled to protect and secondly, whether the action taken properly protected that interest. Again Slade J drew upon the *Eastham* decision, which determined that, the Football Association and Football League had a legitimate interest to protect namely the organisation and administration of professional football in their capacity as 'the custodians of the public interest'. There was a clear parallel here for the ICC and TCCB, even allowing for the fact that the ICC represented countries without any full professional game. Thus, the 'public interest' required a properly organised and administered game, which was a protectable interest within the doctrine of restraint of trade. The issue was whether the proposed bans protected this interest, in effect, whether they were reasonable or not, or realistically to what extent this protectable interest was threatened by WSC. The financial state of the international game was an important part of this argument with the cricketing authorities alleging that the professional game in England depended for its survival on the revenue generated by Test cricket. Consequently if WSC diminished the healthy economic position of official Test matches, the loss of income would harm the professional game. This view was accepted as fact by Slade J; 'conventional first class cricket in the United Kingdom at all levels depends for its financial viability considerably on the profits from Test Matches played in England against overseas teams from the other five Test-playing countries' (*Greig*, 1978, p.349). Wright has vehemently argued that it is the current relationship, between the Counties and the TCCB that is at the heart of the crisis within the game. The County Cricket Clubs depend on the TCCB for income who in turn rely on the receipts from Test Cricket to maintain the pyramid. What then happens if Test cricket declines in favour of the lucrative one day game?

> The next question, then, concerns the future of first-class county cricket if there is no Test cricket for the England team on which the marketing of cricket is structured... Although it is not always obvious at ground level, there is still sufficient interest and belief in first-class cricket to sustain a county circuit, but not on the heavily subsidized scale that has snowballed, providing for big squads of

retained players and generous administrative staffs (Wright, 1994, p.203).

In short, the relationship between Test and county cricket that the cricketing establishment portrayed in their evidence as vital to the health of the national game is viewed, by Wright as the essential problem that the first class game needs to resolve to survive.[22] Test match income has replaced membership subscriptions and localised fund raising but, the result is the same, a national game unable to support itself without subsidy. Wright's view is that the game must fundamentally change its approach and structure in order for the 'soul' of the game to be preserved.[23]

Despite his acceptance of the financial tie between national and county structures (and indeed the lower levels of the game) Slade J was unconvinced that WSC posed a threat to the finances of the ICC members. The comparison was between WSC 'tours' and the thirteen official tours that were already arranged between the Test playing nations for the competing period. The WSC matches were scheduled between the end of November and mid February the following year and accordingly there were only six potential clashes (the Indian tour to Australia 1977/8, England to Pakistan 1977/8, West Indies to India 1978/79, England to Australia 1978/9, Australia to India and Pakistan 1979/80 and West Indies to Pakistan and New Zealand 1979/80). Evidence on the economics of such tours led Slade J to conclude that the only real financial threat of WSC was directed to the ACB as the WSC matches conflicted with the official test series against the Indian tourists. It was suggested by Ross Edwards that the removal of the best Australian players might be of benefit as it would make the series against a weak Indian side closer and therefore a more attractive spectacle, a view subsequently born out by Blofeld (1978, p.188); 'The standard was clearly much lower now, but with two evenly balanced sides desperately wanting to win and the spectators just as involved the players did not have to be the best in the world to attract big crowds'.

Slade J's analysis of cricket's finances was clearly problematic for the authorities. They had argued on an economic basis from the outset, yet the finding was that 'on the balance of probabilities' WSC was only 'likely to diminish the receipts of the ACB'. He did though, accept the defence's view that WSC was acting in a parasitical fashion by capturing the star players who had been nurtured, at cost, by the traditional game. It was also possible that in time WSC would pose a more significant threat beyond that to the Australian game if its programme were extended in terms of the number of games and players contracted. The problem was the depth and breadth of the ban that had been developed by the ICC and the judge appeared to support the lawfulness of a more limited prospective ban:

In general terms I see the force of the proposition that official Test-players should not for the future be permitted to make themselves available to official Test cricket and to privately promoted international cricket in turn and from time to time, as and when they please. There would, I think, have been much to be said for the reasonableness and thus for the validity of a resolution, passed on July 26, 1977, of which the effect had been merely to inform cricketers in clear terms that any of them who thereafter contracted with and elected to play cricket for a private promoter, such as World Series Cricket, could not subsequently expect to be engaged to play in official Test Matches by any of the cricketing authorities of the Test-playing countries (*Greig*, 1978, p.352).

Slade J was considering what restriction might have been more reasonable (and therefore lawful) as the threat of WSC began to impact upon the international game. He suggested that a prospective ban would have dealt with this problem and whilst not suggesting that it would have necessarily have been reasonable, argued that it would have been easier to justify. Having established a protectable interest (the organisation and administration of the international game) the ICC would be permitted to initiate measures, albeit in restraint of trade, that protected those interests. The threat was to the finances of the ACB, therefore action against international players with, at best, an extremely indirect relationship to the ACB would be extremely difficult to justify. Slade J's suggestion that a prospective ban might be reasonable to deal with the presumed wider threat to the game makes it clear that a retrospective and prospective ban together, was beyond justification. The future threat identified by Slade J was highly speculative; that other players might join, that the programme might extend beyond three years and because other promoters might follow Packer's lead. It was the issue of retrospectiveness on the bans that appears to have been the crucial factor. When considering the threat to the cricketers' ability to ply their trade, the judge focused on the issue of players 'who had already contracted' with WSC. The principle was not one based on the freedom of the individual player to contract with any cricket employer but on the unfairness of banning such relationships after they had been formed. In addition Slade J considered that the authorities had not clearly identified what positive benefits might result from such a ban when weighed against the 'injustices to the players involved and the certain detriment to the world public interested in cricket'. If these two points are the yardstick by which any restraint must be measured, it is similarly difficult to see how a prospective ban could be reasonable. Given that the players were perfectly free to sign with WSC there would still be an injustice imposed by such a ban to both the players and the public.

It was clear that if the ICC restriction fell the TCCB's comparable rule change would also be deemed unlawful. Whilst the ICC could seek to prevent participation in Test match cricket, the fundamental loss of revenue for the players would be at County level. Some players would not, in any event, be appearing in the international arena. Aside from those whose Test career was coming to an end like John Snow, there were the South Africans such as Michael Procter who were banned from Test matches. Bailey (1989) argues that the selection of Snow and Proctor as plaintiffs was a carefully thought out decision to accentuate these points. It was at this level of the game that the more familiar arguments concerning the doctrine of restraint of trade were aired. The length of the ban would, thought the judge, 'probably have the effect of driving these two cricketers permanently out of first class cricket', yet the three year period of the WSC contracts had not apparently been a persuasive point when considering their validity. There was also the concept of the public interest in seeing 'star players' and it was suggested by the judge that the ban might lead to a reduction in gate receipts. Ironically, at the time that the TCCB initiated its ban, no action had been taken by the ACB with respect to Sheffield Shield cricket, though there are a number of reasons which explain why the TCCB acted so promptly. First, the closeness of the relationship between the ICC and TCCB along with the position of influential MCC personnel. Although the TCCB had been formed in 1968, until 1974 the MCC was the dominant force.[24] This altered in 1974 with an increase in autonomous power of the TCCB at the expense of the MCC. There were still informal overlaps in terms of personnel between the two organisations, but more important was the overlap between the MCC and ICC. For example, Jack Bailey was Secretary of the MCC but he also occupied the position of Secretary of the ICC and was therefore in a pivotal position with regard to both domestic and international cricket administration despite the growing power of the TCCB.[25] Secondly, it was in professional English cricket that many of the (non Australian) players earned their living, the judge noted that approximately twenty of the WSC cricketers fell into this category. Thus, if financial leverage was to be applied to the players it would be the TCCB that would have to apply it, the non professional structure in the rest of the world would make sanctions less effective though still important. Accordingly the TCCB rule change was also held to be in restraint of trade. In addition to the successful action by the cricketers themselves WSC were granted a declaration that the actions of the authorities amounted to the tort of inducing breach of contract. In short the relationship between WSC and the cricketers was preserved with the court strongly upholding the right of the players to ply their trade wherever possible.

Future relations; hired hand or independent professional?

After two years of competition between WSC and the cricket establishment, the inevitable settlement resulted in Packer obtaining the television rights that he had sought. More crucially, the shape of cricket was irrevocably altered as was the status and earnings of the top players. The agreement provided for a series of Test matches in each season but also a triangular international one day series consisting of Australia and two overseas teams, to be known as 'the Benson and Hedges World Series Cup' comprising fifteen matches. What was of concern to some of the cricketing establishment was that, whilst the ACB would determine the playing conditions of the matches, the Board had agreed to; '...consider favourably the introduction of the 30-yard circle in limited-overs matches, day/night matches and, on an experimental basis, the use of coloured clothing in Benson and Hedges one-day limited-overs international matches' (Bailey, 1989, p.114). These elements of WSC which were now being officially adopted, shocked many following the acrimonious battle with Packer to preserve the very traditions of the game. As Bailey observed, 'above all there was the immediate feeling that the television tail was now wagging the Australian cricket dog and hence the international kennel' (Bailey, 1989, p.116). Such features are now commonplace and there is a readiness to experiment in order to produce a marketable product that captures, not only the public imagination but also, more fundamentally, the interest of the broadcasters.[26] This one day revolution has also extended into the sacred territory concerning the number of players on each side. Cricket has long resisted the use of active substitutes, even for injured players, let alone for purely tactical reasons. A substitute may only field in place of an injured player and neither bat nor bowl. However, the ACB suggested in September 1997 that, in fact, an additional player, who is able to bat or bowl, should be allowed in one day games.

Despite the changes that have taken place, the traditional five day Test match remains largely unaltered notwithstanding that the nature of television coverage has changed. More innovative camera angles and developments such as stump cameras have given viewers previously unseen views and, microphones placed in the playing area, have given unheard commentary - in the case of England's tour to Pakistan in 1987, much to Mike Gatting's chagrin. A further development has been the introduction of the third umpire who is now able to rule on some close decisions, involving run outs, stumpings or hit wicket appeals, along with contentious boundary decisions, in one-day Internationals and Test matches. Recourse is only made to the third umpire at the initiation of the on field umpires, and contact is made via two way radio with a series of lights available to display the results of his deliberations (ICC Regulation 2.2(c)). The third Umpire is to be ensconced in a separate room, with access to a television monitor and direct sound link with the television control unit director, to facilitate as many replays as are necessary to reach a decision, ICC Regulation 2.1(b) provides:

> The third Umpire shall call for as many replays from any camera angle as is necessary to reach a decision. As a guide, a decision should be made within thirty seconds wherever possible, but the third Umpire shall have discretion to take more time in order to finalise a decision (ICC, 1996, p.17).

The major switch has been towards the one day game that has a strong prescence in both the domestic and international schedule. Changes in the relationship between the players and the employers have also developed to produce a far more sophisticated and detailed association between them. The administration of the game has passed through a number of distinct phases; the major splitting of roles occurring in 1968 for purely political reasons. Although the MCC originally retained a prominent position, this change eventually resulted in the loss of power and the beginning of the domination of the game by the First Class clubs, through the TCCB. The struggle between the two continued throughout the 1980s culminating in the resignation of the treasurer and secretary of the MCC:

> This parting of the ways, no wider at first than a hair-line crack, but developing over the years into a schism, had its origins in a flexing of muscles, a thrust for power by the TCCB centre, within the confines of Lord's; and a reluctance by MCC to grant *carte blanche* in their own house to an organization which sought power without responsibility - responsibility vested in the MCC committee by its members (Bailey, 1989, p.142-143).

This problem reflects the historic development of the game that had empowered a private club to run not only English cricket but also the international game. The growing power of the TCCB indicated the changing commercialisation of the game and the desire to shift the administrative structure accordingly. The eventual tripartite formation represented a decisive movement of power but some critics have commented that it still lacked a business structure. There has long been pressure for one amalgamated body that could oversee all aspects of the game and the impetus for the creation of an English Cricket Board (ECB) was provided by the Griffiths Report (1994)[27] which saw benefit in having one supreme organisation. In December 1995 the TCCB established a Working Party chaired by FD Morgan to consider the proposals for the formation of the ECB that had been presented to the TCCB. The resulting report was clear that the current structure was presiding over a failing game; '...despite the high levels of participation apparent in our game, standards at First Class level and below are lower than those in a number of other cricketing nations' (Morgan, 1996, p.2).

This was the prime issue; the improvement of cricket at *all* levels. Clearly administrative changes alone will not improve standards but changes to the First Class game will require the consent of the Counties who will need to be persuaded that such changes are in their long term interests. To be fully effective the ECB needs to be able to convince the County clubs that the broader health of the game is vital.[28] The Board itself is constituted along County lines with thirty eight members (First Class and Minor County) in addition to a place for the MCC, recognising the latter's unique position within the game. There is still a division below the governing Management Board, separating into the First Class Forum (FCF) and the Recreational Forum (RF). The FCF can dominate the Management Board as it effectively controls nine of the fourteen seats. Even within the FCF there may be tensions between the group of First Class Counties that occupy Test match grounds and those that don't. Notwithstanding these administrative changes at the top, the major issue facing the game was its structure. If the only changes were cosmetic, little of real worth would have altered and it is the proposals of the ECB since its formation that are of more significance (MacLaurin 1997). MacLaurin started by showing cricket's structure as a pyramid, at the pinnacle of the pyramid is a successful English Test side, that will stimulate other parts of the game:

> Fine performances by England cricketers make heroes. England heroes are projected on television and in newspapers. These heroes generate enthusiasm and interest amongst children who want to play and get involved in our game. Our future success and prosperity depends very much on our ability to convince each new generation of the enjoyment and lifelong rewards that cricket provides. This can only be achieved if we all work together in pursuit of a common interest (ECB News, January 1997, p.1).

The question is then how to create a more successful England side to provide the impetus for the remainder of the game. In many ways this was the same dilemma that faced the football authorities when the Premier League was formed. The problem for the ECB was how to persuade the Counties to accept fundamental alterations to the structure of the domestic game. Originally, there was some suggestion that a two divisional County Championship could be introduced with promotion and relegation. A system would have to be worked out as to which sides would play in each division. This was likely to be a controversial area as one of the most consistently successful one day sides, Lancashire, has, over the last few years, under performed in the Championship. The fear of some Counties was that such a proposal would immediately create, not just two divisions, but a two tier game. The clubs at the top would attract the best players and increased financial support, which might eventually, lead to some clubs being unable to compete. Accordingly, the Counties rejected the plan and voted to maintain the status quo.

In terms of the national side, the ECB has built on the Acfield Report (1996) which considered the selection, management and coaching of England teams and the position of the players. The issues of selection, coaching and management of the side are not pertinent here but, more importantly, the Report considered the relationship between the Counties, the Test team and the players. This has two dimensions, first the contractual relationship, secondly, the amount of cricket played and for whom; two questions which are inexorably linked. Players for the Test team are drawn exclusively from the County sides and the players are contracted to their County clubs. They are paid for playing for England and there has been a trend in recent years to provide Test players with increased contractual security, a means also of preventing any rival promoter emerging. Given the paymasters, the players are firstly County Cricketers and expected to play in the County Championship and the various one day competitions. This is their prime responsibility, especially given the fact that they will be amongst the best players available. This puts players in a position of playing, continuously without periods for recuperation and practice. A comparison between some of the key English and Australian players demonstrates the point. In the period 1 April 1995 to 31 March 1996 Dominic Cork, Mike Atherton and Jack Russell had completed a total of 239, 241 and 232 days of cricket respectively. The comparison with the core Australians was markedly different, with Glenn McGrath, Mark Taylor and Ian Healy having completed 129, 135 and 127 days respectively, during the same period. Although the English players racked up more days through a heavier winter tour (100 days in contrast to 35 days) the most telling difference relates to the domestic first class game. For example, Atherton played 68 days of domestic cricket whilst his Australian counterpart, Mark Taylor played merely 20. This demand was considered by Acfield (1996, p.10) as a serious issue that needed addressing; 'the Working Party believes that ways *must* be found of giving top players sufficient periods of rest before and after the domestic season and overseas tours; and, if necessary, at other points during the course of the domestic season'.

It is this last point that is crucial and impacts upon the contractual arrangements of the players. Because of the structure of the First Class game, and hence the cricket timetable, domestic games and Test matches overlap which already means that the top players will miss those matches for their Counties. The suggestion from Acfield (1996) is that they should have additional rest periods that will eat further into their availability. The situation has been aggravated by the increase in International one day matches that now accompany every Test series. A five match one day series adds the equivalent of at least one Test match. As the game has adapted to embrace the new format, it has placed an added burden on the players, by requiring further cricket from them, but it also strains the club/country relationship. The key issue remains, to whom are the players contracted? As we note above, Packer's challenge to the established order could only be successful as the players were free agents outside of their County contracts. Acfield (1996) considered the thorny problem of how to get the players to play less for the Counties without permanently contracting them. One solution would, of course, be to reduce the amount of one day matches at both domestic and international level but this would have serious financial implications. An interesting development within the English game has been to consider the two formats as separate, and select accordingly. There has always been some element of this with all-rounders preferred for the one day game, but for the 1997/8 trip to Sharjah the selectors picked, not only a largely different squad of players, but also a new captain. There was however an overlap between the two squads with certain core players appearing in both. The principle of full time contracts for Test players was accordingly rejected by Acfield (1996, p.10), a move which had been supported by the County clubs who were consulted:

> 5 out of 10 Individuals, and a very few of the Counties, are in favour of full-time Board contracts. Among the pro-contract group, the belief of the Individuals is that contracts should be for a calendar year and offered to a larger squad of players, rather than just certain types of player (e.g. fast bowlers); while Counties feel that if these must be offered, this should be done to *leading players only*.

If players were directly contracted to the ECB, the major problem would be how they would be able to obtain the requisite match practice. Counties might be loath to give spaces to players who would not be available for much of the season, displacing the regulars. The players themselves might not be committed to the cause of the team but playing only to achieve the necessary skills. Ironically, this player versus club dispute appeared when professionals first emerged and were criticised for playing for themselves and having less club loyalty than the amateurs. If the England players could not then fit into the existing County structure, a new tier of cricket would have to be created to provide the players with the opportunity to play themselves into form. There would also need to be a squad of contracted players, and those not selected for the Test eleven would need to find an outlet for their talents. The Counties outlined their objections to direct contracts, which would:

> ...deprive Counties of their most able players; affect the standard of the County

game; make it difficult for Counties to run their First Teams if players were 'floating in and out of the side'; lead to conflicts between the Board and the Counties; produce complacency/a lack of incentive within the contracted squad itself; and lead to potential bitterness between players. Some also suggest a danger that Counties' membership would lose interest and that their support for the game would wane (Acfield, 1996, p.10).

This whole problem is accordingly unresolved but a compromise reached whereby the Report recommends that the Chairman of Selectors be given the right to withdraw players from any County or one day match. This was mooted in 1994 by the then Chairman of Selectors, Raymond Illingworth, who wanted the authority to withdraw players and request their selection where appropriate (*The Guardian*, 12 December 1994). The Committee was divided on this issue but prepared to support only the right of withdrawal and not any right to insist that a player be selected. The ECB blueprint, unsurprisingly, followed the Acfield line on contracts although with the distinct caveat that it was not necessary to consider the issue at this point in time. Given the fact that the ECB undoubtedly realised that there was likely to be County opposition, to at least some of the proposals, throwing another extremely controversial issue into the pot would not have been the wisest move. Similarly, the voluntary code on player withdrawal operated by the Counties and the Chairman of Selectors was supported as it; 'seems to be working satisfactorily at the moment, and for as long as that continues to be the case there would seem to be no justification for altering the present arrangements' (MacLaurin, 1997, p.30).

MacLaurin also considered the problem of how to limit the matches played by the top cricketers whilst maintaining the position of the Counties. The relationship between the Counties and the Board is often an uneasy one although the key issue of finance indicates the nature of the problem with the Counties largely dependent on the money generated by the national side. However, changes to the First Class game to strengthen the Test side would require the support of the Counties if they were to be approved. MacLaurin also raised the question of the relationship between the players and the ECB, and the related issue of the powers that could be exercised over these players by the ECB.

The control of professional cricketers

Apart from any contractual constraints that may be placed upon professional cricketers, the governing bodies also exercise a number of regulating and controlling powers. This can cover, not only, who is eligile to play, but also the conduct of players. Players must be registered to play County cricket and Counties are restricted in the players that may play for them. In order to qualify to play County cricket, a player must have been born within the EC, or satisfy the residency requirement. Additionally, the cricketer must be an EC citizen and not have played for another country in the preceding four years. Counties are entitled to register one unqualified player, the dispensation that has allowed for participation by the overseas stars. No player may, subject to the overriding discretion of the Board, be registered for more than one County in the same season, except in the case of a Minor County cricketer playing for a First Class County without cancelling his Minor County registration.

County players are further divided into two categories, List I and List II. List I contains the names of cricketers who have a written contract to play for that County for the forthcoming season. List II consists of those players who were previously contracted or registered with the County. The chief problem, with this system, arises when players wish to transfer to a different County. A player who wishes to leave may still be on List I unless the County concurs, with the move, and withdraws any offer it may have made for the following season. The implications of this are that, if another County wishes to register a List I player, it must give written notice to both the County and the TCCB (now ECB).[29] The Board will not register him for the new County unless there are 'exceptional circumstances', effectively, a player who has been offered a new contract will not be permitted to change Counties. If the player has not accepted the contract offered by his County, the procedure allows for an Investigating Tribunal to 'report on and consider the application'. If the Board approves the switch it will be treated as an 'Extraordinary Registration' and Counties are permitted only one such registration in twelve months or two within five years:

> The majority of county cricketers are offered short-term (one- or two-year) contracts. When these have run their course, a county club has the option to renew a player's contract or release him. If the club releases a player, he is free to approach other clubs to attempt to secure another contract. If, however, the club offers the player another contract, he then becomes a List One player. This means that even if the player does not wish to take up the contract offered, he is often prevented from moving to another county. Counties are only permitted to offer places to two List One players from other teams every five years. As a result, if a county has its full quota of List One players, it is unable to employ anyone else in this category until the five-year period has elapsed (Speight, 1996, p.93).

The Board may hear evidence from either County and the player himself and may also consider whether the terms offered by the original County 'were, in all the circumstances, fair and reasonable'. Thus, if the Board concludes that the terms offered were fair and reasonable, the County who wishes to sign the player will, in all likelihood, be faced with an extraordinary registration and these are strictly controlled. This is a procedure that, essentially, prevents any real transfer market in players developing. However, it was thought that the attempt by Chris Adams to free himself from his contract with Derbyshire might in fact render this system unworkable and that Adams, himself, would become 'cricket's Bosman' (Hopps, 1997). Adams's agent had threatened to sue both the ECB and Derbyshire if the player's demand to be moved from List I to List II was not complied with. In the event, the ECB allowed him to become a List II player (Brenkley, 1997; Marks, 1997) ostensibly on compassionate grounds because of Adams's disaffection with the regime at Derbyshire in the wake of the departure of Dean Jones. However, there was a further reason that the Board was keen to allow his appeal:

> The Registration Committee was anxious to avoid the test case that Adams's agent, Jonathon Barnett, had promised if his client did not receive the right result from Lord's. Barnett and the committee members knew that the ECB's method of trying to restrict player movement in county cricket was unlikely to stand up in a law court. By upholding Adams's appeal the committee won a little more time (Marks, 1997).

Furthermore, the Board has issued strict regulations regarding the process of negotiations between Counties and players. No County can be involved in discussions with any player or agent or other representative during the season, offering him employment or even a trial, without the written consent of the County that has registered him. This also applies during the close season although, players on List II can be contacted if prior notice is given to the County holding the registration and to the Board. If the player is on List I but without a contract, negotiations may take place after 31 October, again providing that written notice has been given. The emphasis is not just placed on the Counties to avoid negotiations but also on to the cricketers themselves who undertake that neither they, nor anyone on their behalf, will be engaged in prohibited discussions. Further to this, the regulations contain a draconian paragraph that presumes that any negotiations are taking place on behalf of the County concerned:

> In order to discourage informal approaches including approaches through a County's registered Cricketers, if an employee or agent (including another Cricketer) or official or member of the Governing Body of a County approaches or is involved in discussions with a Cricketer or any agent or other person on his behalf, such approach or discussions shall be regarded for the purposes of this Regulation as an approach or discussion on behalf of that County, except in circumstances where the County satisfies the Board that this was contrary to a

written instruction received by the employee or agent or official or member of the Governing Body concerned and that the employee or agent or official or member of the Governing Body concerned had not been authorised to make the approach or to be involved in the discussions (ECB, 1997, p.10)

This clearly covers the scenario that arose during the Packer affair when Tony Greig (then registered with Sussex) acted to recruit players. Any County side that relies on informal player contacts, to recruit may fall foul of this regulation and may be subject to action by the Disciplinary Committee of the ECB. This Committee has jurisdiction over all registered cricketers and the Counties. There has long been debate about the potentiality of a transfer system in cricket. Perhaps the sport looks enviously at the amount of coverage garnered by football during the cricket season concerning the various comings and goings before the start of the football season in August (Wisden, 1968, p.87). It is unlikely that a more open transfer system can be endlessly resisted; 'I know that art, unlike life, is supposed to be perfect, but do we really have the right to demand that cricket - a business like any other to its employers and employees, after all - be above the social and economic restraints that fetter the rest of us?' (Steen, 1987, p.17).

In addition to these restrictions concerning who cricketers may play for, the Board regulations also contain a number of further restrictions that may affect players. In particular, the Board require that (registered) cricketers under its jurisdiction behave in a certain way both on and off the field; regulations that have produced disputes both in terms of discipline and the relationship with the press.

Discipline and punish

In the past the TCCB exercised this 'paternal' function in a number of instances. Tom Graveney is a prominent early example of the power of the Board to direct players under its auspices. In 1968, Tom Graveney was playing for Worcestershire and had been awarded a benefit for the following year. Whilst having a quiet drink in the Cricketers' Club he met a businessman, Tony Hunt. Hunt, a keen sportsman and Chairman of Luton Town FC, offered him a four figure sum if he were to come and play cricket at Luton one Sunday. The figure was substantial and equivalent to a fifth of the previous total of a benefit Graveney had received whilst at Gloucestershire. The problem was finding a day to stage the match, as the recently initiated John Player League took up most Sundays during the cricket season. There was, however, one possible date, the Sunday of the Old Trafford Test match against the West Indies. Whilst Sunday play in Test matches is now *de rigeur*, it was only as recently as 1981 that Sunday play in Tests was permitted. Graveney informed Alec Bedser (Chairman of Selectors) of his plans, and when told that he could not play in both matches, told Bedser that the Luton 'benefit' would have to take precedence. However, Graveney was named in the team for the Old Trafford Test, and he presumed that the matter had been sorted out. On the evening of the first day of the Test, Bedser then informed Graveney that he would be unable to play in the Luton game on the Sunday, Graveney retorted that it was now too late to pull out of his commitment. He duly played the game at Luton and returned to Old Trafford the next day, where England completed a ten wicket win. However, during the Monday whilst fielding, Graveney heard over the loudspeakers that he had been summoned to appear at Lord's on the Thursday to explain his action. At his hearing, Graveney was severely reprimanded for 'a serious breach of discipline' and banned for the next three Test matches, effectively finishing his Test career and causing much debate with the cricketing press (Bannister, 1969 and anon, 1969).

Other cricketers have similarly been disciplined for misdemeanours committed both on and off the field. In 1971, England fast bowler, John Snow, was not selected for the Old Trafford Test against India due to an incident involving Indian batsman, Sunil Gavaskar. Ian Botham was banned for two months in 1986 after he admitted to smoking cannabis, while David Gower and John Morris were both censured by the tour management during the England tour of Australia in 1990/1991. Here, in what was to become known as 'The Tiger Moth Affair', the two 'buzzed' the Carrara Sports Oval on Australia's Gold Coast in Tiger Moths during England's innings against Queensland (Martin-Jenkins, 1991). They were fined £1,000 each by Peter Lush the tour manager. Cricketers of other nations have also been subject to disciplinary action in the past with, for example, Dennis Lillee fined for his role in a spat with Javed Miandad during a Test Match in Perth (Blofeld, 1982, p.7) and Salim Malik originally suspended (though later reinstated) by the Pakistan Cricket Board following allegations of bribery (Selvey, 1995). Similarly, Richard Stemp, the Yorkshire left arm spinner was fined £500 by the TCCB; 'Stemp, dropped from England's Test squad on Sunday after being named in the 13 for the first two Tests of the summer, was found guilty of using 'crude and abusive language' to Somerset's opening batsman Mark Lathwell. He was also severely reprimanded and warned about his future conduct' (Hopps, 1994). Perhaps the most infamous example of the operation of TCCB provisions in recent times was the treatment meted out to the then Sussex fast bowler Ed Giddins who was banned by the TCCB for a period of almost two years after he was found guilty of using the recreational drug cocaine.[30] The Board's regulations were, however, seen by some to be seriously flawed due to the length of time between the failure of the drug test and the hearing itself:

The Giddins' case exposed a fundamental flaw in the disciplinary regulations. A competitor who failed a drugs test on 2nd June was able to carry on playing until nearly the end of August and a week before his ban, Ed Giddins turned in a career best performance. This situation arose because under the previous Regulations, the wheels turned rather slowly. The investigating Doping Control Panel could not be assembled until 23 July and the Discipline Committee took place on 19 August. This delay exacerbated the problem. The player continued to be selected for his county and although the sword of Damocles was hanging over him, it appeared that you could fail a drugs test and carry on regardless (O'Gorman, 1996, p.24).

Philip Tufnell (Middlesex and England left arm spinner and *enfant terrible*) also ran the gauntlet of the Board's provisions with regard to drugs when he failed to submit a random urine sample, after Middlesex's last game of the 1997 season. Tufnell's explanation was accepted by a five man disciplinary panel and he was given a suspended 18 month ban, a £1000 fine and ordered to pay £250 costs ('Forgetful Tufnell given suspended ban' *The Independent*, 25 October 1997). No doubt this decision was welcomed by those involved with the winter touring party.

The cricket authorities are committed to maintaining the highest standards of behaviour and conduct of those subject to their jurisdiction. All players must comply, at all times, with the rules, regulations and resolutions of the Board. In particular, a player must 'conduct himself fairly and properly' both on and off the field. This includes the prohibition of verbal or physical abuse (including sledging), the disputing of umpiring decisions or generally conducting 'himself in a manner or do any act or omission which may be prejudicial to the interests of cricket or which may bring the game of cricket or any Cricketer or group of Cricketers into disrepute' (ECB, 1997, Reg. D).

In addition, compliance was required with the Board's anti doping regulations and the guidelines on Cricketers' benefits. What became even more problematic however, was the controversial paragraph 3 that limited the freedom of players to comment on the game. Many players have lucrative contracts with various media in the form of newspaper columns etc and this clause effectively fetters the ability to comment, with impunity, on various cricketing matters. Statements that are termed as 'public statements'[31] were proscribed for any registered cricketer or indeed anyone subject to the jurisdiction of the TCCB if the statement:

(i) is of a derogatory nature; or

(ii) may be prejudicial to the interests of cricket; or

(iii) likely to bring either the game of cricket or any cricketer or group of cricketers into disrepute, or

(iv) without proper authority discloses any matter which is confidential to the Board or to any of its committees (TCCB, 1995).[32]

This prohibition also extended to details of negotiations between Counties and cricketers. Before making any statement concerning the game or any players, a cricketer must obtain the consent of his County Cricket club and furthermore, any registered cricketer must obtain consent from the County club prior to the publication of any material. The onus is on the cricketer to ensure that a book contract permits the process of monitoring of the material by the club. Drafts or proofs must be supplied as and when they are prepared, and before they are submitted to the publisher. Any refusal of such consent will constitute a breach of the cricketer's obligations and a disciplinary offence. The cases of Raymond Illingworth and Allan Lamb are prime examples of the operation and ambit of such a provision, and also of the potentially serious effects that such a requirement can have.

Illingworth was the Chairman of England Selectors when the *Daily Mail* serialised his (then) forthcoming book 'One Man Committee' (1996) which incurred the wrath of the TCCB. In particular, his book, and the excerpts reproduced in the tabloid press, were critical of England fast bowler Devon Malcolm and '[t]he timing of the publication of the articles, as well as their nature, so incensed Derbyshire and Lancashire that they called on the TCCB to refer Illingworth to Gerard Elias QC, chairman of the Disciplinary Committee. Elias considered there was a case to answer and in turn ...referred the matter to the full committee to determine whether there (had) been any breach of the Board's Regulations or Directives' (Selvey 1996). Illingworth was not bound by the same contract, as the players, that instructed them to submit any publication to the Board for vetting. He was, nevertheless, brought before a disciplinary hearing on 18 June 1996 and fined £2000 (with a further £500 in costs) for bringing the game into disrepute. Many commentators found the decision unjustifiable, Christopher Martin-Jenkins in the *Daily Telegraph* for example (quoted in Illingworth, 1996, p.322) noting that 'once again it is the Board and their hopelessly muddled mode of governance, which come out worst from this business. The affair might more justly and wisely have been knocked on the head by a private reprimand and a brief decisive statement of public admonition'. Initially Illingworth considered resigning his post but decided instead to appeal against the committee finding, especially when he saw the sympathy and support he was receiving from players and commentators alike. The appeal saw him totally vindicated.[33]

The eventual outcome of Allan Lamb's dispute with the TCCB was even more severe than the original fine imposed on Illingworth. Lamb's first problem arose over an article that appeared in the *Daily Mirror* which dealt with the controversial issue of alleged ball tampering by the touring Pakistani side, during the fourth one day International in August 1992. This was eventually to lead to two libel actions. Lamb didn't clear the article with his County, Northamptonshire, or the TCCB, in breach of his contract. Northamptonshire acted quickly, fearing that he might be suspended for the forthcoming Nat West final; and fined Lamb the maximum permitted (one twenty-sixth of his salary) and suspended him from a Championship match and a Sunday league game. He eventually appeared before a TCCB disciplinary hearing to consider the breach of contract issue. Lamb's solicitor was 'amazed and relieved' that he was not also charged with bringing the game into disrepute or making derogatory statements. Lamb was fined a total of £5000 with £1000 costs although this was reduced on appeal to a £4000 fine of which half was suspended for two years, whilst the costs element was reduced to £500. Even this pales into insignificance when it is considered that Lamb's wish to publish his biography (Lamb, 1997) led to his enforced retirement from cricket. In essence Lamb had signed a contract in 1993 to deliver his autobiography in 1996 and he was unable to sign the playing contract offered to him by Northamptonshire as he would then be in breach of the (then) TCCB regulations concerning clearance of published material. As the publishers were keen for the book to be delivered during that season and for serialisation to take place as a precursor to this, Lamb was in a 'Catch 22' situation in that something would have to give:

> ...on Friday 12 April I went to the club offices and told Steve Coverdale that I was going to accept the inevitable and suffer a retirement that I believe was forced on me from Lord's. They can argue all they like, but it can't be natural justice to make me break a contract with my publishers that I signed well before they changed their rules in the player's undertaking. I always believed you can't move the goalposts in legal matters, but the TCCB did just that with me (Lamb, 1997, p.289).

Lamb gave up First Class cricket because of this conflict and his autobiography makes it clear that he feels bitter at the way in which the governing body of his sport had tried to control him. It is undoubtedly the case that these battles will become more pronounced in the future.

Towards a new cricket culture

Cricket has many developments to deal with; the changes that have confronted cricket over the last twenty years or so have been formidable, but perhaps the 'battle for cricket's soul' that has been played out against a shifting commercial backdrop symbolises the new issues that confront it. With one day Internationals and injections of glamour in a television friendly format, we have witnessed the rise of the 'barmy army'. Undeniably, the culture of cricket supporting has changed immeasurably, particularly since the Packer revolution which sought to attract a new type of supporter. Much of what McLellan calls the new cricket culture is undoubtedly part of an attempt to unshackle the game from the burdens of its history whilst celebrating parts of that very history. What though of the players, the central figures in the game? In England the PCA have continued to push for a number of basic rights and there has been talk of forming an International Players Union to forge some collective spirit. The suspicion remains, however, that such moves are very much centred on the pinnacle of the game with only a few cricketers actually gaining much real benefit. Whilst money has come into cricket from a variety of sources, sponsorship and television are increasingly important. This may not have benifitted a large number of county professionals. Despite the fact that it is, theoretically, a full time profession, many players will be forced to find other work during the winter months. Those players who are selected for overseas tours, either with the full Test team or the 'A' side, represent those who could be viewed as the full time professionals. Similarly, other players may find cricket related employment in Australia or South Africa but there still remains a large group for whom cricket is essentially a summer job.

The current regulations regarding cricketers' contracts and the lack of a 'real' transfer market (for fear of creating a monster akin to that involved in association football) demonstrate the restrictions placed on player movement. In the aftermath of the 'Adams judgement', some commentators (Marks 1997, Brenkley 1997) posited that a restructuring in the way players are contracted was not only inevitable, but actually more fundamental to the future of cricket than the so-called revolutionary 'two tier championship':

> Greater freedom of movement is inevitable and poses a far more serious threat to ill-run counties than any plans for two divisions. There may be a few casualties along the way as clubs squander much of their annual hand-out from Lord's. In the end market forces will prevail. As several rugby union clubs are now discovering, the books have to balance (Marks, 1997).

All of this must be couched, however, in terms of the fact that whilst cricket, at its pinnacle, is a highly competitive and marketable commodity, at many levels of the professional game its attractions are less marked. This promotes a view that perhaps players at this level should in many ways be grateful for what they have at present; 'You might get someone coming in and saying "I want this and this" and you think "hang on, what have you done for the club?" Cricketers are very well paid, considering 100 people come to watch them play' (Dave Gilbert, quoted in Longmore, 1997). It seems increasingly likely, that the structure of professional cricket will be the subject of radical reorganisation. Despite the rejection of

MacLaurin's original proposals, it appears that greater support is developing for a two tier structure. Eventually, this may lead to a reduction in the number of professionals engaged by the Counties, and a concentration of the better players at fewer clubs. In many ways, this mirrors the changes within association football that led to the formation of the FA Premier League, and the consequent financial domination of that League by an elite of clubs. It is unlikely, given the legal dimension, that such a restrictive contractual regime can be maintained and it is probable that the restructuring of the game will be accompanied by greater player freedom.

Notes

1. A prominent example of the conservative values embodied in the game was the relationship between the English cricket establishment and South Africa, see for example the excellent account by Peter Hain (1996).

2. There is the danger, as we observed in the football chapter, of generalising about sport when there are enormous internal variations. Most obviously there is a great difference between the professional and amateur sides of cricket. The recreational game has undoubtedly provided an important recreational opportunity for ordinary people, regardless of social divisions. Our analysis relates primarily to the professional game and the attitudes and beliefs prevalent within this sector of cricket. That it has, at times, exhibited reactionary views is borne out by the South African debate though this was not dissimilar to the view taken by the Rugby Union authorities. Thanks to Roy Greenfield for his observations on this point.

3. The social historian GM Trevelyan, is said to have noted that, if the French noblesse had been capable of playing cricket with their peasants, their chateaux would never have been burnt.

4. The World Cup was first played in England in 1975.

5. England's recent decline as a Test playing nation reached its nadir during the 1996 overseas series with Zimbabwe which was drawn. Their performance led the Zimbabwe captain Alistair Campbell to suggest that these two sides plus New Zealand were the three weakest cricketing nations. The other test playing nations are Australia, India, Pakistan, South Africa, Sri Lanka and the West Indies.

6. For example, Tony Greig (Queenstown), Ian Greig (Queenstown), Allan Lamb (Cape Province), Robin Smith (Durban) and Chris Smith (Durban) were all South African. England has also relied on the talents of the Zimbabweans, Graeme Hick (Salisbury) and Neil Radford (Luanshya). There have also been many examples of distinguished English players born outside of England such as Douglas Jardine (Bombay), Tony Lewis (Swansea), Mike Denness (Lanarkshire) and Colin Cowdrey (Bangalore).

7. McCague was born in Ireland but emigrated with his parents to Australia at the age of one; he played for Western Australia before joining Kent and playing for England. Craig White was born in Yorkshire but brought up and educated in Australia before playing for Victoria, Yorkshire and England.

8. Obviously the same restrictions do not apply to multi channel broadcasters such as BSkyB, who have three dedicated Sports Channels, which require filling and for which cricket provides good programming potential. The BBC has always been able to utilise its two terrestrial channels to offset the problems of overload, though during Wimbledon fortnight non-sports fans may find

that the BBC offers a more limited choice of viewing than normal. The digitalisation of broadcasting, and the consequent explosion in the number of channels, should enable more sports specific channels to be developed.

9. Brookes provides a good excavation of these early stages of 'cricket' with games such as 'trap-ball', 'tip-cat' 'cat and dog', and, 'stool ball'; '[stool ball] consists in simply setting up a stool on the ground, and one of the players takes his place before, while his antagonist, standing at a distance tosses a ball with the intention of striking the stool, and this it is the business of the former to prevent by beating it away with the hand...' (Strutt J (1801), quoted in Brookes, 1978, p.11).

10. A 'benefit' is a financial incentive that is offered to many professional cricketers as a reward for a long period of service to a county; this may now be a very lucrative event for the leading players.

11. Correspondents to The Times took a whimsical view of the situation;

> Sir, Will you please refrain from dignifying Mr Kerry Packer's commercial adventure through your continued description of his proposed artificial cricket matches as a 'Test Series'?
> 18 July 1977
> Sir, Will you please refrain from dignifying Mr Kerry Packer's commercial adventure with the title of such a traditional and honourable form of entertainment as the Circus?
> 20 July 1977
> Sir, Will you please refrain from dignifying Mr Kerry Packer's commercial adventure through your continued description of his proposed activity as 'cricket'?
> 22 July 1977

(Cricketing Letters to the Times; Williams, 1983, p.125).

12. The first one day game took place in 1971. By the time of the 1975 World Cup nineteen international games had been played. 1996 saw a highpoint of 125 international one day matches being played (*The Cricketer* February 1997).

13. A good example of shot creation is the emergence of the 'reverse sweep' which takes a traditional shot and plays it the opposite way around into an area that may well be unguarded by a fielder.

14. Haigh (1993, p.32) notes that from 1973-1976 sport rose from five per cent of commercial network time to eight per cent.

15. The touring Packer signatories were: Greg Chappell, Jeff Thomson, Rick McCosker, Ian Davis, David Hookes, Doug Walters, Rodney Marsh, Richie Robinson, Kerry O'Keefe, Max Walker, Mick Malone, Len Pascoe and Ray Bright. The additional Australians were Ian Chappell, Ross Edwards, Dennis Lillee, Ian Redpath and Gary Gilmour. The Rest of the World side comprised Tony Greig, John Snow, Alan Knott and Derek Underwood (England), Asif Iqbal, Majid Khan, Imran Khan and Mushtaq Mohammed (Pakistan), Viv Richards, Clive Lloyd, Michael Holding and Andy Roberts (West Indies) and Barry Richards, Mike Procter, Eddie Barlow, Graeme Pollock and Denys Hobson (South Africa) (Blofeld, 1978, p.22).

16. *The Daily Mail* (9 May 1977), which had more information than most, used the headline 'World's Top Cricketers Turn Pirate'.

17. Blofeld (1978, p.95) argues that the apparently small majority of 14 in favour of the ban understated the case as it didn't include the votes of the Somerset or Hampshire players who apparently suppprted such action.

18. Bailey (1989, p.90) commented on not only the threat, as the authorities saw it, of Packer to the traditions of the game but also to 'the self-esteem of those representing established cricket'.
19. The statement of the Cricket Council read:

> The Cricket Council's emergency executive committee met at Lord's today to consider the involvement of England players in the proposed series of matches between Australia and the Rest of the World during the coming winter. The Council have today received a communication from the International Cricket Conference asking Test Match countries whether they feel that, in view of recent developments, a special meeting prior to the ICC full meeting in July would be required. The Council have informed the ICC that they strongly support the proposal for such a meeting as soon as possible. Pending the outcome of these discussions, the Council intend to take no action in respect of the availability of any of the England players to represent their country. As far as the captaincy of England is concerned, the Council will be instructing the chairman of selectors, Alec Bedser, that Tony Greig is not to be considered for this position for the forthcoming series against Australia.

In reaching this decision the Council took into consideration the current England captain's clearly admitted involvement, unknown to the authorities, in the recruitment of players for an organisation which has been set up in conflict with scheduled series of Test Matches. His action has inevitably impaired the trust which existed between the cricket authorities and the captain of the England side (Blofeld, 1978, p.49).
20. The original company, which had signed the cricketers, was J.P.Sport Pty. Ltd, which became World Series Cricket Pty. Ltd. On the background to J.P.Sport and the subsequent relationship with the Packer organisation, see Haigh (1993).
21. Haigh (1993, p.317) notes that the first pay dispute between WSC and its cricketers took place in 1979 during the tour to the West Indies when the players agreed a pay cut that was reversed by Packer himself.
22. The tension between the traditional five day game and the newer, brasher one day version was summed up by Paul Weaver commenting on England's tour to Zimbabwe and New Zealand in 1996/7; 'The purist will tell you that Tests are the real thing, which is true, but the purist is a minority through the turnstiles' (*The Guardian*, 5 March 1997).
23. Wright's ultimate conclusion over the future for the English national summer game is pessimistic; 'Overall self interest will prevail, which is why the struggle for cricket's soul is a struggle being lost' (1994, p.212).
24. In fact, during those six years, cricket was still controlled to a great extent by the MCC. The Secretary of the MCC was also the Secretary of the Cricket Council and of the TCCB and to all intents and purposes of the NCA. The MCC employed all the assistant secretaries working on behalf of the TCCB, the NCA and the Cricket Council (Bailey, 1989).
25. Wright (1994, p.208) comments that whilst the influence of the MCC has waned; 'Their committee, however experienced and honourable, contains too many who enjoy cross dressing in MCC tie and TCCB sweatshirt...'.
26. In 1997 two English counties Surrey (whose game was washed out) and more successfully, Warwickshire, experimented with the idea of day/night cricket. According to Sports Marketing (25 July 1997) the latter event was a financial success with the county attracting over 15,000 spectators and a profit of £70,000.

27. The remit of the Griffith Committee was to examine the functions of the Cricket Council, TCCB and NCA; consider the role of the MCC and make any recommendations as appeared necessary.

28. The functions of the ECB were described as:

> To be the governing body of cricket in England and Wales.
>
> To promote and develop the wellbeing and enjoyment of cricket by encouraging maximum participation and interest in the national summer game from the playground to the Test arena.
>
> To ensure the achievement of the highest standards of playing excellence throughout the game and to attain success at all levels of international competition.
>
> To uphold and build upon the long established traditions and spirit of the game.
>
> To nature the interdependence and common interests of both the First Class game and Non-first Class game (Morgan, 1996, p.4).

29. Although, as we have noted, the ECB has superceded the TCCB, the regulations which we are quoting from relate to the previous regime. We have used the 'Board' to cover the functions of both the TCCB and the ECB.

30. Giddins was sacked by Sussex although eventually offered a contract by Warwickshire.

31. The first part defines what is meant by the phrase 'public statement':

> any statement which becomes or is made, or the gist of which becomes or is made public whether in its original or in an edited or serialized form and whether in a newspaper, magazine, periodical or book, or in any form of radio or television broadcast, or in any other manner whatsoever, regardless of the circumstances in which the statement was first made, and includes any repetition of any such statement.

32. These regulations are now expanded in ECB (1997).

33. See further on this Illingworth (1996), p.307 et seq.

Let the laws of your own land,
Good or ill, between ye stand,
Hand to hand, and foot to foot,
Arbiters of the dispute,

The old laws of England - they
Whose reverend heads with age are gray,
Children of a wiser day;
And whose solemn voice must be
Thine own echo - Liberty![1]
PB Shelley, **The Mask of Anarchy**, *1819*

6 Into the Holy of Holies

In Hollywood, all roads lead...to a studio! So, at whatever pace you want to walk and no matter which direction you choose or how much time you take to get your bearings, any one of these streets intersecting in front of you and taking off in straight lines to the East, to the West, to the South, to the North, ends fatally at a wall.This wall is the famous Great Wall of China that surrounds every studio and that makes Hollywood, already a difficult city to conquer, a true forbidden city - actually, either better or worse than that, since Hollywood is comprised of many interior barriers encircling numerous kremlins and defending access to dozens of seraglios, and I believe it is not only because of the radiance of the stars and the attraction they exert the world over that we have baptized Hollywood...Mecca of the Movies, but, strictly speaking, above all because the entrances to these studios are nearly impassable for the noninitiate, as if, really, to wish to make your way into a studio is to want to force entry into the Holy of Holies (Cendrars, 1995, p.78).

Poised on the precipice: dancing at the edge of heaven

To pass into this Holy of Holies is the aim of most creative artists. To gain entrance into this dream world is beyond all but the few and the lure of success a strong one; offering more than just a dream but often also a means of 'escape'. Beattie (1996, p.19) puts the point succinctly when he notes that 'Fighters from the Bronx in New York, the Gorbals in Glasgow, the Markets in Belfast. They punch their way out of the slum, they dance their way out of the ghetto'. For many these potential escape routes offer the only realistic chance of success and wealth, however, for every successful artist, there are thousands of failed, aspiring, or just plain bitter ones. There may also be the need for enormous personal sacrifice. For sportsmen and women the discipline of training has become ever more onerous as preparation has itself become more professionalised. In order to maximise performance, greater attention is now being paid to pre-match work and certainly, with respect to football, there has been an increasing continental influence. Similarly, in cricket, new coaching methods, including the application of new technology, are being utilised to improve performance. Sports are also aware that they may be able to learn from other areas with respect to fitness and application.

Unfortunately, hard work, even when allied to a natural talent, is insufficient to guarantee success and, particularly in the music business, 'time and place' remain important considerations. One reason why creative artists enter the fickle world of entertainment is because of the chance, however small, that their hard work will result in exposure for their talent. There are of course those performers who are able to exploit the vagaries of the music business market and succeed, albeit for a short period, where those with greater ability have failed.

The preceding chapters all provide instances of some of the sites in the entertainment industry where creative talent is bought and sold. We have indicated some of the concessions (artistic, professional and personal) that are often made, by the performers, to try and achieve their aims. In addition, these chapters have illustrated that there are many common threads that are discernible within the practices adopted by various areas of the industry. Clearly, there are common contractual issues and, in particular, the doctrine of restraint of trade has been a route that has been increasingly used by artists to try and obtain greater levels of contractual freedom. At the same time there are individual idiosyncrasies in all the areas that have shaped the development of that particular branch of the entertainment industry. Part of this development has included the fashioning of the contractual arrangements between the parties. For example, within boxing a key point has been the dual relationship of manager and promoter and the potential conflict of interest that this has brought with it. The managerial dimension has also been an important feature of some of the music business cases and this personal relationship has become an increasingly significant issue in the negotiation of football contracts as agents have assumed a more dominant position. Unsurprisingly, the use of agents is extending into both cricket and rugby as players seek to maximise earning capacity.[2]

In all of these fields a major factor is the attempt to control and commodify the artists. This may be done in a number of ways, but in legal terms the foremost expression is in the contractual terms that underpin their professional careers. Contractual theory has historically posited that a central tenet is 'freedom of contract', a legal dimension of laissez faire economics. As you are free to enter into a contract and are otherwise under no compulsion to do so, if you *choose* to enter into a contractual agreement then you will be strictly bound by the terms. The essence of this model is the exercise of free will. This model is undoubtedly somewhat anachronistic although the basic tenet is still a truism; there are however a number of situations where the courts may now be prepared to release a party from their contractual obligations - the restraint of trade doctrine considered throughout the chapters is one prominent example. The slow historical development of the doctrine indicates judicial reluctance to mount many challenges to the sanctity of contracts. However, the situation is further complicated by the use of 'standard form contracts' which reflect longstanding industry practice. That is not to say that they are unresponsive to external events, though it is interesting to note that some of the inherent problems have survived litigation. For example despite the warnings of *Schroeder* and *Holly Johnson* it was clear that unenforceable agreements were still being offered and signed. In *The Stone Roses,* after the contractual agreement had been concluded, the lawyer for the recording and publishing company expressed concern that there had been no real negotiation; that the contract as it stood very much represented the 'opening position' and he would have expected some amendments had the band been properly advised. In short, the company knew that *The Stone Roses* had a poor deal and in fact tried to vary the contract after the decision in *Holly Johnson* was handed down. Similarly, professional boxing seems unable to solve the dilemma of the manager/promoter. There are, however, examples where litigation has acted as a powerful impetus for change, not least the dramatic effect of both *Eastham* and *Bosman* that shifted the terrain for the most marketable players within football. In cricket, *Greig* forced the game's administrators to radically review their relationship with the players, although in England some of the inherent problems that permitted the emergence of Packer remain.

Aside from the legal challenges, technological and marketing developments have also provided the catalyst for some reformulation of contractual terms. For example, before the 1930s, actors and actresses were essentially 'voiceless'; as the movies were silent, the voice, and control of it, was of little consequence. For this reason many contracts in this period omitted to enact provisions that sought to exert some control over the sound of an actor. Gaines (1992, p.156) suggests that this may still be overlooked; 'the industry's tendency to privilege the image over the voice has historically produced a contractual blind spot, and to this day, the legal provisions meant to pin down every conceivable element of the actor's persona may still omit the voice'. Warner Brothers however were wise to the power and potential use of the voice and Gaines notes the difference in Loretta Young's contracts of 1927 and 1930 as examples of this. Whilst her contract in 1927 reflected the common concerns of the industry at the time and concentrated on preserving the studio's entitlement to 'acts, poses, plays, appearances', the 1930 contract is cognisant of the actress's potentiality as a producer of sound:

> The new wording in the 'results and proceeds' section of Young's contract now acknowledges the studio's proprietal interest in the 'voice and all instrumental, musical, and other sound effects produced by her in connection with such acts, poses, plays and appearances'. In other words, even if Loretta Young played the saxophone in a film, the music produced and recorded on the sound track would now belong to the studio. Anticipating the later development of the sound-track

album and acknowledging the radio broadcast, the post-sound section also gives the studio the right to 'record, reproduce, and/or transmit' the star's sound performance, whether or not in conjunction with the exploitation of a motion picture (Gaines, 1992, p.156-157).

Likewise, recording and publishing contracts have altered as the technological terrain has developed and the ability to exploit music in diverse ways is realised. Contracts will also be adapted to take account of wider developments such as merchandising opportunities. A neat example of this is the shifting stature of footballers, whilst once only players such as George Best (sometimes described as the fifth Beatle!) were marketable commodities, in a media saturated market many players achieve iconic status that can be translated into bedspreads, games and other consumer goods. Contracting parties are understandably keen to tap into this potential source of revenue and terms may be altered to reflect these 'new areas of exploitation'. Indeed, the roles and responsibilities of artists have changed markedly, a point illustrated by the position of Prince Naseem, a professional boxer:

> He was being sucked into the maelstrom of commercial success. [Prince Naseems's brother] Raith explained: 'We monitor all the commercial activities for him. They must not conflict with his boxing career. Everything has to be worked out around his training schedule. We all know that it could get out of hand. Everybody wants him. This week, for example, he is booked every day. On Monday he does an interview with a girl from an Asian TV channel magazine, plus the *Daily Telegraph*. Then on Tuesday there's an all-day fashion shoot in the gym for *Nineteen* magazine. On Wednesday the photographer from the *Sunday Times* is coming up to Sheffield. On Thursday there are talks with a production company that makes fitness videos. And on Friday the Asian TV people are back. We're building an empire around him' (Beattie, 1996, p.260).

As new areas of exploitation emerge, so the contracts will adapt to take account of such changes and attempts made to control these opportunities. Thus the area is contractually colonised and the term becomes standard form for the business. Attempts to retain control over previously uncharted zones will depend upon leverage and the foresight of whoever drafts the original terms. It may be possible through the use of general clauses relating to exploitation to cover new developments providing that they do not fall outside of the general parameters. However, once identified, these new points can be made subject to specific contractual control and become part of the industry standard. The crucial aspect of standard form agreements is that they may preclude any real negotiation and potentially allow parties with a stronger bargaining position to take advantage of this imbalance. The entrance, or the mere chance of entrance, to the 'holy' places are inevitably difficult to find and artists may be so desperate to enter that poised 'on the edge of heaven' they enrol without much regard to the entrance fee. The first part of this chapter looks at how standard form contracts are utilised in tandem with the related issues of 'inequality of bargaining power' and 'independent advice'. Having considered these areas we will conclude by analysing how new areas become ripe for colonisation. In the same way that attempts have been made to exploit all potential areas of the artist (the artist as commodity), whole new fields of dispute also emerge as the process of commercialisation becomes all enveloping. Our study will conclude with a short examination of rugby union and the problems that the sport has encountered in trying to come to terms with professionalisation. Perhaps (un)surprisingly, this case study induces a strong sense of *deja vu*, many of the problems that have appeared in other areas of the entertainment industry are re-emerging as relations rapidly alter.

Take that! The role of standard form contracts

A crucial factor in these types of bargaining situations is that most 'new' artists do not have any leverage to negotiate much variation with regards to the individual terms.This both encourages the use of standard form contracts and ensures that the terms agreed are very similar to the norm. In all the areas we have discussed in the previous chapters, the professional bodies, which act on behalf of their members, have a key function to both advise individually and negotiate collectively as regards the content of such standard form agreements. In addition, these professional bodies may offer a service where they provide an adviser or negotiator to help artists in their contractual dealings. The music industry is a useful vehicle for analysing how standard form agreements are utilised - whilst the music industry does, of course, have many of its own norms and peculiarities, an examination of this area provides rich material that can be used to inform the processes and practices of other areas.

Typically, the company's solicitors or business affairs department sends out a standard form contract either as a final draft or with details for completion after negotiation. Where the artist(s) has instructed a lawyer, the draft will be amended after consultation with the client. In *George Michael*, Parker J considered the nature of these types of agreements and the related issue of whether such contracts were unfairly weighted in favour of the stronger party.[3] This argument had its roots in *Schroeder* where Lord Diplock considered that there were two types of standard form contract. First, there were contracts of ancient origin that were firmly established over a long period of time and subsequently would be deemed to have stood the test of time; these would usually be considered fair and reasonable. The second type of standard form contract:

> ...is of comparatively modern origin. It is the result of the concentration of particular kinds of business in relatively few hands...(t)he terms of this kind of standard form contract have not been the subject of negotiation between the parties to it, or approved by any organisation representing the interests of the weaker party. They have been dictated by that party whose bargaining power, either exercised alone or in conjunction with others providing similar goods or services, enables him to say: 'If you want these goods or services at all, these are the only terms on which they are obtainable. Take it or leave it' (*Schroeder*, 1974, p.624).

The industry places much emphasis on the fact that these initial agreements in 'standard form' are (re)negotiable as the artists' careers progress and that as they become more established, they are able to return to the bargaining table to press more strongly for improved terms. While it may be the case that established artists bargain with far more leverage (see *Schroeder*) any renegotiation which takes place is still within the general parameters set by the industry. It is also against the background that the contract, the terms of which are the subject of the re-negotiation, will still bind the artist. Whether or not record companies believe that the contract could be challenged successfully, it will be in the long term interests of the company to improve the terms for the artist in order to preserve a profitable relationship. Nor need the renegotiation be acrimonious or prompted by fears over the validity of the contract. If the artist is commercially successful, agreements covering partnership, merchandising, and other specialised contracts may be the pretext for a comprehensive re-evaluation of the relationship.

It is undoubtedly the case that, in certain industries, the practice of using standard form contracts is both efficient and expedient. Tillotson makes the point, quoting a United States source, that; 'standard form contracts probably account for more than 99 per cent of all the contracts now made. Most persons have difficulty remembering the last time they contracted other than by standard form; except for casual oral arrangements, they probably never have. But if they are active, they contract by standard form several times a day. Parking-lot and theatre tickets, package receipts, department store charge slips, and gas station credit card purchase slips are all standard form contracts' (Tillotson, 1995, p.120). Tillotson (1995) summarises the important underlying reason for the use of standard form contracts, to facilitate the conduct of trade and to achieve economies in transaction costs. However, it is arguable that standard terms are inappropriate to 'transactions' where the commodity is individual creativity rather than goods or other services. Therefore, artists may make commitments which will tie them for the whole of their creative career in circumstances where they have very little bargaining 'leverage' and where any contract offered is on a 'take it or leave it' basis. The relationship between lawyers and clients, or indeed the Musicians' Union,[4] is therefore a potentially critical safeguard against unfair agreements and provides some protection for the creative artist.

A more extreme example may be found with regard to boxing where all the contracts are strictly prescribed by the controlling body, the British Boxing Board of Control. For example, by virtue of Regulation 6.1, any person wishing to manage a boxer must be the holder of a valid BBBC issued manager's licence, and must then enter into a contract in accordance with Regulation 7 for every boxer managed:

> All contracts between Boxers and Managers shall be in writing and executed by the parties thereto upon the BBBC printed standard form of Boxer and Manager contract set out in the First Schedule hereto ('Form 36') or otherwise such contract that shall have been previously approved in writing by the BBBC. Such approval not to be unreasonably withheld providing that such contract shall not be inconsistent with any provision of these Rules and Regulations (BBBC, 1996).

This is subject to Regulation 7.3 that permits previously made contracts to continue. The contract that is described as an 'Approved Boxer/Manager Agreement' is fairly short containing seventeen basic clauses. Similarly, all contracts made between Promoters (or MatchMakers or Agents) and Boxers (or Managers) subject to existing agreements, must be made on the 'BBBC Standard Form of Promoter and Boxer contract'. This strict contractual regime allows the regulatory body to exert a strong measure of control over the participants on two levels, through licensing as well as the contracts themselves. It could also be argued that this regime plays a protective function for those with little leverage or business knowledge. This has not, of course, prevented challenges to such agreements that crucially depend upon unilateral exclusivity. The position of the BBBC is such that it should be able, theoretically, to react to such challenges and alter the whole contractual practices of the industry. Whilst there have been positive responses, the Board cannot act with a complete free hand as its reactions to the problem of coterminous management and promotion show. Football also has to some extent a standard form contract for professional players. Although the fundamental terms, relating to remuneration, are open to negotiation, the contract is basically fairly short (around four pages) with scope for further provisions to be added. These will be the individual financial terms. Standard form contracts are therefore in many ways expedient - especially where the professional bodies have advised, or helped, in determining the content. However, any defence of standard form contracting must be couched in terms that these contracts take on the status of something of a 'holy grail' for many artists and this factor may be used against the artist to extract a deal that is more favourable to the other contracting party.

Inequality of bargaining power and the creative artist

The legal relevance of the existence of inequality in the bargaining process itself depends on the extent to which restraint of trade is concerned with process, and/or outcome. Whilst restraint of trade is a doctrine concerned with the resulting 'paper' terms, there has been consideration of the relationship between the process of bargaining and the terms themselves. In *Schroeder* (1974, p.623) for example, Lord Diplock stated that; 'what your Lordships have in fact been doing has been to assess the relative bargaining power of the publisher and the songwriter at the time the contract was made and to decide whether the publisher had used his superior bargaining power to exact from the songwriter promises that were unfairly onerous to him'. This approach was further developed, in *Clifford Davis* (1975, p.240), where Lord Denning cited dicta of Lord Diplock from *Schroeder* as supporting his own views on unconscionability that had been expressed in *Bundy*:

> Reading those speeches in the House of Lords, they afford support for the principles we endeavoured to state at the end of last term about inequality of bargaining power...[*Schroeder's*] case provides a good instance of those principles. The parties there had not met on equal terms. The one was so strong in bargaining power and the other so weak that, as a matter of common fairness it was not right that the strong should be allowed to push the weak to the wall.

Prior to *George Michael*, the decisions in other 'music cases' suggested that inequality remained an important factor (Greenfield & Osborn, 1992). While the rhetoric of the courts was often that it was the objective lack of reasonableness of the terms which rendered the contract unenforceable, the nature of the bargaining process which produced the terms, was often considered in detail (see *Schroeder,* 1974, p.623). Therefore, inequality in the bargaining process is an undercurrent in many of the decisions on restraint of trade concerning the music industry. By the same token, in all the key cases in boxing, cricket and football, this element is also present although the point is not made as forcefully or as eloquently as in the music cases. In *Watson,* for example, when considering boxing, Scott J noted that whilst the contracts were in standard form the Board's role was explicit; 'The Board's concern is to protect boxers from exploitation. Negotiations between a boxer and a manager might not be negotiations between persons bargaining on an equal footing. Both in experience and in financial power the manager would normally be the dominant party in the negotiations' (*Watson*, 1993, p.297).

The actual remit of what is meant by inequality is difficult to define, but arguably 'ignorance, vulnerability to persuasion, desperate need, lack of bargaining skill or simple lack of influence in the market place' are all potential factors (Beale, 1986). The presence of these factors, combined with sale at an underprice and a lack of advice, may be circumstances justifying the court's intervention. It is therefore arguable that, in terms of formulating rules for such a doctrine, the emphasis should be on the process and not just the outcome (Thal, 1988). In *George Michael*, Parker J suggested that inequality of bargaining power is relevant only to the extent that the court would be more vigilant as to the reasonableness of the agreement if 'the contracting parties were negotiating on other than equal terms'. This contrasts with cases where the unfairness of terms appear to have opened an inquiry into the process of bargaining (Thal, 1988). Obviously conscious of this problem, Parker J approached the case on the footing that there are two jurisdictions of possible relevance; the common law jurisdiction to declare a contract unenforceable for restraint of trade and the equitable jurisdiction to grant relief in certain circumstances against unfair and unconscionable bargains. The equitable jurisdiction arose where the defendant took unfair advantage of the weak and vulnerable and acted in a 'morally reprehensible' way such that the bargain, or some of its terms, was unconscionable. Such agreements, he said, had to be legitimised as fair, just and reasonable. However, Parker J thought that, based on the pleadings, the equitable jurisdiction was not invoked in this case. By contrast, the restraint of trade jurisdiction arose out of a public policy approach that held agreements that restricted free trade were void unless they were reasonable as between the parties, and with reference to the interests of the public (*Nordenfelt*). By implication, Parker J suggested that the two jurisdictions had become confused in *Schroeder* where Lord Reid founded his decision on restraint of trade on the principles set out in *Esso*, and Lord Diplock, purporting to agree with Lord Reid, held that the public policy implemented by the court was the protection from unconscionable bargains of those whose bargaining power was weak. Side-stepping this apparent conflict Parker J concurred with Lord Pearce's point in *Esso* (1968, p.331) that restraint cases took into account; 'the wider aspects of commerce... as well as the narrower aspect of the contract as between the parties'. Some contextual enquiry is necessary because the terms of any specific contract cannot be judged to be objectively fair without reference to the commercial context that gave rise to it.

Because of the limited basis for the decision, what was said in *George Michael* regarding bargaining power is undoubtedly *obiter dictum*. Nevertheless, the facts themselves offer a critical distinction from previous cases in that the contract between George Michael and Sony had been renegotiated at a time when George Michael was able to bargain from a position of greater strength. This is a material distinction between George Michael's case and a number of other restraint of trade cases, where the artists have entered into contracts at an early point in their careers. This could be an important factor if process is to continue to be a feature of these cases because the actual restrictions on George Michael and the other terms of his contract, are remarkably similar to those of the artists who have managed, through judicial intervention, to escape their contractual commitments.[5]

While the successful litigants in the previous cases had subsequently achieved notable fame (Holly Johnson, The Stone Roses) their position at the time of signing the contracts in issue was markedly different to that of George Michael. In *Holly Johnson* (1993, p.65) Dillon LJ noted that 'the members of the group were in 1983 young men in fairly humble circumstances and of little business experience. Some of them were apprentices and others on supplementary benefit'. In *The Stone Roses* (1993, p,161), Humphries J made a similar observation; 'The Stone Roses themselves were not highly educated, had no legal experience, little or no business experience, and were very much under the experience of Mr Evans. They had little or no income. Some indeed I think were on social security'. George Michael's 1988 contract was signed when he was already an international 'Superstar' and the terms of the contract were intended to reflect this status. *George Michael*, therefore, throws into sharp relief the tension between outcome and process. Whilst the end product is arguably equally restrictive, it is the position of the parties in relation to the negotiation of the critical agreements which distinguishes George Michael's unsuccessful claim from those of his successful predecessors. The difficulty of equating an unequal bargaining process with unfair terms was noted in *The Stone Roses* (1993, p.163):

> I find that as between the parties negotiating and entering into the agreement there was immense inequality in bargaining power, negotiation ability, understanding and representation. It is, however, possible even if one person has superior knowledge and bargaining power for a fair agreement to be reached. Not everyone who was in a position to do so misuses his power to take advantage of the weaker party.

Indeed both Beale (1986) and Waddams (1976) argue that it is a combination of large inequality of exchange and inequality of bargaining power which suggests a case for relief. Thus, even worldwide restrictions might be justified, as in *Nordenfelt*, where the consideration payable represents adequate compensation. While George Michael's contract was of a potentially similar duration to both The Stone Roses' and Holly Johnson's, an important compensatory element in *George*

Michael was his earnings. Perhaps because of his admittedly huge income the writ based the argument, regarding remuneration, not on the overall size of the consideration but, on the allegation that the royalty payments paid to his service companies represented an inequitable division of profits. Nevertheless, the argument for 'equitable apportionment' was rejected as was the argument that a restraint cannot be justified by reference to the amount paid for it. Parker J was of the view that the size of the consideration for the restraint was material to the issue of reasonableness between the parties. Therefore, Parker J's view that 'eight album deals' are not necessarily overly restrictive has to be seen in the context of the rewards which George Michael secured by agreeing to this. Such a finding also has the effect of adding further uncertainty to the ongoing bargaining processes within the industry.

Since the amount of revenue an artist generates is itself unpredictable at the time the agreement is signed, its relevance to the reasonableness issue suggests that courts would find it difficult to operate the restraint of trade doctrine by reference to the contract alone. If, therefore, extraneous factors must continue to play a part in the consideration of restraint of trade cases it is necessary to consider which other features of the pre-contractual context may also be relevant. While other common law jurisdictions have been disposed to develop a more general doctrine of unconscionability (Enman, 1987), the previous willingness of the courts to strike down contracts which satisfy the objective test of agreement apparently runs counter to the general development of the law of obligations in the United Kingdom (Atiyah, 1995). However, Waddams (1976) argues that English courts covertly exercise control over unfair agreements in a number of contexts (see also Thal, 1989) and the restraint of trade cases provide the strongest support for the view that 'unconscionability' operates, albeit covertly, within English common law. However, inequality in the bargaining process arises in the restraint cases in a curious and contentious way, that is, as part of the inquiry into whether the agreement is reasonable as between the parties. While this inquiry is capable of giving rise to a fairly limited exercise in determining whether the agreement itself is objectively reasonable, a number of the judgements look at the process (of bargaining) in judging the product (the agreement). The apparent failure of the bargaining process itself has continually undermined music contracts and it is arguable that, even within the constraints of the common law, it is in the interests of justice that this should continue to be so.

The panacea of independent advice?

....unlike in most other commercial areas the commercial sophistication of the client does not necessarily follow the commercial sophistication of the deal. For that reason, even though you are dealing with a high profile negotiation, you cannot assume the client will know or understand the points and you can take it from there... You can be doing a deal worth, quite possibly, millions of pounds for an individual; if you were doing that for a company director, you could assume that as he had managed to get his company to that level, he has a level of commercial acumen. But in terms of the artist it may be solely because he writes good songs and has no commercial acumen whatsoever; nor do they wish to have any. So you are relied on there to distil it into a very straightforward explanation (EL).[6]

One feature that distinguishes music and sports contracts from other areas, is the potentially large sums at stake for naive contractors with a short prospective career. At the start of his or her career, an artist might be invited to enter a number of agreements covering recording, management and publishing. In most commercial transactions of similar scale a lawyer is instructed by a business person who is familiar with common problems in the commercial situation. Where problems are novel the commercial client is a rich resource for identifying and testing solutions. In contrast, artists are usually new to the commercial milieu and faced with complex agreements they have never before encountered. The artist therefore will often depend on a lawyer to identify and protect their best interests although artists are in many cases concerned solely with cutting a record and getting the product into the shops; 'Like most musicians into their thing, I'll just fucking sign anywhere like a moron. I don't think sincere Rock 'n' Rollers are business oriented' (Steve Jones (The Sex Pistols) in Lydon, 1993). The role of the lawyer in ameliorating this problem has become more prominent as recourse to legal solutions has become more widespread in the music industry. It is not clear whether the courts believe that representation is any protection against the consequences of unequal bargaining power. There are some indications that the absence of adequate representation has assisted the courts in finding that agreements are unreasonable as between the parties, and was argued in *Clifford Davis* (1975, p.241); 'One thing is clear from the evidence. The composer had no lawyer and no legal advisers. It seems to me that, if the publisher wished to exact such onerous terms or to drive so unconscionable a bargain, he ought to have seen that the composer had independent advice'. The availability of advice may be used to refute or substantiate a claim that the artist was a victim of bargaining weakness (Thal, 1989; Beale, 1986) and particularly so when the burden is on the party in the stronger position. However, advice can only protect against certain kinds of weakness such as, lack of knowledge and experience. In practical terms, the ability of the lawyer to offer protection from poor bargains is limited. There may be considerable pressure on the artist to forego negotiations and enter the contract immediately in the haste to enter the 'holy of holies'.

Indeed, the use of standard forms encourages positional bargaining because the record company's position, as represented by the standard form, is the starting point for bargaining. Negotiators using this bargaining paradigm have in mind an opening bid, a set of positions which are a credible but exaggerated representation of the negotiator's true aspirations (the 'target'), and a 'bottom line' (a position or set of positions below which the negotiator is unwilling or unauthorised to go). The literature on bargaining suggests that positional bargaining can be conducted either competitively or cooperatively. Competitive strategies seek to maximise gain for the party deploying that strategy while cooperative strategies seek to achieve a reasonable agreement for both sides. While competitive bargaining strategies have the potential to turn bargaining leverage into one-sided deals, in general cooperative strategies facilitate amicable continuing relationships. One feature of cooperative bargaining is the attempt to achieve goals, not by pressure tactics but through attempts to build a relationship with the other side, the offering of concessions in the hope of reciprocation and the expressed aspiration of a fair agreement. However, these very features mean that cooperative bargaining can be exploited by dogged competitors; because the use of a competitive strategy by one side frequently evokes competitive responses, the use of competitive strategies may rebound on the artist's lawyer. The offer of cooperation is therefore a rational strategy in a buyer's market:

> [you]... have to have in mind throughout the strength of your client's bargaining position - how hot a piece of property they are - and have an idea about possibly the company on the other side and how desperate they are, going on past results or existing products they have in the charts, how keen they are to acquire an artist such as this. As with any industry you need to have an idea of how they are suffering in this economy - you can't press too hard and risk losing the deal (EL).

In a first recording contract negotiation, the artist and lawyer are in a disadvantaged position. The lawyer must rely on an assessment of the marketability of the artist, the level of interest in the particular act from the recording company in question and from other companies. The lawyer must also have some awareness of what artists of similar standing are commanding, and the situation in the industry generally. However, the adviser will be painfully aware that the company may lose interest at any moment and that the client is often more interested in a deal on any terms rather than no deal at all. The artist's lawyer is also burdened by the fact that the artist usually needs the contract more than the company needs the artist. A corollary is that there are generally many artists aspiring to a recording career and relatively few record companies prepared to offer contracts. Further, it would be naive to think that when concessions are made this signifies genuine negotiation or leads to fair agreements. Particular clauses may be routinely included in the draft agreement in order that they may be jettisoned during negotiations. This may give the appearance that a fair bargaining process has been completed when, in fact, the final agreement represents the record company's target position as one entertainment lawyer noted; 'When you're negotiating with wording in a contract as opposed to money that is also horse trading. Sometimes you will delete things that go beyond the number of clauses that you would ordinarily delete so that you can then, as it were, back down, hopefully on something that you wouldn't have necessarily deleted, in the hope that other clauses you do want deleted will be accepted' (EL). Later in an artist's career circumstances might mean that bargaining is conducted on a more equal footing, Nelson (1995, p.262-263) notes the following as regards football:

> 'Freedom of contract' has made it possible for players to let their contracts expire and yet put themselves in an enhanced bargaining position. Consistently good form should clearly earn appropriate reward - no problem, you would think. But in many cases clubs offer even on-song players the legal limit they are obliged to - the same terms the players are already on. The Board's hope in such instances is that, not attracting any interest from other clubs, the player will be forced to re-sign on the old terms. But if there is outside interest and the player has more than one option, the club's gamble is more than likely to misfire. The player has leverage. He can wait to see what is the best offer on the table; even play both ends against the middle.

Representation therefore provides a safeguard against perhaps only the most blatant exploitation. Further to this, whereas the unrepresented participant in a manifestly one-sided agreement has a reasonable chance of having the agreement overturned; the fact that 'informed bargaining' has occurred potentially places the represented party in a weaker position before the courts. The use of standard form contracts, and the underlying culture of negotiation, are considerable barriers to a form of dealing which attempts to meet underlying needs. While the present bargaining culture within the industry prevails it is foreseeable that some artists will continue to be dissatisfied with their recording and publishing agreements and the industry will continue to try to modify its standard terms so as to reduce the risk of challenge. This will lead to the continuation of the practice of re-negotiation, and in cases where this fails, to legal conflict. If the courts were to pursue the tendency to view the formal agreement in the whole context which produced it, they may broaden their criteria for evaluating the fairness of agreements by reviewing how far the process of bargaining was capable of satisfying the short and long term interests of the artist. Judicial consideration of agreements on this basis would undoubtedly be difficult and it is therefore suggested that this emphasis should not involve any consideration of whether or not the agreement was the best arrangement possible; that decision is essentially a matter for the parties. However this limited enquiry reduces process considerations to an issue of whether appropriate mechanisms were used. This would remove the misleading reliance on the naivety of the artist or concessions or legal representation as indicators of fair process.

Having examined some of the common themes that have pervaded the areas covered in the previous four chapters we now turn finally to examine how these issues all impinge upon an emerging area of contestation and to look at how the problems have been dealt within the game of rugby union.

From blind side to open side

We have tried, throughout this work, to express not only the historical context to much of what has occurred, but also the dynamism of the entertainment business. The concluding part to this work also seeks to look at the relationships and problems within the entertainment industry, but from the perspective of an area that has only recently begun to appreciate and address the ensuing problems. An important divide, in both football and cricket, concerned the battle over professional status, with the amateur supposedly denoting a link to a more 'glorious' sporting tradition. Both football and cricket had difficulty coming to terms with the changing player status and the struggle was particularly marked in cricket where the authorities persisted with the increasingly artificial division. In both sports there was a need to deal with the new administrative arrangements and both sought to retain a high degree of control over the wage earners, most notably through the maximum wage provisions in football. We are now able to witness similar dramatic change taking place within the game of rugby union. Ironically, the original amateur/professional divide had far greater consequences for rugby than it had for either football or cricket. This lead to a most acrimonious split between the two Codes on 29 August 1895, when twenty one clubs broke away from the Rugby Football Union over the issue of broken-time payments. The rugby authorities faced two distinct problems that arose from the split in 1895. First, how to deal with those who had played the professional game and wished to return in some form to union, and secondly, the issue of payments to players who were avowedly amateur. Although the historical split was over the issue of payments, the authorities have found the question of pay for players problematic; 'although they have long practised a form of professionalism at the higher levels, union administrators cannot bring themselves to acknowledge the fact, for that would force them to surrender the moral superiority that forms their basis for their loathing of league' (*Independent on Sunday*, 20 October 1994). The authorities had also at times blatantly ignored payments to preserve the structure of the game. Money was an issue that had always proved difficult to resolve as Frank Keating noted in 1996:

> Ninety nine years ago ...on September 16 1897 the RFU committee munched with melancholy on the same dish of hot potato and humble pie and abjectly agreed to ignore the blatant open-and-shut case of professionalism against the celebrated Welsh captain AJ Gould (*The Guardian*, 30 September 1996).

Treatment of those players who had dabbled with rugby league began to soften for two reasons. First, other countries took a far more relaxed approach to the matter and permitted players to quietly return to union without much fuss. Secondly, players who had been subject to a ban started to make threatening noises concerning their exclusion and this proceeded as far as a writ being issued. Even those players who had not been paid to play rugby league were subject to a ban, Adrian Spencer was originally banned from a Cambridge University rugby union tour to America for having a trial for the London Bronco's Rugby league side (Mitchell, 1997d).[7] The two matters, of playing league and professionalism, were closely linked for if players departed to rugby league to be paid, they could not return to the amateur game, but the ban for those who were not even paid was designed to prevent any flow from rugby union. If players could try out league, as amateurs, and not face any sanction they would be free to dabble before making the final move, a situation that the union administrators were keen to discourage. However, there seemed to be something rather incongruous about banning players who were still amateur, or players who had decided that their professional days were over and wished to return to social rugby. This appeared to be a vindictive and mean spirited approach based on events that had long since passed and, given that it was well known that payments were being made to union players, unsupportable.

That leading players were being paid was undoubtedly one of the worst kept secrets in the game and the issue would, periodically, be brought to the fore by statements from players and clubs. When a delegate to a district meeting of the Welsh RFU complained of one club offering inducements to players, the chairman's realistic response indicates the unspoken oneness of the matter; 'What were Treorchy doing that had not been done by other clubs, including the delegate's own, in the past and indeed the present?' (Plummer, 1994). At times, international players such as David Sole, Scott Gibbs and Murray Mexted have revealed the nature and extent of payments. The larger sums could be gained by players moving to play for foreign clubs (Agnew, 1994).[8] Once the (official) move towards professionalism started it proved unstoppable though it does indeed seem incredible, given the deep and longstanding nature of the split, that the parts to the game should come together so rapidly with the two leading clubs from the different codes (Bath and Wigan) even meeting each other in two inconclusive exhibition matches. It was the politics of the matches taking place that was so significant rather than the results. It remains to be seen whether the new friendship between the two halves of the game will grow into something more permanent:

> The tantalising thought occurred more than once in recent weeks that, although the historical baggage that separates the rugby codes remains stubbornly on board, and while commercial rivalry is a new factor in the equation since the clumsy introduction of professionalism in rugby union, we might be moving towards a period of enlightenment that one day will deliver us an even more exciting hybrid version of the game' (Mitchell, 1997d).

When the end of amateur status arrived, via the decision of the International Board in August 1995, it caused severe problems for those parts of the game who had fought to maintain amateur status. In England, the RFU announced a moratorium in order to give the game time to adapt. Waiting in the wings, or perhaps more accurately in the front row, had been Kerry Packer who was prepared to launch a professional circus by signing up the world's leading players. An earlier attempt had been made in 1983 but had failed because of the lack of support from the terrestrial broadcasters.

After such a long period of amateurism, or at least superficial amateurism, it was apparent that the switch towards the paid game would lead to a revolution. The effect has been startling and caused a number of internal and external divisions. First, inside the RFU itself there was dissent over the change and acrimonious battles with the major professional clubs who formed their own representative organisation, a limited company, the EPRUC. This dispute eventually led to the clubs instructing their contracted players not to attend an England training session. There was serious talk of a breakaway from the Rugby Football Union and the selection of an independent English XV outside of the auspices of the traditional authorities. After all, the leading players were now under contract to the clubs and therefore not 'free' to play for the national side. Contemporaneously to its internal problems, the RFU also opened up a second front over the sale of the television rights to England internationals. This led to moves to exclude them from the premier Northern Hemisphere competition, the Five Nations Championship. At the heart of the entire dispute was the control of the game but, more importantly, access to the television income that could be generated. This source of revenue was vital to the clubs who were facing the wage demands of professional players. According to Robert Armstrong (*The Guardian* 28 March 1996) Bath were anticipating costs in the region of £1.5m. The dispute over the exclusive deal for England matches with BSkyB led to further friction with the clubs when the RFU sought a compromise in the face of expulsion by the other nations.

Within the game the structure and ownership of clubs has begun to radically alter, Ian Malin for example noting cynically; 'And now for Fantasy Rugby. Once rugby union turned professional, a new breed appeared: the rugby club owners. Some leading clubs, notably Leicester, continued to be member clubs. Others, notably Sir John Hall's Newcastle, took on the character of the businessmen that had taken them over' (Malin, 1997, p.28). Aside from a change in status some clubs have moved grounds in order to provide a more attractive option for the much needed spectators. The clubs need to generate more than television income and to move from the status of 'club' to 'business' as one of the new breed of owners observed:

> We had to drag this club into this new era. Bedford had debts, it was poorly run and had sponsorship deals that were rubbish. Club rugby is excellent value. It's not expensive. We have a core of fans but it is quite small and our job now is to market the club regionally. We had over 6,000 to watch us play Newcastle. There were only a hundred or so people from the North East, so there is a potential audience there. But we need a bigger stadium with better facilities. People like to be pampered nowadays; they are more sophisticated. They want something to eat and drink, and merchandise (Frank Warren of Bedford Rugby Club, Malin, 1997, p.43).

Part of this change has seen links develop between rugby and football clubs for a sharing of facilities which is possible as 'grass' technology has improved. This crossover was starkly illustrated during the autumn of 1997, following an England rugby international against the All Blacks at Old Trafford, Wales played the same side at Wembley stadium a week later. What is evident is that rugby has become ripe for colonisation and that this in turn has led to rugby having to confront the same issues and problems that we have seen throughout the other chapters of this book. It seems clear that issues over terms and conditions, the use of agents, transfers and numbers of overseas players are arising in much the same way as they have done in the other areas. However, the rugby market is developing at great speed and issues that have previously taken some time to surface (such as the formation of a professional players body) are now happening almost instantaneously. The question remains as to how well rugby takes on board the experiences of these other areas, and how well it adapts to the constantly changing environment.

Into the max zone: the changing position of creative artists

> Used to scrimping and saving in the lower divisions, Bill [Shankly] did not want to see Liverpool's finances destroyed by a wage explosion however. Allegedly, he, Bill Nicholson at Spurs, Don Revie at Leeds, and Matt Busby at United got together and decided on a wage structure that no-one would exceed. The four top clubs ensured that there would be no superstar wages in the game, for the best would rarely consider a move to many clubs beyond those four (Bowler, 1996, p.245).

The above quote, concerning the legendary Bill Shankly, is an example of what has happened within the entertainment industry with respect to the terms and conditions of artists. The elimination of the maximum wage allowed footballers to obtain greater reward yet such manoeuvring referred to above set other limits. What have not changed are the fundamentals of the relationship between the buyer and seller of the talent in question. The nature of the relationship is an important issue that will determine the extent and nature of the control that can be exerted over the artist. The key element in all the areas that we have considered is exclusivity, being bound for a defined period that may be the career length. Despite the changes that have been brought about by collective pressure and legal action, this element generally remains, though in a more limited form. A good historical example of a very restrictive relationship is that of the American film industry; originally contracts for 'stars' were of virtually unlimited duration with actors expected to work continually to service the increasing demand for pictures. The actors were tied to their studio and unable to work on other projects, a situation which is now completely reversed with the major actors able to pick and choose films and other work at will. The interesting point is that the film industry has shifted so dramatically whilst other areas have maintained the basic position on exclusivity.

In a footballing context, the right to be free to ply one's trade, regardless of contractual obligations, arose in a dispute between Middlesborough Football Club and the talented international footballer, Emerson. During the 1996-7 season Emerson attracted extremely favourable reviews for his early performances on the pitch. He appeared to be settling in well, until he returned home to Brazil three times without permission from the club. At the same time there were rumours that the Spanish giants Barcelona wished to sign him; much to the chagrin of the Middlesborough officials who made clear that they would not allow him to walk out of his contract with them:

> If he does not play for us, he can sit on the beach in Brazil or on the quayside in Barcelona watching the ships sail by. We can afford to write Emerson off. But I am not sure whether the player can afford not to play football for four years. That is how long he is under contract (Keith Lamb, Chief Executive of Middlesborough).

The issue of the enforceability of contracts such as this attracted widespread comment; could players tear up lucrative contracts when it suited them leaving the clubs apparently impotent in the face of such action?[9] In the event Emerson was fined six weeks wages (reportedly this amounted to £96,000) but the case raised interesting points about both the amount of control and the way in which this control could be exercised.

Perhaps the central element to all these deals is the length of the contract that ties up an artist or performer - there are a number of considerations that come into play all of which must be seen within the context that an artist's career is usually 'cruelly brief'. First, on the part of the employer, some estimation needs to be made of the likely career length and at what point the 'artist' is in his career to determine how long a contract period is appropriate to realise the investment. This may be a difficult balancing act that needs to ensure that the artist still has incentive to perform. For example a footballer on a lucrative four or five year deal has little pressure apart from personal motivation or international representative considerations to perform as the income for that period is guaranteed. Providing he fulfils the terms of the contract by keeping himself fit and being available to play, he is entitled to be paid. This point may not apply to younger players who have the longer term to consider but a player towards the end of his career may not have similar motivation. In the light of *Bosman*, many employers have a further consideration to take account of; that their investment may be free to move elsewhere without commanding a transfer fee at the end of the contract, and so may seek longer term contracts to best utilise their investment. However, long contractual terms are not without their own problems and, especially when paying high wages, can represent a financial risk. In music contracts a common strategy has been the use of option periods that can prolong the contract and are 'low risk' on the part of the employer. Ironically, it was this type of option contract that existed prior to *Eastham* with only year long security plus retention at the club's behest. Similarly, in boxing, the option period that could be exercised by the manager should the boxer win a title has been reduced to allow the boxer greater freedom to move elsewhere.

This freedom to sell one's services to a higher bidder (we accept of course that there may be non pecuniary reasons for moving) is clearly of major benefit to those who skills are in demand. Yet as we have noted several times duration is crucially important as the career may be cut short at any time, the injury to Michael Watson is a tragic and poignant reminder of this. The situation may be similar with footballers and cricketers when injury strikes, whilst musicians may find that they have gone past their market peak and are unable to exert much leverage in the market. Thus this ability to move may be seen as a purely individual advantage dependent upon worth and in many other cases that we have examined such freedom was resisted on the grounds that it would damage the interests of the game/business as 'a whole'. The claim was that the existing order would be threatened and that chaos would result. In the music business for example it was alleged that the successful artists needed to be retained in order to subsidise the failures. In one sense the selfishness of the individual was destroying the collective, and this view might perhaps be supported by an analysis of the British film industry after the studio system had been broken. Certainly the trend has become one of oligopoly with many minor players facing extinction, overhaul or simply being bought up by a bigger player. This process is certainly ripe within film and music, and sports such as football are also beginning to exhibit such characteristics. Interestingly we are also seeing suggestions that new collective controls could be introduced to protect areas from the effects of the removal of previous restrictions. For example it was proposed in *Bosman* (1995, p.139) that the transfer rules were justified to preserve the 'financial and sporting balance between clubs' though Lenz argued that this could be achieved in different ways:

> Basically there are two different possibilities....Firstly, it would be possible to determine by a collective wage agreement specified limits for the salaries to be paid to the players by the clubs...Secondly, it would be conceivable to distribute the clubs' receipts among the clubs.

Similarly in Rugby Union which is only just seeing the effects of commercialisation there has been discussion over the same issue, with the suggested use of salary caps to maintain some equilibrium between clubs and prevent the wealthier ones from dominating (Llewellyn, 1996). To return to the theme of our introduction, this work has essentially concentrated on the stories of the players in a number of spheres of the entertainment industry. The stories are often complex and often without a happy ending; what the case of rugby shows is that as with all good stories, the plot can be used again and again and that although we might sense we know the outcome, we still feign surprise when we hear it. Perhaps, for all the debate about the nature of the various relationships and the legal principles we have outlined during the course of the book, the relationship in fact has only one common denominator:

> *...They said we'd be artistically free*
> *When we signed that bit of paper*
> *They meant let's make a lot of mon-ee*
> *An' worry about it later...*
> **The Clash: 'Complete Control'**[10]

Notes

1. Foot (1984, p.183) makes the point that Shelley had little faith in the law being used in such a way; 'This was preposterous - and Shelley knew it. He was an ardent reader of the work of "down-to-earth" reformers like Francis Place, and other ancestors of what became the right wing of the trade union movement. The most powerful contribution these people made to the politics of the time was to dispel sentimental notions about the "good old days" when "the old laws of England" looked after the common folk. There had never been such laws, nor such a "wiser day". The law had always been an instrument in the hands of the people with property who controlled the government. The "old laws" had been just as cruel and unfair as the new ones'.

2. The role of the Professional Association has also assumed a greater importance in order to represent players in the sports industries who are facing disciplinary action but also to provide some input into the standard terms that may be offered.

3. Parker J also argued that contracts within the music industry were a kind of hybrid, although with a different perspective; '...a commercial organisation may choose to adopt a particular structure for its contracts, while being prepared to negotiate detailed terms within that structure. To take an example from the record industry, a record company may be willing to negotiate royalty rates with an artist, on the basis that the agreement is to provide for royalties rather than a share or profit; but it may not be willing to offer the artist any kind of profit-sharing arrangement' (*George Michael*, 1994, p.334).

4. The Musicians' Union provides a number of services for their members including an excellent scheme for helping with contractual matters. Our thanks to Horace Trubridge for giving us details of this during one of his many excellent talks to our Entertainment Law students.

5. For example the terms relating to exclusivity, assignment and duration would all seem to be in line with the other cases.

6. As part of previous research (Boon et al, 1996) we interviewed a number of entertainment lawyers to cast more light on the practices that are utilised in the music industry. References to this will be suffixed with (EL) for 'Entertainment Lawyer'. We have used some of these quotes in this section and are most grateful to Andy Boon for allowing us to use this previous work

7. This incident also provoked a private member's Bill that was designed to prevent such discrimination, although the measure didn't progress through Parliament.

8. Agnew suggests that Italy was a country where clubs were prepared to pay well for the services of international stars; 'Informed sources say that the Australian wing David Campese received an annual fee of 200 million lire (£83,000) from his Italian team Mediolanum'.

9. For example the headline in the double page spread in the *News of the World* of December 8th 1996 'If Boro don't make a stand there will be....ANARCHY. Why Robbo must make Emo stay'.

10. From 'Complete Control' Strummer/Jones (1977, Nineden/Virgin Music (Publishers) Ltd from the LP 'The Clash'. There is a rich vein of songwriting, especially since the advent of

'punk' in the mid 1970s, that critically evaluates the relationship between artists and the music industry. Other notable examples include; 'EMI' Jones/Cook/Matlock/Lydon etc (1977, Stephen Philip Jones/Warner Chappell Music Ltd/Rotten Music Ltd from the LP 'Never Mind the Bollocks...Here's the Sex Pistols' Virgin Records); 'Rough Trade' Fingers/Ogilvie (1979, Rigid Digits Music from the Stiff Little Fingers' LP 'Inflammable Material' Rough Trade Records), 'Paint a Vulgar Picture' Morrissey & Marr (1987, Warner Music UK Ltd from The Smiths' final LP 'Strangeways Here we Come' Warner Music). Whilst we have exclusively given examples from the post-punk period, there are a number of earlier examples by luminaries such as Ray Davies of The Kinks.

References

Bibliography

ABA (1996) *Medical Aspects of Amateur Boxing* ABA Publication.

Acfield Report, The (1996) TCCB Working Party: Lord's, London.

Adams, J. & Brownsword, R. (1987) 'The ideologies of contract' *Legal Studies* Vol.7, p.205.

Agnew, P. (1994) 'Crossing the lire gain-line' *The Guardian* 3 August.

Allen, D. ed. (1984) *Arlott on Cricket. His Writings on the Game* Fontana/Collins: Great Britain.

Anon/editorial (1969) 'MCC not dictators: Graveney supsension was TCCB decision' *The Cricketer* Vol. 50, No. 7, p.12.

Anon (1992) 'A New Spin on Music Sampling: A Case for Fair Play' *Harvard Law Review* Vol. 105, p.726.

Armit, E. (1997) 'USA boxing on the ropes' *Boxing News* 4 July.

Atiyah, P. (1995) *An Introduction to the Law of Contract* Clarendon: Oxford.

Bailey, J. (1989) *Conflicts in Cricket* Kingswood: London.

Bailey, S. & Gunn, M. (1996) *Smith and Bailey on the Modern English Legal System* Sweet and Maxwell: London.

Baldwin, M. (1995) 'The Graveney Train' *The Cricketer*, p.23.

Bannister, A. (1969) Tom Graveney Lesson needs to be in black and white' *The Cricketer* Vol. 50, No.7, p.13.

Bannister, J. (1968) 'The Cricketers' Association' *The Cricketer* Vol. 49, No.7, p.2.

Barrett, E. (1997) 'True Faith' in *Arena* No. 66.

BBBC (1996) *Rules and Regulations* BBBC: London.

Beale, H. (1986) 'Inequality of Bargaining Power' *Oxford Journal of Legal Studies* Vol.6, No.1, p.123.

Beattie, G. (1996) *On the ropes. Boxing as a way of life* Indigo: London.

Benaud, R. (1984) *On Reflection* Collins Willow: London.

Biederman, D. et al (1992) *Law and Business of the Entertainment Industries*

Praeger: New York.

Birley, D. (1993) *Sport and the making of Britain* Manchester University Press: Manchester.

Blofeld, H. (1978) *The Packer Affair* Collins: London.

Blofeld, H. (1982) 'A disgrace to the game' *The Cricketer*, No.1, p.7.

Boon, A. Greenfield, S. and Osborn, G. (1996) 'Complete Control? Judicial and practical approaches to the negotiation of commercial music contracts' *International Journal of the Sociology of Law* Vol. 24, pp.89-115.

Bowler, D. (1996) *Shanks* Orion: Great Britain.

Brenkley, S. (1997) 'Malcolm poised to gain late movement' *Independent on Sunday* 16 November.

Brookes, C. (1978) *English Cricket. The Game and its players through the ages* Weidenfeld & Nicolson: London.

Callahan, T. (1991) 'Iron Mike and the allure of the "Manly Art"' in Coleman & Hornby (1996).

Cendrars, B. trans Garrett White (1995) *Hollywood. Mecca of the Movies* University of California Press: Berkeley.

Chester Report, The (1968) *Report of the Committee on Football* HMSO: London.

Cloonan, M. (1996) *Banned! Censorship of Popular Music in Britain: 1967-92* Arena:Aldershot.

Coleman, N. & Hornby, N. (1996) *The Picador Book of Sports Writing* Picador: London.

Cranford, H. & Johnson, W. (1996) 'UEFA back down on stand against Bosman ruling' *Daily Telegraph* 5 March.

Coulthard, A. (1995) 'George Michael v Sony Music - A challenge to artistic freedom?' *Modern Law Review* Vol. 58, pp.731-744.

Dabscheck, B. (1986) 'Beating the off-side trap: the case of the Professional Footballer's Association' *Industrial Relations Journal* pp.350-361.

Dabscheck, B. (1991) 'A Man or a Puppet?': The Football Association's 1909 attempt to destroy the Association Football Players' Union *International Journal of the History of Sport*, Vol.8, No.2, p.221.

Dannen, F. (1990) *Hit Men. Power brokers and fast money inside the music business* Vintage: London.

Deflem, M. (1993) 'Rap, Rock and Censorship. Contesting Moral Limits in Musical Settings' Paper presented at *Law And Society Association* annual meeting, Chicago.

Denselow, R. (1990) *When the Music's Over. The Story of Political Pop* Faber & Faber:London.

Durant, A. (undated) 'A New Day for Music? Digital technologies in contemporary music making' in Hayward, P. ed (1993).

Duxbury, N. (1995) 'Football: Premiership scraps foreigner rule' *The Independent* December 23.

Ebsworth, J. (1996) 'Kicking misinformation out of football' text of speech made at House of Commons, 6 November 1996, unpublished.

ECB (1997) Registration Regulations.

Edwards, M. (1971) 'Cricketers' Association' *The Cricketer* Vol. 52, No.11, p.9.

Enman, J. (1987) 'Doctrines of Unconscionability in Canadian, English and Commonwealth Contract Law' *Anglo-American Law Review*, p.191.

FA (1991) *The Blueprint for Football.*

FA (1996) *The FA Premier League Handbook.*

FA (1997) 'Parry Comments on Bosman Effects' FA Press Release 22 January.

FA/FL (undated a) 'Code of Practice and Notes on contract for FA Premier League & Football League Contract Players and trainees'.

FA/FL (undated b) FA Premier League and Football League Contract.

Feldman, D. (1993) *Civil Liberties and Human Rights in England and Wales* Clarendon: Oxford.

Fleischer, N. & Andre, S. (1979) *A Pictorial History of Boxing* Hamlyn: London.

Foot, P. (1984) *Red Shelley* Bookmarks: London.

Frith, D. (1977) 'The Packer Affair' *The Cricketer* September, pp.4-5.

Frith, S. (1987) 'The industrialisation of popular music' in Lull (1987).

Frith, S. (1993) 'Music and Morality' in Frith S ed (1993) *Music and Copyright* Edinburgh University Press: Edinburgh.

Frith, S. & Goodwin, A. eds (1990) *On Record. Rock, Pop and the Written Word* Routledge: London.

Fynn, A. & Guest, L. (1994) *Out of Time. Why Football isn't Working* Simon & Schuster: Great Britain.

Gaines, J. (1992) *Contested Culture. The Image, The Voice, and the Law* BFI Publishing: London.

Garfield, S. (1986) *Expensive Habits. The Dark Side of the Music Industry* Faber and Faber: London.

Giannetti, L. & Eyman, S. (1986) *Flashback: a brief history of film* Prentice Hall: New Jersey.

Gorman, K. (1997) 'Dying on its feet' *Daily Mirror* 14 July.

Greenfield, S. & Osborn, G. (1992) 'Unconscionability and contract: the creeping shoots of Bundy' *Denning Law Journal* p.65.

Greenfield, S. & Osborn, G. (1994) 'The sanctity of the village green: preserving Lord Denning's pastoral vision' *Denning Law Journal.*

Greenfield, S. & Osborn, G. (1996) 'Oh to be in England? Mythology and Identity in English Cricket' *Social Identities. Journal for the Study of Race Nation and Culture* Vol 2, No.2.

Greenfield, S. & Osborn, G. (1997) 'Good technology? Music and the challenge of technology towards the fin de siecle' *Information & Communications Technology Law* p.77.

Griffiths Report, The (1994) *Report of the Griffiths Working Party* Lords: London.

Guest, A. (1984) *Anson's Law of Contract* Clarendon Press: Oxford.

Gunn, M. & Ormerod, D. (1995) 'The legality of boxing' *Legal Studies* p.181.

Guttmann, A. (1986) *Sports Spectators* Columbia University Press: New York.

Haigh, G. (1993) *The Cricket War* The Text Publishing Company: Melbourne Australia.

Hain, P. (1996) *Sing the Beloved Country. The struggle for the new South Africa* Pluto Press: London.

Harding, J. (1991) *For the Good of the Game. The Official History of the Professional Footballers' Association* Robson Books: London.

Haynes, R. (1995) *The Football imagination. The rise of football fanzine culture* Arena: Aldershot.

Hayward, P. ed (1993) *Culture Technology and Creativity in the Late Twentieth Century* John Libbey Press: London.

Henderson, R. (1995) 'Is it in the blood?' *Wisden Cricket Monthly* June.

Higham, C. (1981) *Bette. The Life of Bette Davis* Macmillan Publishing: New York.

Hill, J. (1963) *Striking for soccer* Sportsmans' Book Club: London.

Hirsch, P. (1972) 'Processing Fads and Fashions. An Organisation-Set Analysis of Cultural Industry Systems' in Frith & Goodwin, (1990).

Hogdson, G. (1995) 'Kelly appeals for calm after Bosman verdict' *The Independent* 16 December.

Holden, D. (1993) 'Pop go the censors' *Index on Censorship* Vol.5&6.

Hopps, D. (1994) 'Fine and warning for Stemp outburst' *The Guardian* 29 June.

Hopps, D. (1997) 'Adams awaits the day of judgement' *The Guardian* 11 November.

Hornby, N. (1992) *Fever Pitch* Victor Gollancz: London.

Hugman, B. ed. (1994) *British Board of Boxing Control Yearbook.*

ICC (1996) *International Cricket Council Code of Conduct, Standard Playing Conditions and Regulations* Lord's Cricket Ground: London.

Illingworth, R. & Bannister, J. (1996) *One-man committee* Headline: London.

James, C. (1994) *Beyond a boundary* Serpents Tail: London (first published 1963).

Johnson, H. (1994) *A Bone in My Flute* Century: London.

Jones, K. (1997) 'Tyson license revoked as he is fined $3m' *The Independent* 10 July.

Lachtman, H. ed (1981) *Sporting Blood* Presidio Press: Novato, CA.

Lamb, A. (1997) *Allan Lamb. My autobiography* Collins Willow: London.

Larwood, H. with Perkins, K. (1982) *The Larwood Story* Allen: London.

Leaming, B. (1992) *Bette Davis. A Biography* Weidenfeld & Nicolson: London.

Llewellyn, D. (1996) 'O'Reilly calls for Union solidarity' *The Independent* 23 July.

London, J. (1911) 'A Piece of Steak' in Lachtman (1981).

Longmore, A. (1997) 'Gilbert looks back with anger' *Independent on Sunday* 28 September.

Lull, J. (1987) *Popular Music and Communication* Sage: London.

Lydon, J. (1993) *Rotten. No Irish. No blacks. No dogs.* Hodder & Stoughton: London.

MacLaurin Report, The (1997) *Raising the Standard. ECB Management Board Blueprint* Lords, London.

McArdle, D. (1995) *Policing prize fights in nineteenth century England* Unpublished conference paper, North American society for the Sociology of Sport, Sacramento.

McCutcheon, J. (1997) 'Negative enforcement of employment contracts in the sports industries' *Legal Studies* Vol. 17, No.1, p.65.

McFarline, P. (1977) *A Game Divided* Hutchinson: Victoria, Australia.

McLellan, A. (1994) *The Enemy Within* Blandford: London.

McLellan, A. ed (1996) *Nothing Sacred. The New Cricket Culture* Two Heads Publishing: London.

Mailer, N. (1975) *The Fight* Penguin: London.

Malin, I. (1997) *Mud, Blood and Money* Mainstream: Great Britain.

Marks, V. (1990) *The Wisden Illustrated History of Cricket* Queen Anne Press: London.

Marks, V. (1997) 'Freedom for Adams drops dead bat on transfer system' *The Observer* 16 November.

Marqusee, M. (1994) *Anyone But England* Verso: London.

Martin-Jenkins, C. (1977) *The Jubilee Tests* Macdonald and Jane's: London.

Martin-Jenkins, C. (1984) *Twenty Years On* Collins Willow: London.

Martin-Jenkins, C. (1991) 'The Tiger Moth Affair' *The Cricketer*, No.3, p.11.

Mee, R. (1997) 'Savage Tyson must be thrown out on his ear' *Boxing News* 4 July.

Meister, R. (1996) 'Battling for a Boxers' Union' (http://www.uhu.com/boxing).

Melly, J. (1996) 'Cricket 2000: How the media reinvented the game' in McLellan ed. (1996).

Mitchell, K. (1997a) 'Only a ban can save Mad Mike' *The Observer* 6 July.

Mitchell, K. (1997b) 'Tyson gets the maximum' *The Guardian* 10 July.

Mitchell, K. (1997c) 'Lewis sparks revolt of the moguls' *The Guardian* 14 July.

Mitchell, K. (1997d) 'Free spirits bridge the old divide' *The Observer* 23 November.

Morgan Report, The (1996) ECB Working Party Report: Lord's, London.

Mullan, H. (1997) 'Darkest alley for a street animal' *Independent on Sunday* 6 July.

Negativland (undated) 'FAIR USE. The Story of the Letter U and the Numeral 2' reproduced at http://www.negativland.com.

Nelson, G. (1995) *Left Foot Forward. A year in the life of a journeyman footballer* Headline Publishing: London.

Oates, J. (1987) 'On Boxing' in Coleman, N. & Hornby, N. (1996).

O'Gorman, T. (1996) 'Ed Giddins vs. TCCB' *Journal of Sport and Law*, p.23.

Parpworth, N. (1994) 'Boxing and prize fighting: the indistinguishable distinguished' *Sport and the Law Journal* Vol.2, Iss.1, p.5.

Parpworth, N. (1996) 'Parliament and the boxing bill' *Sport and the Law Journal* Vol.4, Iss.1, p.24.

Pawson, T. (1974) *The Football Managers* Readers' Union: Newton Abbot.

Plummer, D. (1994) 'Wales unfurl the white flag on amateurism' *The Guardian* 3 August.

POCA (1996) 'Players Charter' Players Out of Contract Association: London.

Pontremoli, A. (1995) 'Amateur boxing:is it dangerous?' ABA Booklet.

Popplewell (1985) Cmnd 9585 (1985) *Committee of Inquiry into Crowd Safety and Control at Sports Grounds. Interim Report* HMSO: London.

Popplewell (1986) Cmnd 9710 (1986) *Committee of Inquiry into Crowd Safety and Control at Sports Grounds. Final Report* HMSO: London.

Rawling, J. (1997) 'A gutless act of premeditated cowardice' *The Guardian* 30 June.

Redhead, S. (1994) 'Media culture and the world cup: The last World Cup?' in Sugden & Tomlinson (1994).

Redhead, S. (1995) *Unpopular Cultures. The Birth of Law and Popular Culture*

Manchester University Press:Manchester.

Robb, J. (1997) *The Stone Roses and the resurrection of British pop* Ebury: London.

Robinson, P. (undated) Justified and Ancient History. The Unfolding Story of the KLF.

Robertson, G. & Nicol, A. (1992) *Media Law* Penguin: London.

Schatz, T. (1988) '"A Triumph of Bitchery": Warner Bros., Bette Davis, and *Jezebel*' in Staiger (1995).

Selvey, M. (1995) 'Pakistan sack Salim Malik' *The Guardian* 8 March.

Selvey, M. (1996) 'Illingworth on the carpet' *The Guardian* 28 May.

Sissons, R. (1988) *The Players. A Social History of the Professional Cricketer* Kingswood Press: London.

Speight, M. (1996) 'A Bit like sex: Life on the county circuit' in McLellan (1996).

Staiger, J. (1995) *The Studio System* Rutgers University Press: New Brunswick.

Steen, R. (1987) 'Is the price right?' *The Cricketer* March, p.17.

Sugden, J. (1996) *Boxing and Society* Manchester University Press: Manchester.

Sugden, J. & Tomlinson, A. (1994) *Hosts and Champions. Soccer cultures, national identities and the USA World Cup* Arena: Aldershot.

Taylor (1990) Cm 962 (1990) *The Hillsborough Stadium Disaster. Inquiry by the Rt Hon Lord Justice Taylor. Final Report* HMSO: London.

TCCB (1995) Discipline Committee Regulations.

Thal, S. (1988) 'The Inequality of Bargaining Power Doctrine: the Problem of Defining Contractual Unfairness' *Oxford Journal of Legal Studies*, p.28.

Thomas, R. (1996) 'Hands off English system, Uefa told' *The Guardian* 21 February.

Thorpe, M. & Ross, I. (1997) 'Given deal to test transfer system' 31 May.

Tillotson, J. (1995) *Contract law in perspective* Cavendish Press: London.

Tomlinson, A. (1991) 'North and South: the rivalry of the Football League and the Football Association' in Williams & Wagg (1991).

Vahrenwald, A. (1996) 'Am I so round with you as you with me? The Bosman case before the European Court of Justice' *Entertainment Law Review* Vol.4, p.149.

Waddams, S. (1976) 'Unconscionability in Contracts' *Modern Law Review*, Vol. 39, No. 4, p.369.

Weatherill, S. (1989) 'Discrimination on grounds of nationality in sport' *Yearbook of European Law*, p.55.

Weatherill, S. (1996) 'Article 177 reference by the Cour d'Appel, Liege, on the interpretation of Articles 48, 85 and 86 EC. Judgement of the European Court of Justice of 15 December 1995' *Common Market Law Review*, p.991.

Webber, R. (1957) *County Cricket Championship* Phoenix Sports Books.

Wiechula, F. (1997) '$200m bite of the century' *Daily Mirror* 10 July.

Williams, J. Dunning, E. & Murphy, P. (1989) *The Luton Town Members Scheme. Final Report* Sir Norman Chester Centre for Football Research: Leicester

Williams, J. & Wagg, S. (1994) *British football and social change. Getting into Europe.* Leicester University Press: Leicester.

Williams, M. (1983) *The Way to Lord's. Cricketing Letters to the Times* Willow: London

Williams, R. (1997) 'Demeaning and disgusting' *The Guardian* 30 June.

Wright, G. (1994) *Betrayal. The struggle for cricket's soul* Collins Willow: London.

Cases

Allcard *Allcard v Skinner* [1886-90] All ER Rep 90.
Bette Davis *Warner Brothers Pictures Incorporated v Nelson* [1937] 1 KB 209.
Binder *Binder v Alachouzos* [1972] 2 QB 151.
Bosman *Union Royale Belge des Societes de Football Association ASBL v Bosman, Royal Club Liegois SA v Bosman and others, Union des Associations Europeens de Football v Bosman* (Case C-415/93) [1996] All ER (EC) 97.
Bundy *Lloyds Bank v Bundy* [1974] 3 All ER 757.
Clifford Davis *Clifford Davis Management Ltd v WEA Records Ltd and another* [1975] 1 All ER 237.
Colchester *Colchester Borough Council v Smith* [1992] Ch. 421.
Coney *R v Coney* (1882) 8 QBD 534.
Dona *Dona v Mantero* (Case 13/76) [1976] ECR 1333.
Eastham *Eastham v Newcastle Football Club* [1963] 3 All ER 139.
Esso *Esso Petroleum Co. Ltd. v Harper's Garage (Stourport) Ltd.* [1968] AC 269.
Evans *Evans v Llewellin* (1787) 1 COX 334.
FA v FL *R v Football Association Ltd, ex parte Football League Ltd; Football Association Ltd v Football League Ltd* [1993] 2 All ER 833
George Michael *Panayiotou and others v Sony Music Entertainment (UK) Limited* [1994] EMLR 229.
Gibson *R v Gibson* (1991) 1 All ER 439.
Greig *Greig and others v Insole and others* [1978] 1 WLR 302.
Holly Johnson *Zang Tuum Tumb Records Ltd and another v Johnson* [1993] EMLR 61.
Kingaby *Kingaby v Aston Villa FC (1912) The Times 28 March.*
Mason *Mason v Provident Clothing and Supply Company Limited* [1913] AC 724.
McInnes *McInnes v Onslow-Fane and another* [1978] 1 WLR 1520.
Miller *Miller v Jackson* [1977] All ER 338.
Mitchell *Mitchell v Reynolds* 10 MOD 132, 660, (1711).
Morgan *National Westminster Bank v Morgan* [1985] 1 All ER 821.
Nagle *Nagle v Feilden and others* [1966] 2 QB 633.
Nordenfelt *Thorsten Nordenfelt v The Maxim Nordenfelt Guns and Ammunition Company, Limited* [1894] AC 535.

Page One *Page One Records, Ltd and another v Britton and Others (trading as "The Troggs") and Another* [1967] 3 All ER 822.

Pallante *Pallante v Stadiums Pty Ltd (No 1)* [1976] VR 331.

R v Brown *R v Brown and other appeals* [1993] 2 All ER 75.

Saxelby *Herbert Morris Limited v Saxelby* [1916] AC 688.

Schroeder *A. Schroeder Music Publishing v Macaulay* [1974] 3 All ER 616.

The Stone Roses *Silvertone Records Ltd v Mountfield and others* [1993] EMLR 152.

Walrave *Walrave v Association Union Cycliste International* (Case 36/74) [1974] ECR 1405.

Warren *Warren v Mendy and another* [1989] 3 All ER 103.

Watson *Watson v Prager and another* [1993] EMLR 275.